GREAT PUBLIC SQUARES

AN ARCHITECT'S SELECTION

GREAT PUBLIC SQUARES

AN ARCHITECT'S SELECTION Robert F. Gatje

W. W. Norton & Company

NEW YORK | LONDON

This book was supported by a grant from **Furthermore**: a program of the J. M. Kaplan Fund
It received additional support from the Scaler Foundation.

For information about permission to reproduce selections from this book, write to
Permissions, W. W. Norton & Company, Inc., 500 Fifth Avenue, New York, NY 10110

For information about special discounts for bulk purchases, please contact W. W. Norton
Special Sales at specialsales@wwnorton.com or 800-233-4830

Manufacturing by KHL Printing Co.Pte Ltd
Book design by Vivian Ghazarian
Production manager: Leeann Graham
Electronic production: Sue Carlson

Library of Congress Cataloging-in-Publication Data

Gatje, Robert F.
Great public squares : an architect's selection / Robert F. Gatje.—1st ed.
p. cm.
Includes bibliographical references and index.
ISBN 978-0-393-73173-6 (hardcover)
1. Plazas. I. Title.
NA9070.G37 2010
711'.55—dc22
2009034019

ISBN: 978-0-393-73173-6

W. W. Norton & Company, Inc., 500 Fifth Avenue, New York, N.Y. 10110
www.wwnorton.com
W. W. Norton & Company Ltd., Castle House, 75/76 Wells Street, London W1T 3QT

1 2 3 4 5 6 7 8 9 0

To Sue and Alex

CONTENTS

ITALY

ACKNOWLEDGMENTS

This book literally began as I rummaged around sources after busy workdays on planning commissions, finding and filing and losing statistics. Now that I have them all in order, I have to admit that friends who note my spending six years on a book as a way to justify lots of marvelous travel are not all that wrong.

The first person to offer significant help was John Reps, an old friend and former professor of mine at Cornell, who pointed me to the essential giants in the field—Sitte, Hegemann & Peets, and Zucker—and who, from a lifetime in the planning field, has been a source of further support. Cornell classmates Gerry Pook and Jan White have been guiding my graphics from the beginning, while Ken Frampton and Barry Bergdoll of the Columbia University faculty have been willing critics, as have Isabelle Hyman and Carol Krinsky of New York University. Eric Quell and Alberto Izzo provided me with valuable background material from Italy. My Breuer associate Allen Cunningham drove me through the *bastides* country as we were choosing Monpazier, and my partner Mario Jossa measured the roof deck at the Place Vendôme and put me in contact with Pierre Prunet. Ian Arnott and Leland Ludington gave me photographs along with their appreciation of home and adopted home in Scotland and Spain. My associates at Richard Meier's office, John Eisler and Wolfram Wöhr, who had returned to their native cities in the Czech Republic and Germany, respectively, were able to answer questions and make necessary introductions, particularly to Milos Drdacky in Prague and Telč. A chance meeting in the archives of Florence led me to Niall Atkinson who, acting as my local rep, tracked down additional cadastrals and pointed me to Marvin Trachtenberg's *Dominion of the Eye*.

Among the institutions that have been most graciously helpful are the American Academy in Rome, whose chaiman Adele Chatfield-Taylor arranged for guest privileges; Pioneer Courthouse Square Inc., particularly Jennifer Polver, Doug Macy, and Marc Bevans; Tishman Speyer and Beyer Blinder Belle, the architects for Rockefeller Plaza; and the always dependable Avery Library of Architecture and Fine Arts at Columbia University.

Tony Schulte introduced me to my publisher, W. W. Norton, where Nancy Green has guided me through the thickets of putting this book together and selected my multitalented editor, Johanna Zacharias, and inspired designer Vivian Ghazarian.

Furthermore, the publishing arm of the J.M. Kaplan Fund, and the Scaler Foundation, with the sponsorship of the Architectural League of New York and the Architectural Foundation of New York, provided grants in support of the book's publication. Joan K. Davidson, Ann Birckmeyer, Rosalie Genevro, Marvin Wurzer, and Catherine Boissonnas Coste were my loyal backers.

I started with the idea that my enjoyable talents as a draftsman would provide the drawings for this effort. After experimentation with pen and ink, watercolor, and Zip-a-tone, I deferred to the guidance of my graphic artist–daughter, Alexandra Lord Gatje, who taught me everything I know about Adobe Illustrator and Photoshop and has made endless contributions and corrections to the use of my Apple computer.

And, finally, I thank my partner and best friend of twenty-five years, Susan Rentschler Witter, who has held my camera, my papers, and my hand while conducting a first run-through during the entire marvelous adventure.

INTRODUCTION

This book has grown out of my fifty years of experience as an architect and planner, and it builds upon three great books about urban space by Camillo Sitte, Werner Hegemann and Elbert Peets , and Paul Zucker.

In 1889, Sitte critiqued the quality of urban planning in the Europe of his day and accompanied the text of his *Der Städte-Bau* (The Design of Cities) with a hundred-plus small plans of the squares he liked (such as his St. Peter's, at right). His plans were all drawn at the same scale, for comparative purposes. They became well known to the American architectural profession when they were included in a 1922 publication entitled *Civic Art: The American Vitruvius* (known simply as "Hegemann & Peets"). The German-born Zucker, a prolific writer who taught in New York City at the New School and the Cooper Union, updated thinking about urban space with his comprehensive *Town and Square* in 1959. Following what may be considered a forty-year cycle, the book you have in your hands builds upon their thinking with new insight, computer-generated graphics, and color photography.

I have selected forty squares, some paired, and analyzed thirty-five ground plans. All the plans use the same visual language and scale so that, like Sitte's, they can be easily compared.

Sitte's drawings were about one-eighth the size of the drawings in this book—compare his St. Peter's to mine on pages 90–91. Sitte was also limited to printing in black and white. My scale is today's standard of 1:1000. Color allows me to give much more information about the squares.

Most but not all the squares I have chosen were designed with some knowledge of those that had been built before them, sometimes located nearby, so I have arranged them by country in rough chronological order. Since the use of outdoor space developed first in warmer climates (and continues to be best used there), my list unsurprisingly begins with and is dominated by twenty squares from Italy; two each from Germany and the Czech Republic, one from Greece, and five from France follow. Spain and Portugal each provide one, and there are four each from Britain and the United States.

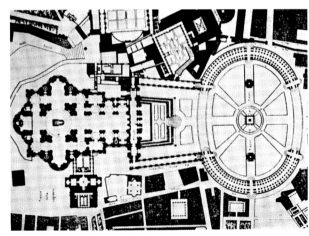

Piazza San Pietro, Rome (Sitte)

Defining the Square

If *architecture* is the product of the art of building self-contained structures, then *urban space* refers to what is left between the structures. Put another way, architecture can be defined by the three dimensions of *volume*; urban space is formed by three dimensions of *void*. As we move through such spaces we may also experience the fourth dimension of time. This book is not so much about architecture as it is about space, albeit space that is usually shaped by architects as enclosed between their buildings.

A single building sitting all alone in the midst of a field is neither urban nor capable of defining the limitless space surrounding it. Put three or four buildings together at a crossroads and you begin to have something urban, or citylike, in the composition. Roads, which up to that point may only have been defined by compact surfaces, hedges, or trees, take on the character of a street. Its space is linear and directional. If the buildings that define a street are sufficiently distinguished by beauty or history they give it a special character. Some of these streets are so well known, or pleasurable to walk along, that they may justifiably be called great, as Alan B. Jacobs did in his fine book *Great Streets*, which was, in many ways, an inspiration for this one.

Long before the motor car, but after the arrival of chariots and the horse-drawn carriage, there was need for spaces within city or town that were more than a street or a crossroad—places for commercial exchange and public assembly. Call them squares, piazze, places, or plätze, the essential elements of success are those of a sense of enclosure and pleasant usefulness. Zucker writes: "The square represents . . . a psychological parking place within the civic landscape. If one visualizes the streets as rivers, channeling the stream of human communication . . . then the square represents a natural or artificial lake."

Many squares started out linear—a widening of the main street to accommodate market activity. Some that bulged off to one side remain a happy eddy space like the Place des Vosges in Paris. Others, in classic times, were meant to be a static destination such as the Campidoglio in Rome. But then the four-wheeled vehicle tore things apart. Baron Haussmann, encouraged by Napoleon III, was permitted to plow straight through the previously placid Place Vendôme.

If most squares can be thought of as gigantic rooms (Napoleon famously called San Marco "Europe's grandest drawing room"), it is no surprise that, in describing their shape and proportion, we often speak of walls, floor, and furnishing. (Some squares ended up overfurnished with trees at the same time society's drawing rooms were being overstuffed with ferns.)

Squares that developed during the Middle Ages, and often over a long period of time, tend to be irregular, but they should not be considered as lacking in design just because we don't know the names of those who decided what to build, keep, and replace. During the Renaissance, with its well-known architects, most squares were designed with some shape in mind. The roster includes rectangles (Jardin du Palais-Royal), squares (Place des Vosges), circles (Bath), ovals (Saint Peter's), and octagons (Place Vendôme), plus some very interesting trapezoids (San Marco). It is clear that greatness can be found in each of the categories. (I don't agree with Sitte that a true "square" square is bound to be less stimulating than a longish rectangle, and many of the best spaces in this book are close to this eponymous shape.)

The squares that follow range in width from well under 100 feet (30 meters) to just over 500 feet (150 meters). Anything smaller is probably not public, and beautiful courtyards are left to another book. Anything larger risks becoming a playing field rather than a room. I rejected Mexico City's Zócalo because its distant walls give no sense of enclosure, protection, or comfort. The rule of thumb cited by Sitte and others is that for the observer an opposite wall should be close enough for one to recognize its architectural details and, therefore, be able to judge its scale instinctively. (The "recognizable" details can be distorted, as was done by Maderno in his façade for St. Peter's, to horrific effect—reducing the pope in his Easter window to a little white dot.) Sitte reported the average dimensions of Europe's great old squares to be 190 × 465 feet (58 × 142 meters). The forty squares in this book average 265 × 410 feet (80 × 125 meters)—not too different.

Regarding my dimensions, please remember that these are to be generally useful rather than precisely accurate; they have been scaled from drawings and photographs rather than measured in the field.

Judging the Squares

Twenty centuries ago, the Roman architect Vitruvius gave us the best standard for judging architecture, usually rendered in English as "Commodity, Firmness, and Delight," or, less elegantly, as "utility, structural dependability, and physical beauty." Space too can be judged à la Vitruvius by its "utility, integrity, and delight."

UTILITY

A great square should have served, and continue to serve, some useful purpose such as commerce or public assembly. It may also provide the foreground of an important building. While some were conceived as stage sets to enhance a speculative real estate scheme, those that have grown to greatness are the few that have been welcomed into the real life of the community, surrounding their citizens to good purpose.

INTEGRITY

If a successful building is supported by a secure structure, space needs another standard of reliability. We can think of squares as vessels or containers of space. If the lip of a vessel is low, or its walls full of holes, the space contained will "leak out."

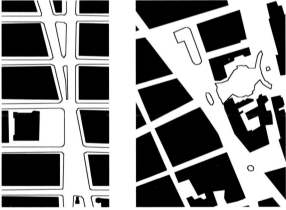

Times Square, New York   **Piazza di Spagna, Rome**

Times Square and the Piazza di Spagna are both drawn at the same scale and represent "squares" of a remarkably similar size and shape. I considered both for inclusion in this book. Why did one make it and the other not? Most important, the Piazza di Spagna is essentially a pedestrian area, whereas Times Square is full of roaring traffic morning, noon, and night. Few of the Piazza's streets go all the way through the space; most are "stopped" by buildings or stairs. In other words, the space of the Piazza is largely "contained" whereas that of Times Square leaks out all over the place. This does not make the illuminated display of Times Square undeserving of a visit—in fact, it is active all year long while the Spanish Steps work best in the summer sun. But Times Square doesn't fit my definition; the Piazza di Spagna does.

Integrity also concerns that magical moment when façades stop shaping surrounding buildings and join hands to become the outer surface of the space they enclose. Depending upon their relationship, the façades so established by design or accident may result in a consistent harmony of dimension, proportion, and material that make up a whole. (Zucker uses a rather weak pun: "Is a square a 'whole' or a 'hole'?")

DELIGHT

People on foot must be so pleased to be in a square as to give it life. They may have come from afar to marvel at its beauty, or they may walk through it daily on the way to work or shopping. The square may invite them to stop for a drink, a meal, or a suntan. The point is that they want to be there because it pleases. It looks good and feels right. No amount of persuasion, false pride, or phony history will fill a square with people. And no such space can claim greatness without the presence of people. Just as the pleasurable space of every square in this book has dimensions that are easy to define but often hard to replicate, the space is also defined by surfaces of color, texture, and complexity that we find beautiful. Finally, perhaps, the most difficult quality to measure, evaluate, and appreciate in a square may be its share in some slice of human history that has marked the place in memory forever.

Choosing the Squares

In selecting squares to write about, I obviously had to set some limits. For the purposes of this book, I chose squares that are all in use today, are generally admired, and will be familiar to many. The ruins of ancient Greece and Rome are not included, and the selected squares are all in Western Europe and North America. Each square included here has something to show that is all its own. Gramercy Park in New York is a fine Georgian square—perhaps the best Georgian square in the US—but the gems of its type are Edinburgh's Charlotte Square and London's Bedford Square. When I started work on this book, I intended to cover twenty-five "greats" and ten "near greats" for comparison to make my pedagogic points. By the time I had finished, the line between the twenty-five and the ten had become very fuzzy, and a few squares had jumped from one group to the other.

Every reader will find favorites missing, but I invite you to measure them against my choices.

Drawing the Squares

GROUND PLANS

I have followed the lead of Sitte in showing all the squares at a common scale and with comparable graphic treatment so readers can make direct comparisons. The drawings are big enough to illustrate a lot about each square's enclosure and surroundings; even San Marco fits within the 11-inch-square format of the book. The "footprint" or closed section of each building is rendered in black. (Beaux-Arts architectural terminology calls this *poché*.) The interior floors of important public buildings that influence the square outside are rendered in color to suggest a continuity from inside to out. Shared characteristics and dimensions are noted in the text and averaged in a table at the end of the book. Color helps to define contents and quality, and shadows suggest the third dimension.

SURFACE TEXTURES

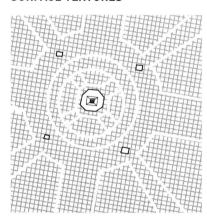

I use a square grid of fine gray lines in most places to indicate sidewalk and pedestrian surfaces. These represent joints just over 6 feet (2 meters) apart, fairly close to reality in most places.

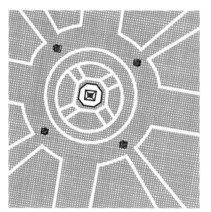

In Rome, however, the typical pavement stones (basalt San Pietrini cobbles) measure only 6 to 12 inches (15 to 30 centimeters) on a side, and if they were drawn to scale they would be unprintable. Therefore, I simply halved my usual grid in order to indicate something in smaller scale.

SHADOWS

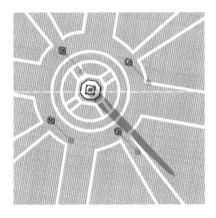

Convention puts north at the top of maps and plans, but the shadows on my plans point down and to the right. My training as a topographic computer in the United States Army demonstrated that buildings "jump up" when you view aerial photography if the shadows point down, so my plans assume a sun that is illogically high in its northwest quadrant. Architects long ago decided to live with this convention.

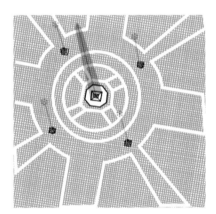

If the drawing is rendered realistically, with the sun below and to the south, the upstanding shadows look like the objects themselves. (Jacobs decided to live with the real sun's upward pointing shadows for his *Great Streets*, and it is the only thing in his book with which I find fault.)

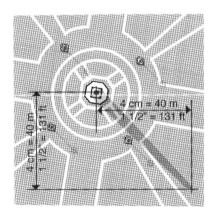

With a ruler you can determine the height of a building or other shadowed object, such as a fountain, by measuring the width or depth of its 45-degree shadow at the scale of 1:1000, or 1 inch = 83.3 feet, as shown in the plan of St. Peter's obelisk, which is 131 feet (40 meters) high.

I must repeat that while I have tried to make the drawings as close to truth as possible, there are places where I simply had to wing it. Either the information was not available, or sources disagreed. More to the point, some things were too small to be seen at the scale of 1:1000. So I either left them out or exaggerated their size, as with the Roman stones described above.

The fine white lines that crisscross each of my ground plans represent the 100-meter grid that is to be found in many of the official cadastral plans (records of property ownership) that underlie my new drawings. These plans were usually easy to obtain in or from the building departments of each city, but like my other two nemeses (weather and scaffolds), they presented occasional problems. For example, the map covering the site of the Campo dei Santi Giovanni e Paolo in Venice was in a remote branch of the building department where very few people spoke English. I arrived there on a busy Monday morning when plumbers and real estate agents, who knew to take a number, had been waiting on line for some time. Such is the grace of the Venetians that, once my needs had been established, everyone generously stood aside to let a foreign architect go to the head of the line.

Considering the squares as outside rooms, the ground plans overemphasize the "floor" of each square because that is our principal subject. The photographs are intended to show the "walls" of each room as best they can. They are mostly my own, some taken years ago as a student or tourist, some especially for this book. (Other sources are noted in the Credits.) I shot the spaces in use, rarely waiting for people to get out of the way, and at ground level or from some viewpoint accessible to the public. The "ceilings" are a variable sky. Perhaps Italy has produced so many great squares because its sky so often offers a deep blue ceiling in comparison to those gray skies in northern Europe.

I begin each section with a set of data for comparative purposes, followed by my opinion about the character and quality of each square and a brief description of how and when each of the squares happened to be built.

Other authors have suggested categories, rules, and standards in analyzing squares. (Zucker uses an elaborate set of classifications for which I find no use: "closed," "dominated," "nuclear," "grouped," and "amorphous.") My purpose is simply to provoke and enhance your judgment of urban spaces by comparing one with another so that they may be enjoyed, appreciated, and preserved.

The Greeks used space *around* great buildings in order to show them off to best advantage. The Romans used buildings to *surround* and define great space. Vehicles were initially forbidden but ever since the fourth century, when chariots and wagons were admitted, pedestrians have had to dodge increasing traffic.

After the Second World War, when so much of Europe had to be rebuilt, enlightened planners recognized that there were alternatives to having their cities dominated by the needs of cars and trucks, and the pedestrian zone in combination with public transit began to take over more and more of the inner city's ground plane. Jan Gehl and Lars Gemzoe have recorded so many excellent, largely European examples, in their *New City Spaces* as to make the rest of the world, and particularly the United States, shudder in shame. When the land seemed endless and gasoline was cheap, no one *had* to cater to the pedestrians who voluntarily stayed in town. Now that this is no longer the case in the Western world and, as the people of the East move into cities predicted to double and treble in size, pedestrians in the great cities of the world must be recognized as those to be satisfied in future planning.

Does the study of successful squares of the past make sense at a time when conditions are so very different? Absolutely—because the determinant factors are still the same. People have the same set of eyes; they want to sit down when they are tired; they either welcome the sun or demand shelter from it; splashing water and rustling leaves still enhance outdoor dining; marketing in the fresh air with the chance of meeting neighbors increasingly competes with the air-conditioned mall. No one expects to find a great space around each street corner, nor can we demand great architecture in view of every outdoor bench, but cities can and will vie with one another to offer attractive pedestrian experience.

In planning city squares, it may be useful to note the following characteristics found in most of the great squares included in this book.

Learning from the Great Squares

PLAN DIMENSIONS

In order to appreciate the good architecture that we can hope will envelop a fine square, its walls need to be at a comfortable distance, where they can be seen without craning one's neck, but not so far away that they are unreadable to the naked eye. Most of the spaces in this book begin to turn from a wide street to a narrow square at about 200 feet (60 meters). Beyond 500 feet (150 meters), the details that give its walls their scale have disappeared. These dimensions are balanced in a square square, stretched with some tension up to the proportion of one to five, and beyond that constitute more a boulevard than a space.

HEIGHT

Rockefeller Plaza demonstrates that no outdoor room can be too high; most failures are too low. Old Europe surrounded its pre-elevator spaces with three- and four-story walk-ups (about 50 feet or 15 meters high). With one's back to such a wall, the top of the other side of the square will be at a comfortable 25 degrees above the eye at a distance of just over 100 feet (30 meters) away. This proportion of 2:1—width to height—is not a bad norm with which to start. Many of the squares in this book range from 3 or 4 to 1. At 10 to 1, St. Peter's is more like a ballpark; Bernini tried unsuccessfully to convince the pope to pay for a two-story arcade. The upper part of any building wall that is above 25 degrees contributes little to its role as enclosure.

FAÇADE MATERIAL

Uniformity (Place des Vosges) has been just as successful as harmonious complexity (Old Town, Prague) in rendering a square whole, but the latter is both more difficult and more rewarding.

ROADWAYS

It is best to keep vehicles outside, or at least off to the edges and moving slowly.

PAVEMENT

The variety of pattern, texture, color, and finish that are to be found in the central part of many a square's "floor" suggest that its composition is a great challenge for the imagination of its designers and plays a very important role in bringing the space together. Grass requires more care than hardscape but it allows for a greater variety in use and is "friendly" to people.

FURNITURE

Fountains and sculpture, chairs and benches, cafés and music stands all enhance the pleasure and usefulness of urban rooms.

ARCADES

There has never been a square whose usefulness was not enhanced by covered walkways. They're obviously not absolutely necessary but should always be considered. Santa Fe didn't really have a plaza until it added its *portales* in 1966. The fear of criminals hiding behind columns in the 1980s seems to have faded away.

MONUMENTAL BUILDINGS

Architecture has always had a dominant role to play in urban space, but the power can be positive or negative. Rittenhouse Square in Philadelphia has been ruined by tall, nondescript apartment houses and office buildings. The small, elegant space that Mies van der Rohe put in front of the Seagram Building worked as a gate in the unbroken wall of Park Avenue until Citicorp tried to share the glory next door by extending the break. There are centuries of squares that relied upon simple, repetitive, rhythmic façades that seem to belong to the space rather than the occupants behind, and this magic is easily replicated.

TREES

The "emptiness" that many consider the essential mark of a square has become a point of debate in modern times. The spaces originally reserved for jousting matches, royal weddings, and public meetings would be largely useless if open only to activities that have died away. Markets continue in force and green markets are making a comeback, but their umbrellas risk crowding space. Boston's City Hall plaza was praised for its wide-open urban setting, but the same citizens chose not to use its windy, barren surface. So trees have taken over more often than not and most of them work very well, cooling the space in the summer and letting the warm sun enter in winter. Still, the purists are unhappy.

PEDESTRIANS

The marvelous thing about squares is that the very reason they are made provides for their own success. The more people in a square, the better it feels. No one complains about crowding at San Marco. But the simplicity of the goal belies the difficulty of achieving it. More and better urban spaces will be needed in the very near future as society reorganizes itself all over the world, and we know from the successes that it can be done. It is a worthy aim.

Key to Colors and Textures Used in the Drawings

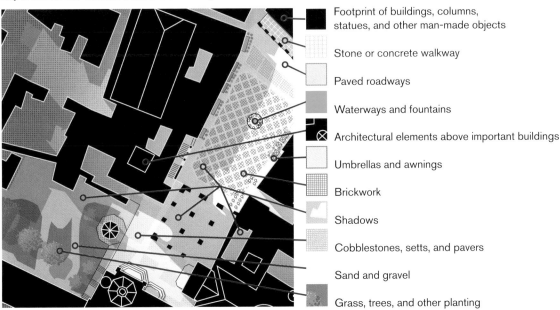

Footprint of buildings, columns, statues, and other man-made objects

Stone or concrete walkway

Paved roadways

Waterways and fountains

Architectural elements above important buildings

Umbrellas and awnings

Brickwork

Shadows

Cobblestones, setts, and pavers

Sand and gravel

Grass, trees, and other planting

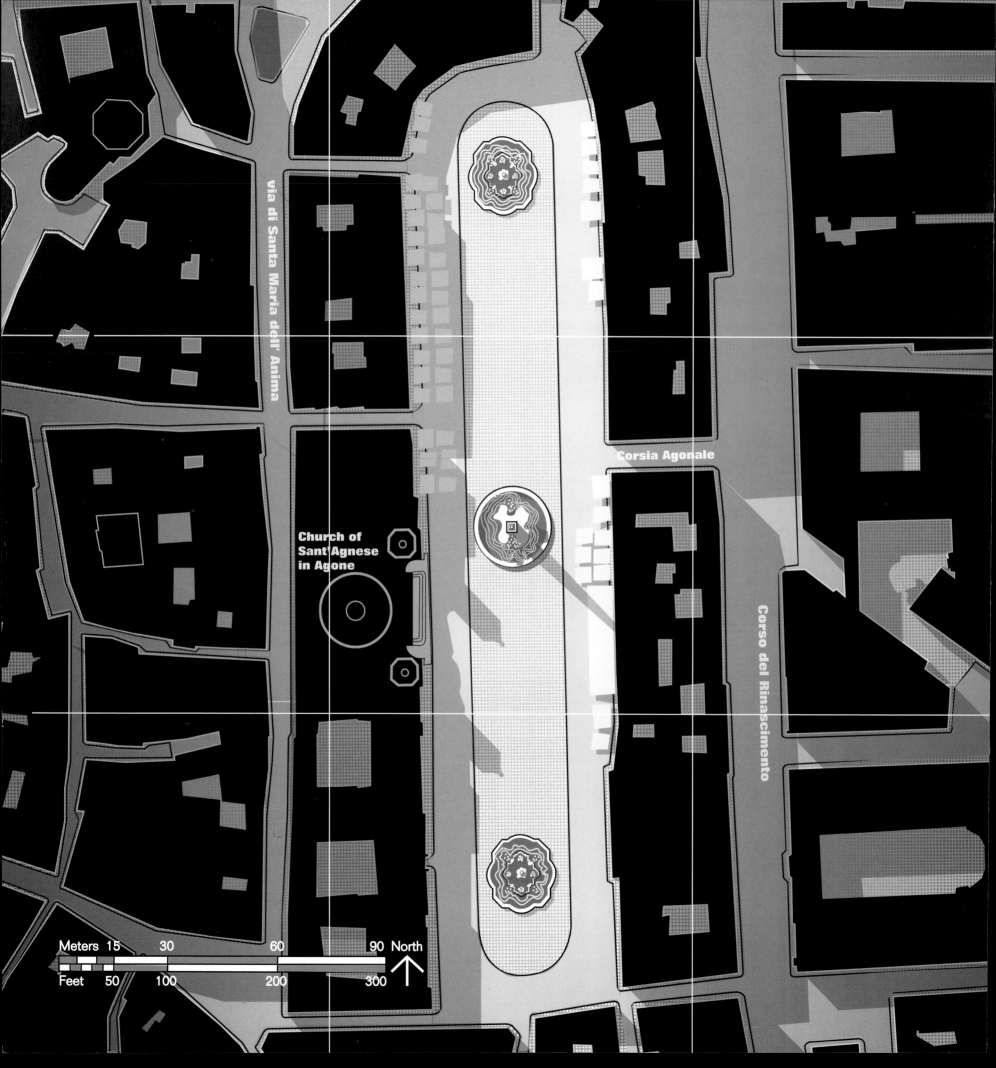

via di Santa Maria dell' Anima

Corsia Agonale

Corso del Rinascimento

**Church of
Sant'Agnese
in Agone**

Meters 15   30   60   90   North

Feet   50   100   200   300

PIAZZA NAVONA

Rome

PLAN DIMENSIONS	RATIO OF WIDTH TO LENGTH	AREA	TYPICAL HEIGHT TO SKYLINE	HIGHEST POINT	RATIO OF WIDTH TO SKYLINE HEIGHT	ANGLE OF VIEW FROM THE SHORT SIDE TO THE SKYLINE	KEY DATE
180 × 845 ft (55 × 257 m)	1 to 5	3.5 acres (1.4 ha)	65 ft (20 m)	145 ft (45 m), pinnacle of Sant'Agnese church dome	3 to 1	20°	85 A.D., construction of Domitian's circus

Source of drawing data: Cadastral maps from the city of Rome and Kidder-Smith, *Italy Builds*

Though not unique, the great oval urban space that is the Piazza Navona is sufficiently unusual to startle the first-time visitor, particularly if you arrive from the east after the short walk from the Piazza della Rotonda (see page 22). As the crowded Corsia Agonale opens into the square's east side, you look across its center toward a quite uniform row of four- and five-story houses with façades in various Roman earth tones. A few paces more and you see an obelisk, seeming to float in the air, prepared to shoot up to the sky against the backdrop of a church with a distinctive concave façade. Then the great arms of the piazza embrace you from left and right and guide you onto a vast stage.

1 Bernini's Fountain of the Four Rivers and Borromini's church of Sant' Agnese behind it are the first elements to greet one approaching the piazza from the east. 2 The fountain astounded Romans by seeming to support an ancient obelisk "in thin air." 3 Two of Bernini's rivers—the Ganges and the Nile—are prominently studied from the sidewalk cafés. 4 The Rio de la Plata is represented at another corner. 5 The Danube flanks the obelisk at the fourth.

The Piazza Navona is one of the most admired and enjoyable of urban spaces—not just in Rome but in the entire world. A slow walk around its third-of-a-mile (half-kilometer) track provides a wall of wonder that is always moving away or coming closer. The piazza we see today is the work of two giants of the Baroque, Borromini and Bernini, who show us in this space just about everything we need to know about art, stone, and negative space.

The shape of the piazza derives from its original purpose. In the fifth year of his reign, the Roman emperor Domitian (81–96 A.D.) ordered built on this spot a *circus*—a stadium for athletic competitions and other spectacles for a crowd of thirty thousand; remnants of the ancient ticket booth are still on view below street level at the north end of the piazza. The space has been a circus ever since. In the Middle Ages it served as a marketplace for produce, which, in turn, drew jugglers, actors, and singers for a welcoming audience. Architecture and sculpture appeared in the seventeenth century, but to this day you still find the place alive with descendants of those medieval performers, plus artists and vendors in fairground-style tents. While all this mêlée gets in the way of architectural photography, it certainly meets the expectations of happy crowds.

ROME

North

Meters 300 600 900
Feet 1000 2000 3000

Castello di
SAN ANGELO

Piazza di
SPAGNA

Piazza di
SAN PIETRO

Piazza della
ROTONDA

Piazza NAVONA

Piazza FARNESE &
Campo de' FIORE

Piazza del
CAMPIDOGLIO

The most important structures on the piazza's rim went up during the 1600s. At mid-century, Pope Innocent X, a son of the powerful Pamphili family, commissioned a church dedicated to Rome's martyred Saint Agnes on the piazza's western edge next to his family's palazzo. The church of Sant'Agnese in Agone (from the Greek *agon*, meaning contest) was begun by others and completed by Francesco Borromini (1599–1667), a great architect and a great friend of the pope. The church's principal contribution to the square is its concave façade. Some observers say it was shaped this way to enhance the visibility of its dome. Others are content to note the power of the concavity as welcoming churchgoers at an entry. In either case, the church of Sant'Agnese, with its towers and dome, is the major event in the otherwise repetitious façades that surround the square.

The great Borromini competed for a commission to design fountains for the center of the piazza, but he lost out to his rival, the even greater Gian Lorenzo Bernini (1595–1680). While the Piazza Navona is honored for many features, its principal attraction is Bernini's three fountains—particularly the central Fountain of the Four Rivers (*Fontana dei Fiumi*). The rivers represented here symbolize four continents: the Danube, Europe; the Nile, Africa; the Ganges, Asia; and the Rio de la Plata, South America. Most fountains shoot their waters straight up, but Bernini made the water rush out toward us, then splash into basins. What does point upward, at the fountain's center, is a Roman imitation of an Egyptian obelisk carved in the time of Domitian.

In the view of the eminent historian Simon Schama, Bernini's Fountain of the Four Rivers "was surely the greatest water spectacle in any urban space in Europe: the ultimate consummation, not merely of papal Rome's hydraulic revival, but of the entire tradition of fluvial vitality." The water here and elsewhere in Rome still comes from the *Acqua Vergine*, a network of aqueducts that starts in the Alban hills east of the city and runs through most of Rome. It continues to supply many of the city's waterworks with pure drinking water under enough pressure to make the fountains work with splendor.

North and south of the fountain are two other fountains by Bernini and his followers that are of lesser importance: the fountains of Neptune and of a Moor. On hot summer days, children and adults welcome the spray and play in the basins. But even in winter the Piazza Navona is alive with the constant motion of people and water.

1 Three modest villas are carefully placed behind the northern fountain and serve to round that end of the square with strength and dignity. 2 The southwest corner of the square is visually "closed" behind a Moor fighting a dolphin and young Romans gaining summer relief from the waters at its base. 3 Neptune's fountain to the north is not by Bernini and was only completed in the nineteenth century. 4 The oval space sweeps around past Neptune and the central obelisk to close at the far southeast corner. 5 The northeast corner is closed by the way that two streets behind Neptune head off on separate diagonals. 6 Sant'Agnese dominates the western wall as it clasps the space.

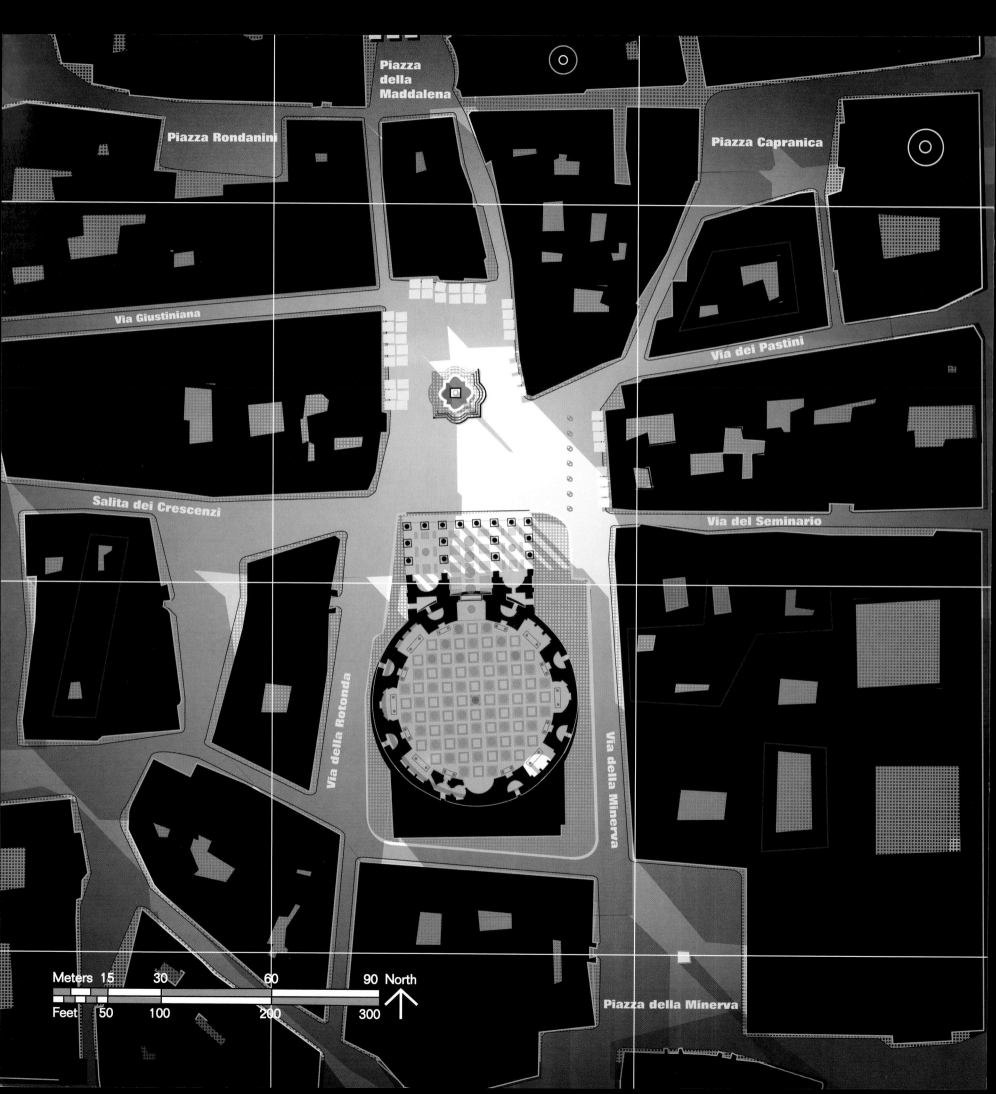

Piazza della Maddalena

Piazza Rondanini

Piazza Capranica

Via Giustiniana

Via dei Pastini

Salita dei Crescenzi

Via del Seminario

Via della Rotonda

Via della Minerva

Meters 15   30   60   90 North

Feet   50   100   200   300

Piazza della Minerva

PIAZZA DELLA ROTONDA

Rome

PLAN DIMENSIONS	RATIO OF WIDTH TO LENGTH	AREA	TYPICAL HEIGHT TO SKYLINE	HIGHEST POINT	RATIO OF WIDTH TO SKYLINE HEIGHT	ANGLE OF VIEW FROM THE SHORT SIDE TO THE SKYLINE	KEY DATE
200 × 220 ft (61 × 67 m)	1 to 1 (approx. square)	1 acre (0.4 ha)	65 ft (20 m)	150 ft (45 m), top of the Pantheon dome	3 to 1	18°	120 A.D., Hadrian's reconstruction of the Pantheon

Source of drawing data: Novelli, ed., *Atlante di Roma*

Most visitors head toward the beautiful Piazza della Rotonda to see the Pantheon, the onetime Roman temple to "all gods" (from the Greek *pan theon*) that dominates the square on the south. The praise that we direct to the piazza in no way diminishes the fame and power of the greatest ancient Roman building still standing. It and its piazza make a perfect pair. Because the Pantheon brought the square into being and draws throngs to it day after day, our story must begin with the building itself.

Construction of the Pantheon started with serious logistic problems. It was begun, around 27 B.C., on soft, marshy land by the then-consul (later, emperor) Marcus Agrippa. It was ravaged by fire many times, starting within decades of its completion. Emperor Hadrian (76–138 A.D.) had the building completely redesigned and rebuilt between 118 and 128 A.D. He may have had doubts about its long-term stability—that is at least one theory as to why he had Agrippa's name and not his own inscribed over the entrance. In 609, Pope Boniface IV had the Pantheon consecrated as a church, which it remains today.

Hadrian's engineers took their time, either by choice or by necessity, in creating the largest unreinforced concrete dome ever built. Using aggregates of varying weights and concrete of differing thicknesses, and paying careful attention to any cracks that appeared, the Roman designers and builders accomplished an extraordinary feat of construction. The Pantheon's shallow dome represents part of the upper half of a globe, of which the imagined lower half fits neatly within the simple cylindrical drum that forms the body of the building (hence the nickname *rotonda*, meaning "round" in Italian). The sum is a building of remarkable power and grandeur.

The exterior, as indicated by lingering remnants of the original façade, was once covered in polychrome marble, but it didn't need such decoration. The long Roman bricks we see today, especially as they define the relieving arches needed to bear some of the thick walls' weight, define a tectonic cylinder of subtle complexity.

If the Pantheon draws crowds to the piazza, its splendid interior can claim much of the credit. The clear internal dimensions—horizontal and vertical—are each 142 feet (43 meters). The architectural details inside the drum are grand, and they bring its scale and surface down to the floor. The sky, seen through the dome's 30-foot (9-meter)-wide eye, or *oculus*, draws the eye up and out. Rectilinear coffers radiate down from the concrete band surrounding the oculus and give it a three-dimensional scale all its own, as opposed to the painted plaster of most other domes. There is a sense of reality and conviction in the recognition that it's the actual inner skin of the dome and the drum that we are looking at—that it is shaped and sized by the outer structural limits of unreinforced, compression concrete as designed by engineers almost two thousand years ago.

Leaving the Pantheon through a pair of bronze doors 21 feet (6.5 meters) high, you cross a portico that looks like an afterthought and was, indeed, rebuilt after it was moved from the south side of the original temple in its reconstruction. While the Pantheon was settling into its marshy site, the ground around it was raised by building atop twenty centuries of accumulated debris. This makes for the unusual experience of climbing up out of an important building. Because the portico faces north it is almost always in shadow, which makes photography difficult and results, for some, in a Darth Vader sort of presence.

When you come up into the sunshine you find yourself in a space that is quite similar in size to the one you've just left. Straight ahead stands a fountain with an obelisk; this one, from Heliopolis and carved to honor the pharaoh Rameses II, is one of eleven ancient Egyptian obelisks carried back by victorious Roman armies that still stand in the city. (Roman stonecutters added a good half dozen imitations to the city's inventory of "Egyptian" obelisks, including the one in the Piazza Navona.) This obelisk was not always here; in 1711 Pope Clement IX had it moved from elsewhere to the center of an existing fountain. There is something just right about the fountain and its surrounding structures. Narrow, bending streets on all sides contain its space, and the piazza's feeling of enclosure was recently enhanced by the prohibition of vehicular traffic.

Michelangelo is widely quoted as having proclaimed the already 1,350-year-old Pantheon "angelic and not of human design." Today, it remains, by all odds, the best-preserved of the great Roman buildings and the most enjoyable to enter. The Piazza della Rotonda forms a splendid setting. Despite its dark aspect, the Pantheon is a welcoming monument and a friendly building to have over your shoulder while you sit by the fountain or at a café or just walk through the square on your way to the Piazza Navona a short distance away.

PIAZZA DELLA ROTONDA

25

1 The break in the eastern side heading toward the Via dei Pastini keeps the space from leaking out as if with a hand clasp. 2 The Pantheon catches some sun in the late afternoon, but it looms over the piazza as a dark presence. 3 Leaving the church through its bronze doors and marble columns, the sunlight on the piazza beyond is a physical and emotional shock. 4 This modest side door set today in the Pantheon's unadorned brick-work speaks with the noble power of ancient bronze and careful relieving arches. 5 Toward the end of the Pentecost mass, twenty thousand rose petals float down from the oculus. 6 The approach from the Maddalena on the north provides one of the few direct views of the Pantheon.

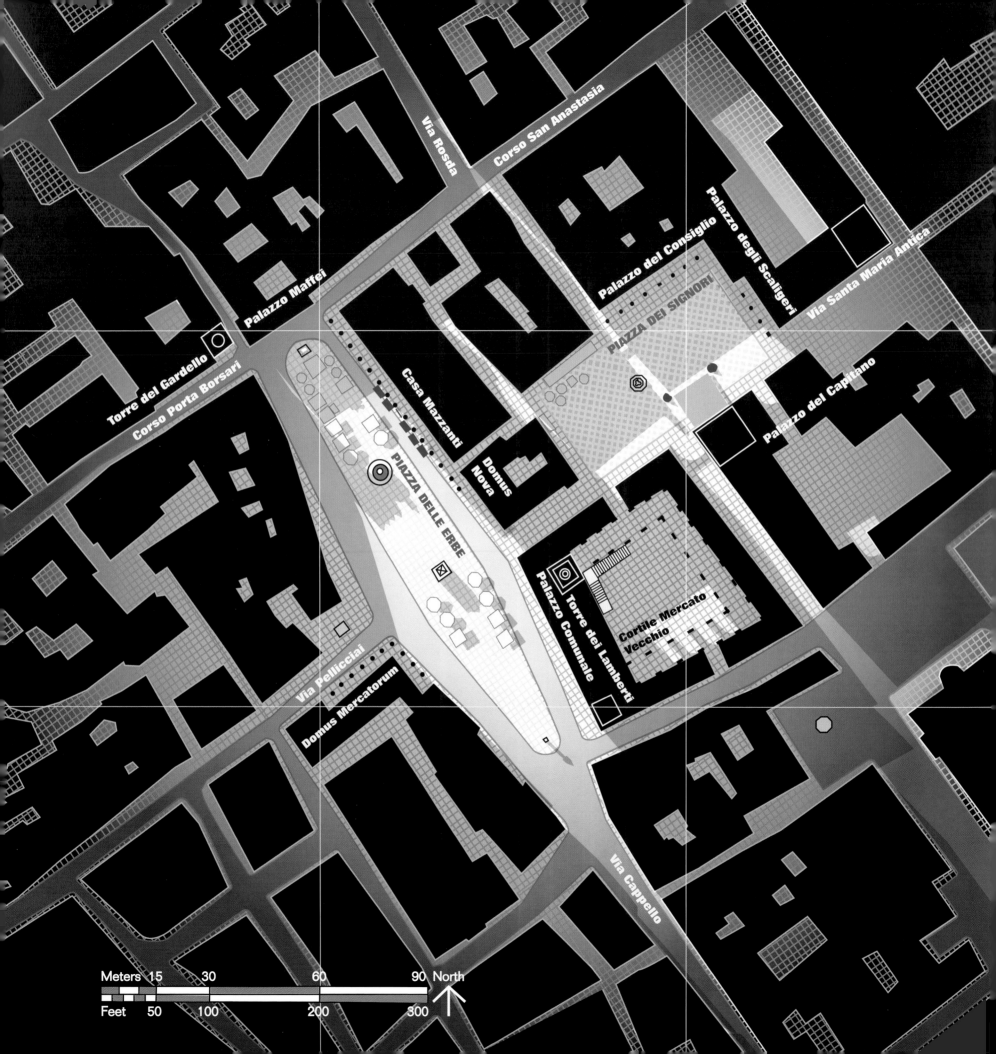

Via Rosda

Corso San Anastasia

Palazzo del Consiglio

Palazzo degli Scaligeri

Via Santa Maria Antica

PIAZZA DEI SIGNORI

Palazzo Maffei

Torre del Gardello

Corso Porta Borsari

Casa Mazzanti

Domus Nova

Palazzo del Capitano

PIAZZA DELLE ERBE

Torre dei Lamberti
Palazzo Comunale

Cortile Mercato
Vecchio

Via Pellicciai

Domus Mercatorum

Via Cappello

Meters 15 30 60 90 North

Feet 50 100 200 300

PIAZZA DELLE ERBE AND PIAZZA DEI SIGNORI
Verona

PLAN DIMENSIONS	RATIO OF WIDTH TO LENGTH	AREA	TYPICAL HEIGHT TO SKYLINE	HIGHEST POINT	RATIO OF WIDTH TO SKYLINE HEIGHT	ANGLE OF VIEW FROM THE SHORT SIDE TO THE SKYLINE	KEY DATE
138 x 475 ft (42 x 145 m); 118 × 210 ft (36 × 64 m)	1 to 3; 1 to 2	1.4 acres (0.5 ha); 0.6 acres (0.2 ha)	65 ft (20 m); 50 ft (15 m)	285 ft (90 m), peak of the Lamberti tower	2 to 1; 2 to 1	25° (Erbe) 22° (Signori)	1172, start of construction on the Lamberti Tower

Sources of drawing data: Cadastral maps from the city of Verona; Gromort, *Choix des Plans de Grandes Compositions Exécutées*); and Google Earth

Even with all the fine squares in Italy, no spatial experience matches the drama of walking through the piazzas and courtyards of the historic center of Verona. Close to each other but not touching, the Piazza delle Erbe and the Piazza dei Signori together provide a singular experience that is extraordinary for its complexity and diversity. Given the difficulty in linking one urban space to another, the success with which the edges of these two squares are joined is remarkable. The intertwining space gives the visitor an incredibly vivid sense of spatial compression and explosion.

1 The eastern wall of the Piazza delle Erbe is seen from the northwest corner—dominated by the great Torre dei Lamberti. 2 The Berlina shrine at the center was used for ceremonies and safeguarded the market units of measurement. 3 Entering the Piazza della Erbe from the south, one sees a long composition of wildly variable elements. 4 The murals of the Casa Mazzanti are used to enhance the beauty of the square. 5 A fascinating combination of colorful façades makes up the western side of the Piazza della Erbe. 6 The Torre dei Lamberti is one of the best in the world and serves to dramatize the knuckle in the spatial shape. 7 The Piazza della Erbe is seen in Lamberti's shadow from the top of its tower. 8 The square is closed at its south end by the Lion of St. Mark in front of the Palazzo Maffei and the Torre del Gardello.

The Piazza delle Erbe lies on the site of an ancient Roman forum, but it takes its present lozenge shape from a series of distinguished buildings that have defined it since the twelfth century. (Not far from here stands the house where, as legend has it, Juliet gave her heart to Romeo.) The oldest structure bordering the present square is the beautiful Torre dei Lamberti, begun in 1172. Building the tower took so long—almost three centuries—that it acquired the stylistic features of several eras. At the top, the enclosure of its two great bells was completed in 1464 in a style that is unmistakably Renaissance. The tower's base, however, has the distinctive Romanesque cladding of striped courses of red brick and white tufa, a soft calcite stone much used by the Romans and still seen throughout northern Italy. One theory holds that this banding provides earthquake protection; another, that it helps resist rising ground dampness. I suspect, though, that it was used here and in the neighboring squares at least partly for its good looks.

The tower marks one corner of the great Palazzo Comunale (city hall), an edifice with medieval origins. The palazzo served as Verona's administrative building through its centuries as a city-state. The building's outer façades have been resurfaced to suit its importance as a governmental center at different times in different styles. Today it presents a nineteenth-century neoclassical façade.

Counterbalancing the august purpose of the Palazzo Comunale, great umbrellas open in front of it six days a week, and the Piazza delle Erbe continues its longtime use as Verona's bustling market. Everyday commerce gives the space joyous legitimacy. So much noisy, historic vitality would have been enough to mark this corner of Verona as a place of honor and delight.

Beyond the Palazzo Comunale, where the edge of the square takes a slight but significant bend to the west, stands the Casa Mazzanti, still covered in sixteenth-century frescoes. Its welcome arcade ends at the beautiful Palazzo Maffei, which has closed the north end of the square since the eighteenth century with a white marble and stucco façade that dresses up its medieval origins. Next to it is the fourteenth-century Torre del Gardello. At the western hinge of the long lozenge, where the Via Pellicciai enters, appears the Domus Mercatorum, a fine brick-and-stone Romanesque building that was redecorated in the nineteenth century and given a Gothic look with a crown of merlons (the solid, square part of a battlement).

A fountain, column, and public shrine ornament the spine of this magnificent square, but you can hardly see them on any day but Sunday. That's when the sea of market umbrellas is neatly folded up and the crowds

PIAZZA DELLE ERBE AND PIAZZA DEI SIGNORI

31

1 Here one is looking west along the Via Peliccial from the Lamberti above. 2 The Piazza dei Signori is approached through this "tight" archway. 3 The "whalebone arch" provides a connection of remarkable spatial compression between the two squares. 4 The Palazzo degli Scaligeri housed ruthless rulers. 5 The Palazzi del Consiglio and degli Scaligeri meet behind the statue of Dante. 6 The northwest wing of the Palazzo Comunale faces the piazza with its original splendid striping of tufa and brick. 7 The southwest side of the Piazza dei Signori is closed by a composition of three arches that meld two passages and a doorway. 8 The Torre dei Lamberti rises from within the Cortile Mercato Vecchio. 9 One leaves the Piazza dei Signori at its northeast corner along the Via Santa Maria Antica.

of sellers and buyers disperse. Otherwise, the overactive Piazza delle Erbe prompts you to explore what urban treasures lie nearby.

Two arches define a short passage alongside the Palazzo Comunale: the link to the dignified Palazzo dei Signori. The spatial compression of passing from one square to the other—from noise to quiet, chaos to order, popular to exclusive—is one of Italy's urban triumphs. At first glance there is not much in the second square to attract the visitor's gaze—some elegant houses built for Verona's ruthless governing families of centuries past (the signori, or lords, for whom the square is named); a lonely statue of Dante, who lived here in exile for thirteen years; and an informal stage. But on careful examination, the care that went into composing the Piazza dei Signori reveals itself.

The north side of the Palazzo Comunale, which forms the square's south side, retains its original striped façade. Like all the buildings on this square, it is linked—in this case, by an archway—to its neighbor, the Palazzo del Capitano, where Verona's mayors lived during the sixteenth century. Part of the Palazzo Comunale was designed by the only big-name architect to have worked here: Michele Sanmicheli (1485–1559). The Palazzo degli Scaligeri, the house of the della Scala family that ruled Verona on and off for two centuries, makes up the square's entire east side. A very fine marble palace for the city council, the Palazzo del Consiglio, dominates the square's north side. It has been attributed to Fra Giovanni Giocondo (1433–1515), a Dominican monk and obviously an excellent architect.

The principal surprise of the Piazza dei Signori comes when you look back toward its two-part entrance. Before you now is the façade of the Domus Nova, which features a powerful trio of arches—two leading back to the Piazza delle Erbe and the central one leading to the home of the podestà, Verona's magistrate.

In the south corner of the square, one more arch leads into the Cortile del Mercato Vecchio—the courtyard of the Palazzo Comunale, where the old market once flourished. A fine staircase leads to the Torre dei Lamberti and its modern elevator. The top of the tower affords a splendid view of all that surrounds it. This three-dimensional spiral of space—Erbe to Signori to tower—is an urban composition without precedent or equal.

PIAZZA DELLE ERBE AND PIAZZA DEI SIGNORI

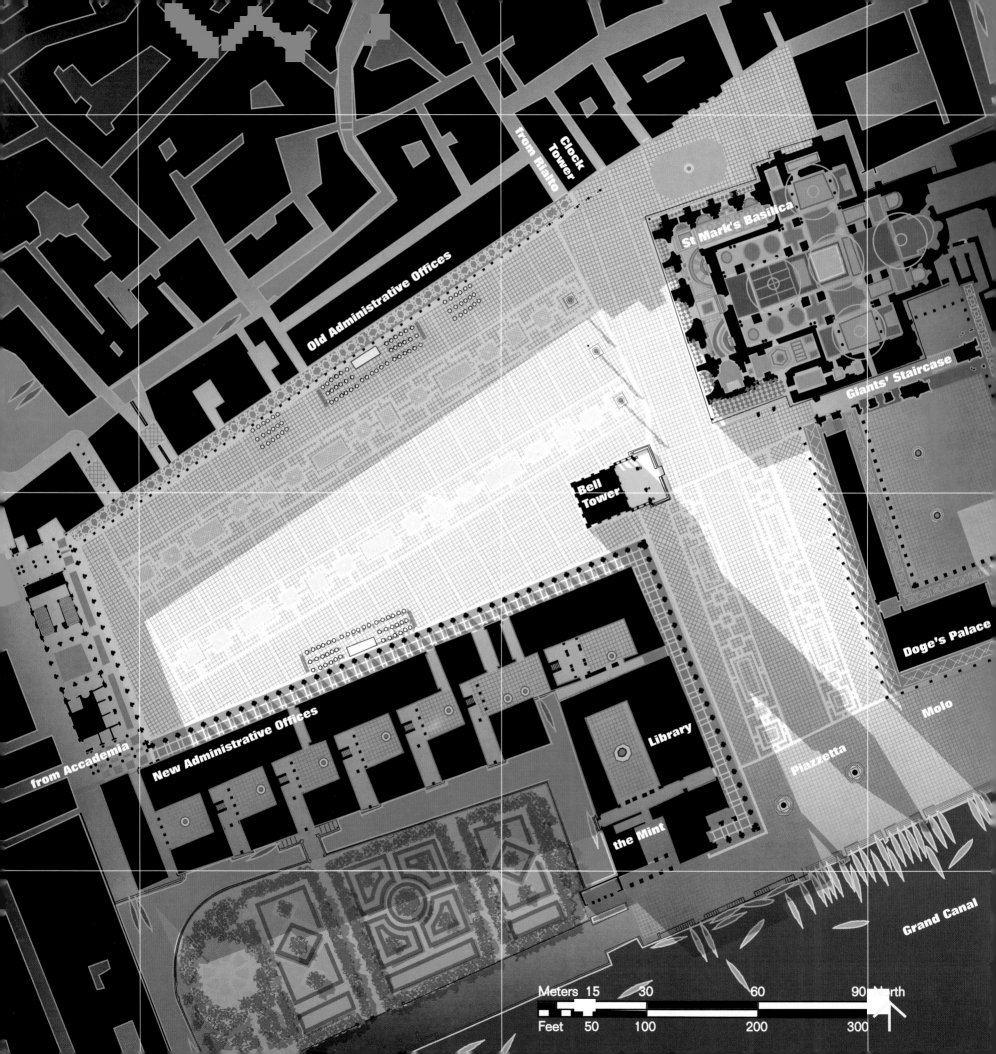

Clock Tower

from Rialto

Old Administrative Offices

St Mark's Basilica

Giants' Staircase

Bell Tower

Doge's Palace

Molo

from Accademia

New Administrative Offices

Library

Piazzetta

the Mint

Grand Canal

Meters 15   30   60   90 North

Feet   50   100   200   300

PIAZZA SAN MARCO AND THE PIAZZETTA
Venice

PLAN DIMENSIONS	RATIO OF WIDTH TO LENGTH	AREA	TYPICAL HEIGHT TO SKYLINE	HIGHEST POINT	RATIO OF WIDTH TO SKYLINE HEIGHT	ANGLE OF VIEW FROM THE SHORT SIDE TO THE SKYLINE	KEY DATE
230 × 560 ft (70 × 171 m); 160 × 290 ft (48 × 88 m)	1 to 2; 1 to 2	3 acres (1.3 ha); 1 acre (0.4 ha)	80 ft (25 m); 80 ft (25 m)	285 ft (90 m), peak of the campanile	3 to 1; 2 to 1	20°; 27°	1063, start of construction of the present basilica

Source of drawing data: Gromort, *Choix des Plans*

The Piazza San Marco, the city square that Napoleon called Europe's most beautiful drawing room, sits on one of the largest, lowest islands in the Venetian lagoon. You can reach the piazza easily in one of three ways: by water, in a gondola or vaporetto (water bus) that deposits you on the Molo of the Grand Canal; on foot via the Rialto Bridge that leads you under the clock tower; or by walking through a winding passage from the Gallerie dell'Accademia that requires you to find your way along a tortuous route from the west and stumble onto a never-to-be-forgotten framed view that includes a corner of the Basilica di San Marco, the base of its bell tower, and a glimpse of its next-door neighbor, the Doge's Palace. As you move into the piazza, the space explodes around you as though you've emerged from a tunnel. If you really want to impress someone, try this by moonlight.

North

VENICE

Meters 100   200   300

Feet   1000

Campo dei
**SANTI GIOVANNI
E PAOLO**

RIALTO BRIDGE

Piazza SAN MARCO

As can be seen more clearly in the plan than in actually being there, the north and south sides of the piazza are not parallel. Like the Campidoglio or Saint Peter's in Rome (see pages 82 and 90–91), the trapezoidal space plays tricks in perspective. Unlike the Baroque designers who chose the trapezoid for optical effect, the architects of San Marco were only lining up the columned sides as best they could. Rather than an enhancing or enlarging effect, the spreading of the north and south sides toward the east shrinks the apparent size of the great basilica. It looks more like an amazing jewel box than a Byzantine monument of the world's most powerful eleventh-century city-state. By contrast, if you look back from the steps of the basilica, a kind of reverse perspective exaggerates the length of the square.

Near the basilica's front steps, the huge grouping of golden archways, marble columns, and fantastic domes with their finials is more than overwhelming. But from the point of view of spatial analysis, the basilica serves principally as the east and north sides of two very complicated interlocking spaces. Before we can even begin to understand the splendid spaces, we need to examine the eight architectural masterpieces that define them.

The basilica that now stands here is the third church dedicated to Saint Mark erected on this spot; fire consumed both predecessors. Construction of the great church began in 1063 and was completed in 1094. Its purpose was to serve as the church of Venice's ruling duke, the doge, when Venice was approaching the peak of its power. The new basilica represents Venice's link to Byzantium and was based on the Church of the Holy Apostles in Constantinople (long since demolished and replaced with a mosque). Accordingly, its floor plan is the Greek cross, and it has five domes. Over time, it was enriched with fabulous mosaics, marble skin, and sculpture, including the famous four bronze horses.

The residence and offices of the doge had occupied the present palace site for centuries, since well before the new church was erected. Along with the square itself, the Doge's Palace took its present form around 1176. It was reshaped and resurfaced in connection with a general enlargement of the square made possible by the filling and rearrangement of several existing canals.

The south and west façades of this splendid palace serve principally to counterbalance the mass of the basilica in architectonic terms. Their use as a pair is apparent in the near-parallel placement of their western façades, separated by a narrow slot. This tense space between the two leads to and up a white marble staircase, the Scala dei Giganti (Giants' Staircase), more

38

1 The very significant "notch" between St. Mark's and the ducal palace leads to the Scala dei Giganti (Giants' Staircase) but was principally designed to dramatically separate the two monumental buildings. 2 Most of the beautiful buildings that make up the Piazza San Marco can be seen from afar on the Grand Canal. 3 The façade of the Doge's Palace is a unique composition of Venetian Gothic décor on the structure of a Romanesque building. 4 Entering the Piazza San Marco through the Piazzetta, the campanile, the clock tower, and the basilica are framed between the library on the left and the Doge's Palace on the right.

famous for the white giants at its foot than its function in giving access to the upper level of the palace courtyard. The unifying façade of the Doge's Palace is set back slightly from the front of the basilica so that the latter's opulence can serve as an invitation to worshippers approaching from the lagoon. The powerful pair not only make up the eastern face of the piazzas but also establish a directional grid that the rest of the space follows to a large extent.

The campanile—San Marco's great bell tower—marks the intersection of the two piazzas and has done triple duty—not only as a bell tower but also as a watchtower and lighthouse—for most of a millennium. It has fallen more than once, in part because of inadequate construction materials but also because of earthquakes. It took its present form only in 1912, after a disastrous collapse in 1902. Regardless of whether the campanile should be considered a pivot or a hinge, or just a vertical accent, as different writers have characterized it, it is certainly in the right spot, angled correctly, and with a height that speaks to all of Venice. But the tower's original designers don't get the credit for its key spatial role: the campanile was there first, and the other buildings grew up around it. So credit for the campanile's success in the piazza should properly go to the designers of its surroundings.

Jacopo Sansovino (1486–1579), certainly the best and best-known architect to have worked on the square, designed the two-story Biblioteca Marciana (Renaissance library) in 1536. He sited it almost parallel to the Doge's Palace, thereby creating a smaller entry square along the quay. He gave the Piazzetta di San Marco, best known simply as the Piazzetta (little square), a subtle perspective exaggeration that seems to some people to encourage the visitor to gaze across the lagoon toward the island church dedicated to Saint George (San Giorgio Maggiore) and designed by Andrea Palladio (1508–1580) in 1560. When Sansovino pushed the library, and also the zecca (mint), southward toward the lagoon, he was essentially saying to anyone strolling westward along the Molo, or quay, "This is the place to turn right." This directional signal is so strong that practically everyone overlooks the lovely garden cul-de-sac behind the mint.

Vincenzo Scamozzi completed the library after Sansovino's death and used the vocabulary of its façade to reface the Procuratie Nuove (new administrative offices), which turn from the piazzetta into the piazza. More important, he moved their façades back to clear the campanile, which had been attached, and added a third floor to give the south side of the square a presence appropriate to confronting the Procuratie Vecchie (old

administrative offices) on the north side. All this is perpendicular to the library and establishes the square's strongest corner.

Although most visitors remember that the piazza is surrounded on three sides by tall arcades, only the most observant detect its complexities, differences, and a few flaws. The north side was refinished in the late fifteenth century, but its three stories are rather low, and Scamozzi's three stories had to match the taller library. The west end, where a church had stood that was torn down in 1797 on orders from Napoleon, presented an architectural challenge: how to close the square with something that could intersect the differing heights of the north and south sides with dignity? Look at the two corners, and you can see the problem. The two-stories-with-frieze solution is rather weak, though probably not conspicuous to most observers.

Nor can much be said of the clock tower that stands at the entry to the square from the Rialto Bridge. Erected in 1499, it is generally considered to be out of scale with the arcade that it ends and the basilica whose colors it tries to match. But it does frame a view into the piazza, across the façade of the basilica and straight out through the Piazzetta, until San Giorgio Maggiore emerges, seemingly afloat on the lagoon.

Notwithstanding a few minor blemishes, the Piazza San Marco is a monument to imagination, respect, and great good luck. Considering the number of rulers who controlled it for ten centuries, it could easily have been ruined. But the square is a marvel of consistent quality shaped by careful addition and subtraction.

In plan, three orthogonal grids provide a powerful presence for their component parts. The basilica and palace determine the first. The second follows the Z-shaped arcade that takes its orientation from the campanile; these angles are separated by only six degrees—a difference that can barely be perceived on the ground but does establish a subtle tension. The third is the incredibly long arcade of the Procuratie Vecchie, twelve degrees off the opposing Procuratie Nuove—just enough to reveal an invisible human hand rather than a mechanical formula. The relationship between the opposing arcades is so strong that it can make a great cathedral look small and a longish square look endless.

Were these effects expected, or did they simply result from the designers having to make do with the irregularities they encountered? There is obviously a bit of both. But planners everywhere have been skewing grids ever since.

1 San Giorgio Maggiore sits on its island directly across the Grand Canal from the entry to the Piazzetta. 2 The northwest corner of the piazza, where three levels crash into two, presents an architectural problem that was not entirely solved. 3 The view of the basilica through one of the faraway western arches, next to its proud campanile, seems diminutive compared to its architectural importance. 4 The clock tower, with its moving bell ringers, is a popular but overdecorated favorite of the public.

3

41

Calle Larga G. Gallina

Fondamente dei Mendicanti

City Hospital

Rio dei Mendicanti

Church of Santi Giovanni e Paolo

Colleoni

Rio di San Marina

Rio di San Giovanni Laterano

Meters 15   30   60   90 North

50   100   200   300

CAMPO DEI SANTI GIOVANNI E PAOLO

Venice

PLAN DIMENSIONS	RATIO OF WIDTH TO LENGTH	AREA	TYPICAL HEIGHT TO SKYLINE	HIGHEST POINT	RATIO OF WIDTH BETWEEN BRIDGE AND CHURCH FAÇADE TO HEIGHT OF TOP	ANGLE OF VIEW FROM THE FOOT OF THE BRIDGE TO THE TOP OF THE CHURCH	KEY DATE
200 × 410 ft (60 × 125 m)	1 to 2	0.9 acres (0.4 ha)	50 ft (15 m)	105 ft (32 m), peak of roof over church nave	3 to 1	14°	1230, start of church construction

Source of drawing data: Cadastral map from the city of Venice building department

The Piazza San Marco is not the only great Venetian square. Somewhat off the beaten track, the L-shaped Campo dei Santi Giovanni e Paolo—named for two fourth-century martyrs (not apostles)—is best known to artists, architects, and art historians. The campo (field) is dominated by three major works of art: a huge church, a hospital (formerly a school), and one of the world's greatest equestrian statues. The spirit of this square is anchored in the orthogonal placement of its principal components, but the bulges and motion of its surfaces give it extraordinary life. Consider the campo as a sampler of parts, and then note how subtly the parts are distributed in the formation of a complex composition that hangs together in beautiful balance.

The church was begun on land donated to the Dominicans in 1230 by Doge Jacopo Tiepolo. After one or two false starts, "San Zanipolo," as the Venetians affectionately call Santi Giovanni e Paolo in their dialect, was finally consecrated in 1430. Its style is about as Gothic as anything ever built in Italy, and it is one of Venice's largest churches. In it are the tombs of twenty-five doges and paintings by such greats as Lorenzo Lotto, Titian, and Giovanni Bellini.

You can approach the campo from the nearest vaporetto stop just behind the city hospital, but it is best seen on axis along Calle Larga G. Gallina. From the bridge over the canal, the church seems to grow with your every step until it swells to life among its notable neighbors. The façade is a powerful composition of red brick trimmed in white stone with great round windows and a few pointed arches to establish its Gothic credentials. The square along its side is greatly enhanced by three round-ended chapels that shape the southern façade of the church.

From the bridge, a multicolored marble extravaganza comes into view, its elaborate arched ornamentation offseting the severity of the church. Begun in 1458, the sculptured wall originally formed the façade of one of a series of grand Venetian schools (Schola di San Marco). A fire in 1485 destroyed all but two of the original bas-reliefs, but a handful of able sculptors got to work, and by 1495 they had reestablished the façade's sumptuous surface. Though its details are Renaissance in style, its spirit is Byzantine. Closed by Napoleon in 1797, the building itself was put to various uses, and today it serves as the city hospital. The façade has suited whatever use was made of the building; its eclectic collection of lions, figures, and architectural embellishments seems able to stand for anything.

When you look to the right past the south side of the church, the equestrian statue of Condottiere Bartolomeo Colleoni by Andrea Verrocchio (1435–1488) captures your gaze. The sculpture radiates such power and hauteur that it dominates its neighbors in controlling the space. Designed for a competition in 1481, the commission was Venice's way of keeping the money that the great mercenary captain had bequeathed to it. With the basilica in mind, the condottiere had asked for a monument to himself "in front of Saint Mark" (see page 45), but the city fathers could not accept that. So they changed the wording of his bequest to read: "in front of the Grand College of St. Mark." The Colleoni equestrian was completed after Verrocchio's death and was unveiled, in full gilded glory, in 1496. Unlike the Marcus Aurelius equestrian on Rome's Capitoline hill (see page 86), the Colleoni has appar-

ently never needed museum protection, and the original stands guard over the Campo dei Santi Giovanni e Paolo in a very imposing dark bronze.

San Zanipoli's square is little more than a yard bordered by a great church, a canal, and a pleasant row of cafés with typical Venetian houses behind them. In so small a space, the decoration can seem to overwhelm it— polychrome marble, Gothic tracery, a bronze horse with an armored rider, and of course the water. The Piazza San Marco uses much the same collection of parts but has a lot more volume to fill with its pieces. In both squares, the sum total is an assemblage of all that is good about Venice.

Being somewhat out of the way, the Campo dei Santi Giovanni e Paolo is usually quite calm—much quieter than its gigantic rival 2,000 feet (680 meters) away along a complex pattern of passages. After making its statement, the space within the campo seems to wander off in several directions—along the canal or down an alleyway and around some trees behind the church. Against the awesome grandeur of San Marco, the campo holds its own, demonstrating that Venice is fine enough to support two great squares.

1 Most visitors first see the church at the end of Calle Larga G. Gallina. 2 The extended space of the Campo funnels down between the church and the statue, past bulbous apses, and ends with a fine old tree. 3 The façade of the hospital with lions and entablatures crowned by arches and St. Mark's winged beast is almost too much for just one out-of-the-way square. 4 The true volume of the space is seen best from the bridge over a canal that marks it as Venice. 5 Verrocchio's great equestrian statue of Bartelomeo Colleoni stands next to the church. 6 The main components of the square come into view while crossing the Rio dei Mendicanti with the college/hospital on the left. 7 From the nearest vaporetto stop, one can approach the square alongside the hospital on the Fondamente dei Medicanti. 8 Water and granite, bridge and marble, church and statue make up a complex but balanced enclosure of space.

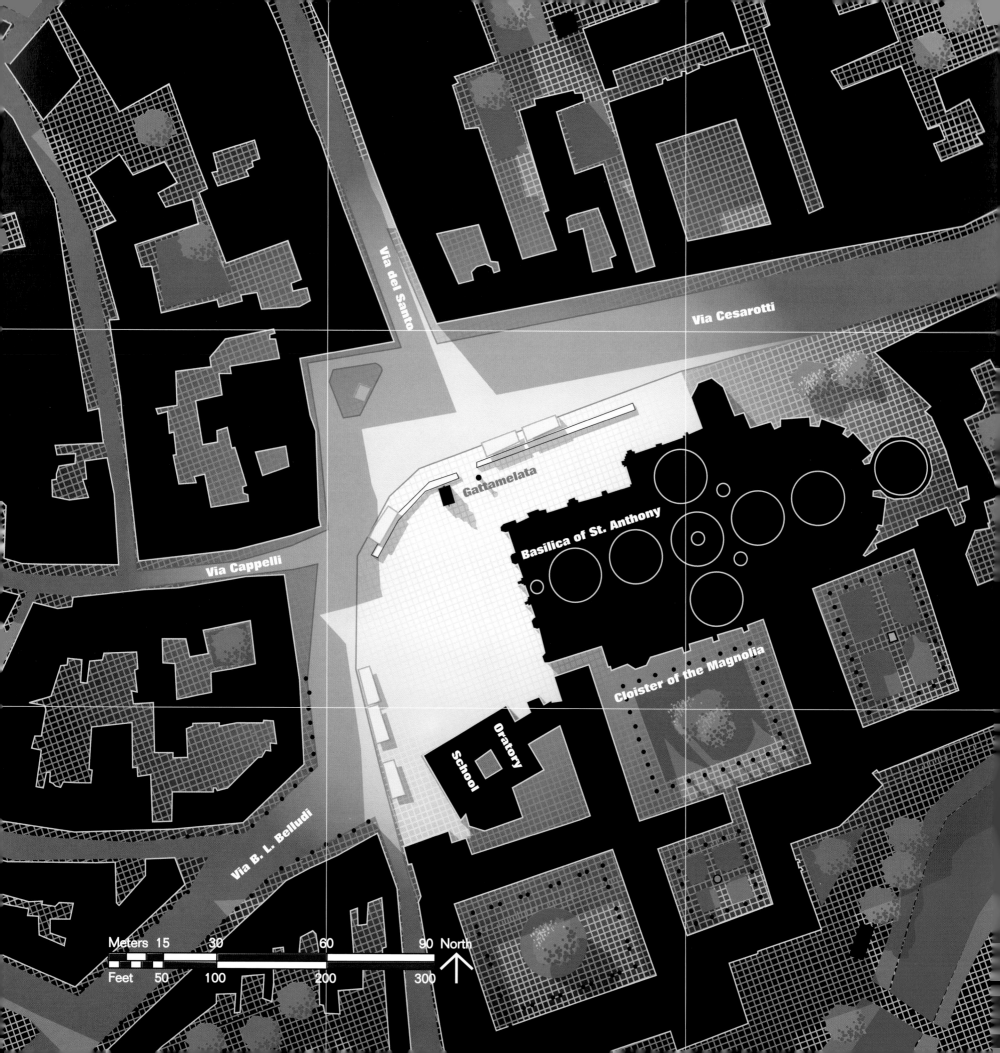

Via del Santo

Via Cesarotti

Via Cappelli

Gattamelata

Basilica of St. Anthony

Cloister of the Magnolia

Via B. L. Belludi

Oratory School

Meters 15 30 60 90 North

Feet 50 100 200 300

PIAZZA DEL SANTO

Padua

PLAN DIMENSIONS	RATIO OF WIDTH TO LENGTH	AREA	TYPICAL HEIGHT TO SKYLINE	HIGHEST POINT	RATIO OF WIDTH TO SKYLINE HEIGHT	ANGLE OF VIEW FROM ANY SIDE TO THE SKYLINE	KEY DATE
330 × 330 ft (100 × 100 m) in an L shape	1 to 1	2 acres (0.8 ha)	65 ft (20 m)	more than 230 ft (70 m), conical cupola of Sant'Antonio basilica	5 to 1	11°	1232, start of basilica construction

Source of drawing data: Cadastral material from the city of Padua and aerial photography from Google Earth

Many odd-shaped squares bypass a monumental building or grasp it on one side, and the Piazza del Santo in Padua is one of these. Its inclusion here is a tribute to Padua's beautiful basilica dedicated to St. Anthony—Sant'Antonio—and the lessons to be learned from the square's size and the placement of its thoroughfare. Particularly instructive is a comparison with the Campo dei Santi Giovanni e Paolo in Venice (see page 42). They were begun just two years apart—1230 (Venice) and 1232 (Padua); the Venetian square was consecrated two centuries later, while its cousin in Padua was under construction for about one hundred and twenty years. I think of them as virtually contemporaneous. Both are in the province of Veneto and just 32 miles (52 kilometers) apart, so their similarities can hardly be a surprise.

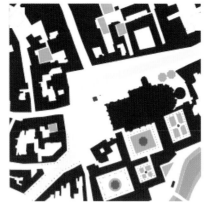

Santi Giovanni e Paolo in Venice   Piazza del Santo in Padua

In terms of architectural style, the two are much alike—blends of
Romanesque and Gothic—plus, in the case of the Piazza del Santo, a strong
flavor of the Byzantine. In fact, the basilica of Sant'Antonio, with its seven
cupolas—domed, pyramidal, and conical—atop a beautifully articulated set of
brick prisms, is one of the world's great ecclesiastical structures. Architectur-
ally, it beats the huge, heavy basilica on Venice's campo hands down. Both
churches back up against fine networks of cloisters and courtyards.

Each piazza is enclosed by a jumble of residential and institutional
structures. Padua's features the Oratory of San Giorgio and the Scuola del
Santo (admittedly no match for the Scuola di San Marco in Venice). The space
of each is bordered by the traffic of public transport. In Venice, gondoliers
slide by on the Mendicanti canal, while pedestrians can cross it on a beautiful
bridge. Those in Padua, however, must heed a traffic light and zebra crossing
to get across two busy streets.

Art historians often compare the two cities' equestrian statues:
Gattamelata (Padua, 1453) by Donatello and Colleoni (Venice, 1496) by Verrocchio. And both, in turn, have been compared to the great Roman equestrian
of Marcus Aurelius that stood, until 1538, in front of the papal church of
San Giovanni in Laterano in Rome. The asymmetrical placement of both
statues in their odd-shaped piazzas serves to animate their spaces.

Although the size and shape of the Padua and Venice squares are
comparable and diagrammed here at the same scale, they part company
when it comes to their sense of enclosure. The Venetian square is wrapped
neatly within its residential surroundings; its canal and walkways are
relatively narrow and bending, making the square a spatial event. But in
Padua modern-day traffic on the now-widened Via Cesarotti tears the
heart out of the Piazza del Santo and leaves it badly shattered, much like
the Place Vendôme in Paris (see pages 144–48).

1 Donatello's equestrian statue of Gattamelata is strong enough to anchor the space in front of Sant' Antonio. 2 There are two great reasons for being interested in Sant' Antonio: the statue of Gattamelata, on the left, and the fantastic church set at the back of the main square, which is otherwise determined by low walls and souvenir stands that barely shut out the traffic. 3 The main cloister behind the church is one of four that surround it and can be considered part of a system of space that encompasses its incredible complexity. Instead of one square, we are offered a total envelope sliced by low arcades. 4 Sant' Antonio's square is hemmed in by busy roads on two of its sides and amounts to a sort of double parvis.

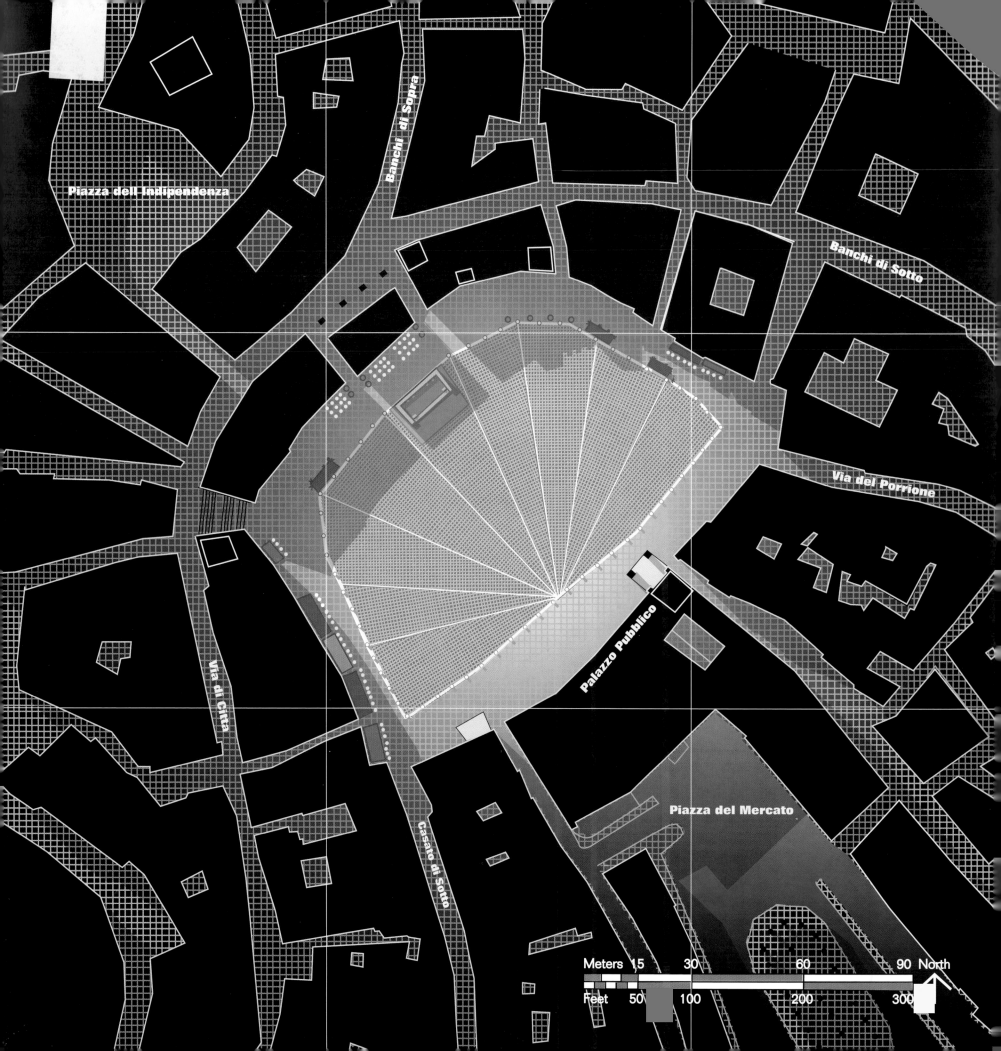

Piazza dell'Indipendenza

Banchi di Sopra

Banchi di Sotto

Via del Porrione

Via di Città

Palazzo Pubblico

Casato di Sotto

Piazza del Mercato

Meters 15   30   60   90 North

Feet 50   100   200   300

PIAZZA DEL CAMPO

Siena

PLAN DIMENSIONS	RATIO OF WIDTH TO LENGTH	AREA	TYPICAL HEIGHT TO SKYLINE	HIGHEST POINT	RATIO OF WIDTH TO SKYLINE HEIGHT	ANGLE OF VIEW FROM THE SHORT SIDE TO THE SKYLINE	KEY DATE
328 × 395 ft (100 × 120 m)	1 to 1 (approx. square)	2.9 acres (1.2 ha)	95 ft (30 m)	334 ft (102 m), top of Torre del Mangia	3 to 1	17°	1292, construction of square and component buildings

Source of drawing data: Cadastral maps from the city of Siena

Siena's Campo, meaning "field," formally called the Piazza del Campo, offers one of the most sculptural and rewarding urban experiences to be found anywhere in the world. Within this extraordinary, scallop-shell-shaped space hardly a line stands still. Every surface is either rising or falling, and always turning. Despite its great size, unique form, and restless visual vocabulary, the Campo manages to be in perfect harmony with the medieval city that surrounds it. A natural dip between several hills was transformed into this city square during a bellicose but remarkably productive century. The result testifies to the genius of human imagination and civic discipline. The Black Death of 1384 stopped the development of the Campo, and since then it has changed very little.

The space, at the junction of several roads entering Siena from farming communities on the surrounding hills, originally served as a marketplace. Its conversion into a town square began during an intense rivalry between Siena's ruling Ghibelline families and the Guelphs of Florence, and the design of the Campo reflects that competition in many of its visual elements: size of space, height of tower, and unity of composition. Demonstrating their civic stability, the Campo's size was big enough at the time to hold the city's entire populace for political events and festivals.

The most prominent building facing into the Campo is the Palazzo Pubblico, Siena's city hall. It is made up of four outsize stories topped by robust crenellation. The Palazzo's curious mixture of sturdy medieval Romanesque and delicate Gothic architectural detail surrounds the space in the façades of the noble palaces (Palazzi Signorili) on the Campo's rim. The city hall has prototypes and counterparts in many other Italian cities, as does its slender, soaring Mangia tower, which was designed to outdo the bell tower in Florence (the Mangia tower's name means "eat," supposedly for a medieval Tuscan sculptor with a gluttonous appetite). Placing the city hall at the bottom of a swale, or dip in the land, was unusual, but the setting creates a back wall like that behind the stage of a Greek or Roman amphitheater.

The Campo's floor, paved in red brick in a herringbone pattern, channels rainwater toward a central drain that helps to prevent flooding in a practical manner. The radiating lines of embedded travertine define nine segments that are said to represent the city's nine predominant Ghibelline families.

Very few architectural intrusions interrupt the Campo's inner walls: the Palazzi Signorili that flank the city hall have only occasional and shallow protruding balconies. The Mangia tower is the only dramatic vertical interruption, and the portico at its base is the only significant horizontal projection. The Fonte Gaia (Joyous Fountain) is little more than a flat patch of water opposite the city hall; its only motion follows the toss of a coin. Like the fountains in Rome's Piazza Navona (see page 20), the Fonte Gaia is fed by distant and ancient aqueducts.

1 This is one of eleven slotted views of the Campo and its tower from the upper road and neighborhood that surround it. 2 Some of the approaches are through gateways. 3 And this is the space to be seen. The great Mangia tower is taller than that of Florence and high enough to rival Siena's nearby cathedral that sits on elevated ground. In form, color, and material this vertical accent tops them all. 4 Some passages are easily bridged over. 5 Others bend gently around diners protected from the sun. 6 The water in the Fonte Gaia forms practically the only horizontal surface in the space.

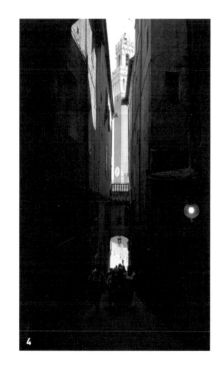

Contributing to the Campo's harmony with its surroundings, the city hall's Gothic windows became a motif that recurs throughout Siena. Happily, the town controlled the manufacture of a handsome brick that, together with local travertine, became Siena's prevalent building materials. Civic discipline, meanwhile, produced a law that limited cornice height, producing Siena's calm skyline (in sharp contrast to the jumpy skyline of nearby San Gimignano (see page 57).

A ring road on high ground above the Campo affords glimpses down the eleven narrow openings that give access to the square. Seen in rapid succession, these openings allow your view of the Campo to develop almost as though through an old-fashioned zoetrope—that slotted cylinder on a central spindle that gave us our first moving images. Any entrance you might choose will provide the same explosive effect of landing amid a whirling space that is genuinely breathtaking.

Twice a year, on July 2 and on August 16, the Campo erupts in a clamor. Since 1701, an outer ring of gray stone in the brick paving has been covered with sand for the Palio, a wild, bareback horse race rich in political symbolism. For ninety seconds, banner-wielding jockeys, clad in brilliant colors representing ten of Siena's seventeen districts or contrade, run their mounts three times around the inner walls of the Campo—a city square big enough to be a hippodrome.

1 A principal entry to the Piazza del Campo is down the steps of the Costarella dei Barbieri. 2 Palazzos north of the city hall have recently been restored and align under a common cornice that brackets their varying materials and sympathetic detailing. 3 The Costarella is wide enough to house shops as one descends to the piazza floor. 4 The central Torrione houses the council chamber and the treasury and sets the architectural standard for the Campo as well as for much of the rest of the city. The blind arcade in stone at its base reflects the commercial nature of the piazza while the semi-machicolation and cutout crenellations that form its crown recall the days of castle warfare. 5 Looking southwest from the front of the portico, the concave floor of the space is resolved in the strong horizontal base of buildings that ring the square and face the town hall. Restoration is continuing around the Campo, and portions were still under wraps when this photograph was taken.

Torri Gemelle

Via San Matteo

Piazza delle Erbe

Il Collegiata

Torre Rognosa

Palazzo del
Podestà

PIAZZA DEL DUOMO

Torre Grossa

Palazzo
Comunale

Loggia del Popolo

Torre del
Diavolo

Torri
Ardinghelli

Via del Castello

PIAZZA DELLA CISTERNA

Arco dei Becci

Torre dei
Cugnanesi

Torre dei Becci

Via Quercecchio

Via San Giovanni

Meters 15   30   60   90 North

Feet   50   100   200   300

PIAZZA DELLA CISTERNA AND PIAZZA DEL DUOMO

San Gimignano

PLAN DIMENSIONS	RATIO OF WIDTH TO LENGTH	AREA	TYPICAL HEIGHT TO SKYLINE	HIGHEST POINT	RATIO OF WIDTH TO SKYLINE HEIGHT	ANGLE OF VIEW FROM THE SHORT SIDE TO THE SKYLINE	KEY DATES
130 × 280 ft (40 × 85 m); 200 × 200 ft (60 × 60 m)	1 to 2; 1 to 1 (approx. square)	0.9 acres (0.4 ha); 0.9 acres (0.4 ha)	65 ft (20 m); 65 ft (20 m)	130 ft (40 m), top of Torre del Diavolo; 170 ft (52 m), top of Torre Grossa	2 to 1; 3 to 1	25°; 18°	1273, La Cisterna; 1239, Palazzo del Podestà

Source of drawing data: Cadastral map from the town of San Gimignano

Crowning a Tuscan hill at the crossroads of historic trade routes and the main pilgrimage route to Rome from the north, San Gimignano and its bristling skyline appear from afar like the Emerald City in *The Wizard of Oz*. The historic center of this town is instantly recognizable by its beautiful towers, though only fifteen of the original seventy-two are still standing. These punctuate a remarkable set of interlocking piazzas and courtyards. While the towers may have been built for a practical purpose—looking out for approaching enemies—most were also vanity gestures by the wealthy families that once controlled San Gimignano.

The town's spatial procession starts at a handsome gate in the town wall named, along with the street that leads up to the town center, for San Giovanni. Just after the street pauses to display the remnant façade of the church of San Francesco, it passes through the gate of the Becci family, which was opened through the inner wall of the town in 1000, and explodes into the square named for the old town well at its center: the Piazza della Cisterna.

The cistern was probably sunk sometime around 1273, and the piazza is surrounded by fine old family palaces with towers from the thirteenth and fourteenth centuries. The square today is filled with the stands and canopies of a very busy morning market, which disappears with almost magical efficiency shortly after noon. The Piazza della Cisterna is visually tightly contained, although a winding road at the far end leads downhill and away.

A narrow neck of space leads off through the northwest corner to the cathedral square—the Piazza del Duomo—and its own competing market. Here are several more towers, the old and new town halls, and the cathedral, called Il Collegiata. Between it and the new town hall, the fourteenth-century tower, Torre Grossa, functions as a spatial joint not unlike San Marco's campanile. The Via San Matteo leads off to another town gate on the north, while the space links at the west to the Piazza delle Erbe.

These elements describe a sequence of wide and narrow spaces that grew up during two medieval centuries of political chaos and artistic achievement. The piazzas then began slowly to deteriorate as the power center of Italy shifted southward and towers fell amid earthquakes and neglect. The competing residential façades that graced the walls of San Gimignano's space were more of an architectural recipe book than they were components of a homogenous urban composition. Then a series of events transformed the town. They are meticulously recorded by D. Medina Lasansky in her paper for the Journal of the Society of Architectural Historians in September 2004: "The Fascist Redesign of San Gimignano."

Toward the end of the nineteenth century, when Italy was unified, the country was looking for visible ways to bind itself together. Locally, a Sienese architect named Giuseppe Partini had been commissioned to begin the "medievalization" of San Gimignano's Palazzo del Comune (town hall); this was being carried out with more concern for theatrical effect than for historic accuracy. By the time the Fascists took over in 1922, most construction, new or old, had to be approved by the office of the town superintendent (podestà). By our great good fortune, despite their politics, the men who worked in Italy and its colonies at the time (see, for example, Rhodes,

page 100) were good designers. The results of their efforts, largely meant to attract tourists, especially Italians in search of a heritage, are still attractive.

A medieval style somewhere between Romanesque and Gothic became the local favorite, and the elaborate trompe l'oeil neoclassical pilasters that had been painted on the front of the Collegiata were stripped off to expose the rough masonry seen today. Much of the restoration was done in preparation for the 1922 celebration of the six-hundredth anniversary of the death of Dante.

The tight intersection between the two piazzas was the subject of much discussion during San Gimignano's twentieth-century revitalization, particularly because of a 1338 document referring to a public loggia that, had it existed, would have predated the late-fourteenth-century Loggia dei Lanzi in Florence. Drawings of the loggia were never found, but the ever-resourceful architect on the job designed a new one based on scratches he found under the stucco of the corner building. No doubt the view of its neighboring piazza through the arches of 1936 is an urban improvement. The phony crenellations and arches over previously flat window lintels, however, were less worthwhile.

The color and texture of stripped-down masonry that gives San Gimignano its visual unity were arrived at after the fact—that is, after the removal of mostly Baroque overlays and sometimes even as fabrication of what was presumed to have lain underneath. The evidence of the Renaissance was stripped off in search of a Gothic that had largely bypassed Italy. Today San Gimignano attracts visitors ranging from Italian day-trippers to serious scholars, but few can count on discerning where the authentic stops and reconstruction begins. If you're going to "improve" a place, it's best to produce a result that's truly an improvement. UNESCO acknowledged this achievement in 1990 by designating San Gimignano a World Heritage Site.

1 The view along the Via San Giovanni shows the first of the town's many towers. 2 The Via San Matteo enters the Piazza del Duomo from the north. 3 The Arco dei Becci leads from the Via San Giovanni into the Piazza della Cisterna. 4 The Piazza della Cisterna winds eastward from the Becci entrance as buildings surrounding the cistern enclose the visitor in a complex composition of fine medieval masonry.

1 The Old Cistern (1273–1346) is at the center of its piazza with the Torre del Diavolo to the right and the porticoed entry to the Piazza del Duomo at the far left. 2 The twentieth-century portico that stands between the two piazze guards a tight, attractive spatial juncture with the Piazza del Duomo barely visible beyond. 3 Carefully composed forms of stone hang over one's head. 4 The Loggia del Popolo, Palazzo Comunale, Torre Grossa, and the cathedral form the southern side of the Piazza del Duomo. Their façades were stripped down to bare masonry and topped with decorative crenellation in the 1920s and 1930s. 5 The eastern side of the Piazza del Duomo was recently stripped of accumulated plaster by talented architects, allowing the Palazzo del Podestà, with the Torre Rognosa behind it, to dominate this dramatic wall facing the cathedral. 6 The buildings surrounding the cistern enclose the visitor in a complex composition of fine medieval masonry.

Via Bartolomeo Colleoni

Civic Library 1684

Piazza Mercato del Fieno

Teatro Sociale

Via Gombito

PIAZZA VECCHIA

Campanone 1200

Baptistery

Palazzo della Ragione 12th C

Torre Gombito

PIAZZA DEL DUOMO

Academy of Science, Letters, and Arts

Colleoni Chapel 1427

Duomo 1459

Via Mario Lupo

Temple of the Holy Cross

Santa Maria Maggiore

Via Arena

Meters 15   30   60   90 North

Feet 50   100   200   300

PIAZZA VECCHIA AND PIAZZA DEL DUOMO

Bergamo

PLAN DIMENSIONS	RATIO OF WIDTH TO LENGTH	AREA	TYPICAL HEIGHT TO SKYLINE	HIGHEST POINT	RATIO OF WIDTH TO SKYLINE HEIGHT	ANGLE OF VIEW FROM THE SHORT SIDE TO THE SKYLINE	KEY DATE
115 × 230 ft (35 × 70 m); 66 × 132 ft (20 × 40 m)	1 to 2; 1 to 2	0.6 acre (0.2 ha) 0.2 acre (0.1 ha)	65 ft (20 m); 115 ft (40 m)	100 ft (30 m), top of the library; 175 ft (54 m), top of the tower	2 to 1; 1 to 2	30°; 64°	1300, start of the construction of the Piazza Vecchia

Note: The irregular shape in plan of the Piazza del Duomo makes most of its dimensions and proportions irrelevant.
Source of drawing data: Cadastral maps from the city of Bergamo

The charm of the space contained within Bergamo's pair of piazze derives initially from their being in a beautiful medieval town atop a high hill. The features of the Piazza Vecchia (old square)—regular surrounding structures, a tower, a fountain, a grand stairway—resemble those of many other Italian squares. What is unique is its peek-a-boo relationship to the Piazza del Duomo next door. Crossing the former to approach the latter through the open base of the Palazzo della Ragione, the visitor experiences a sense of discovery. This effect is quite unlike what you feel in other paired spaces such as those of San Gimignano and Verona (pages 56 and 28). In those, the tight passage is lateral and quite straightforward, rather than under a massive building's supporting vertical vaults.

I agree with Frank Lloyd Wright, who declared that "Bergamo is a city of marvels. [It] stuns whoever comes near it" (quoted in *Bergamo—the History and the Art*). Approaching historic upper Bergamo (the Città Alta) is best done via one of two funiculars. Surrounded by a sprawling modern city, medieval Bergamo sits atop a prominence where the foothills of the Alps abut Italy's vast, flat Po Valley. Upper Bergamo has served as a heavily fortified lookout for various peoples as long ago as 2000 B.C.—well before Rome absorbed the area into the empire around the third century B.C. The city's most significant date is 1428 A.D., when Bergamo became part of the Venetian city-state and its urban fabric took on a medieval quality. Venice controlled Bergamo for the better part of four centuries. The massive walls that still form upper Bergamo's skyline were the work of military men from 1560 to 1623. Present-day Bergamo clearly treasures its heritage, and a preservation-and-improvement project has been in progress since 1934.

The principal funicular, which pierces the city wall just below the Piazza Mercato della Scarpe, has been the most used since it was installed in 1886. A short walk along Via Gombito and past its tower brings you into the northeast corner of the Piazza Vecchia in front of the library (biblioteca). The old square is intimately connected to the smaller, more crowded Piazza del Duomo beyond; you get a hint of it from the daylight that shines through the piers under the Palazzo della Ragione, which forms the southern edge of the old square. In other respects the Piazza Vecchia is very simple in its conception: three- and four-story buildings on either side with cafés at their bases, a fountain, and the civic library along the northern edge. The square is clearly marked by its paving, a strong pattern of dark red bricks set within diagonal stripes of stone.

If the Piazza Vecchia's identity was set by the Venetians in the fifteenth century, this doesn't mean that its parts stayed in place. The Palazzo della Ragione was turned around to face the old square and the vaults below were given their Gothic groins in 1520 after the grand staircase leading to the palace's upper rooms was put in place. The civic theater was built in 1806 on the grounds of the former Venetian headquarters right next to the 177-foot- (54-meter-) high civic tower, which is named after its largest bell, the Campanone. The present library occupies the former city hall and received its current façade only in 1928. The Fontana Contarina was a gift to the city in the seventeenth century by a departing Venetian rector.

While the old square kept its basic simplicity, the same cannot be said of the smaller space to be seen through the vaults of the palazzo.

The Duomo, which gives the piazza its name, was started in 1459, and the baptistery that closes the Piazza del Duomo at the opposite end was moved there in 1898. To the south, across from the palazzo, is a perfectly fine and substantial twelfth-century basilica, which originally housed the baptistery.

Then came Condottiere Bartolomeo Colleoni, the great gun-for-hire who had freed the city for the Venetians and was to be honored by Verrocchio's equestrian statue of him in Venice. Planning his mausoleum, he chose Giovanni Antonio Amadeo, an up-and-coming architect already admired for his work at the Certosa di Pavia, and Colleoni forced his hometown to carve out a corner of the basilica for him and his daughter. The sacristy that stood in one corner of the Greek-cross basilica was torn down in 1427 to make way for a building that was noted in 1609 as "the absolute masterpiece of the first Lombard Renaissance" with just a touch of "Gothic Florentine taste" (quoted in *Bergamo—the History and the Art*).

The chapel's façade of polychrome marble and extraordinary sculptural ornamentation is right in front of you as you walk through the vaulted approach under the palazzo, and it could use a lot more space for proper viewing. It makes the Piazza del Duomo, as it winds around and between all its superabundant architecture, look like a colorful jar of candy. If it had to be done to satisfy the great condottiere, however, at least it was done well. The tower and cupola of the basilica line up with the dome of the chapel and the baptistery in a diagonal that couldn't be accidental.

With two linked squares of such interest and variety, no one can be surprised to find the rest of the upper city full of delight. Behind the basilica are its own fine porch and apses as well as the delightful tenth-century Temple of the Holy Cross, which you encounter on the way to Via Arena, declared by Le Corbusier to be "one of the most beautiful streets in the world."

1 The leonine fountain is a central feature of the Piazza Vecchia. 2 The Palazzo della Ragione closes the south end of the Piazza Vecchia but allows a bit of the Piazza Duomo to be seen through its vaulted base. To the right, a grand staircase climbs the side of the Teatro Sociale with the Campanone tower beyond. 3 The library dominates the typical approach to the piazze walking along the Via Gombito up from the funicular. 4 The Via Mario Lupo leads up to the Torre Gombito from the east and is typical of medieval Bergamo as it approached the top of the old city. 5 The library closes the Piazza Vecchia to the north with cafés to either side.

1 The Palazzo della Ragione stands between the two piazze with the Duomo to its right. 2 One passes the Temple of the Holy Cross behind Santa Maria Maggiore if approaching from the south. 3 The grandiose Colleone Chapel competes with the Duomo for attention and wins. 4 The vaults and bridge of the palazzo frame the library beyond. 5 The chapel and the baptistery are anchors to the Piazza Duomo as seen through the vaults of the palazzo. 6 The civic tower, called the Campanone, rises from the corner between the two squares. 7 The baptistery is handsome enough to stand on its own.

Via dei Calzaiuoli

Via della Condotta

Via de' Cerchi

Piazza S Firenze

Via Vacchereccia

Borgo dei Greci

Palazzo Vecchio

Loggia dei Lanzi

Galleria degli Uffizi

Via della Ninna

Meters 15 30 60 90 North

Feet 50 100 200 300

PIAZZA DELLA SIGNORIA

Florence

PLAN DIMENSIONS	RATIO OF WIDTH TO LENGTH	AREA	TYPICAL HEIGHT TO SKYLINE	HIGHEST POINT	RATIO OF WIDTH TO SKYLINE HEIGHT	ANGLE OF VIEW FROM THE SHORT SIDE TO THE SKYLINE	KEY DATE
295 × 395 ft (90 × 120 m)	1 to 1 (approx. square minus the cutout)	2 acres (0.8 ha)	65 ft (20 m)	310 ft (94 m), top of tower of the Palazzo Vecchio	4 to 1	12°	1299, start of Palazzo Vecchio; 1386, final alignment of the western wall

Sources of drawing data: Cadastral maps in the archives of the city and slightly different drawings from Gromort, *Choix des Plans*; and from Boroi and Pampaloni, *Monumenti d'Italia, Le Piazze*

The Piazza della Signoria may be the most sophisticated urban space in Italy. Despite its peculiar L shape, it works as a great square because of the remarkable collection of building façades around and within it and the exceptionally interesting, carefully placed statues that seem to shape the space that surrounds their own sculptural power. While the nearby Piazza della SS. Annunziata (see page 74) induces a calm repose, the Piazza della Signoria sends you racing about, peering around corners, always expecting another surprise. Each of the principal entrances to the square gives a different impression. Once you're inside the square, its calculated visual harmony seems always about to slide into visual cacophony.

This space has been in a state of almost constant adjustment since the region was settled in the tenth century B.C. Bellicose contests for power both among and within city-states left their mark on just about every corner of historic Florence. The Piazza della Signoria (Signoria means lordship) first staked out its space from 1299 to 1314, when a site for a city hall was chosen and a building was commissioned and constructed. The palace, which today is usually called the Palazzo Vecchio, honored Florence's ruling townsmen.

The monumental Palazzo Vecchio is one of the quirkiest compositions in all of architecture, making its own rules as it twists, turns, and finally shoots upward. The structure originally covered only about half of its present footprint, when a sturdy tower was added, created by the great architect-sculptor Arnolfo di Cambio (ca. 1245–1302). The main façade and entrance to the town hall then turned west. The crowning cornice of corbelled crenellations was deep enough to accommodate an arsenal of projectiles and a lot of boiling oil. Today it serves principally to create shadows that give its form architectural strength in the harsh Tuscan sunshine. Indeed, the overwhelming, top-heavy tower can be seen for miles and is never lost in the haze.

At first the space in front of the palazzo—called the Platea Ubertorum (street of the Uberti) for a family that lost its property to the powers that were—was purposely kept quite small. A square large enough to accommodate large crowds was considered risky in times of political instability and possible rebellion. The several decisions to enlarge the building—the palazzo was renovated and added to first in 1308, then at least three more times before the end of the sixteenth century—represented a communal confidence that finally settled over the great Florentine city-state. The placement of sculptures to embellish the palazzo and the square it dominates continued well into the Renaissance.

Enhancing visitors' first view of the Palazzo della Signoria from the several street entries to the square required the removal, reconstruction, and replacement of many important buildings. The façades of their replacements form the present boundaries of the square. The art historian Marvin Trachtenberg has observed that, instead of being formed by the careful placement of buildings next to each other, the Piazza della Signoria seems carved out of a dense group of competing palaces. The L shape that resulted from all these modifications is very unusual—almost inconceivable. In fact, the line of fountain and statues that crosses the angle of the L divides it into two almost-rectangles.

A huge arcaded porch, the Loggia dei Lanzi, was placed next to the palazzo for sheltered events (1376–82); today it serves as a large outdoor sculpture gallery. Between them, the Uffizi Gallery heads toward the River Arno. Important statues were also placed in front of the palazzo and to its side; some of the more precious, such as Michelangelo's David, have been removed for protection to indoor displays, and copies substituted for them in the piazza.

The finishing touches that gave the square its nearly ideal shape required the straightening of the north and west façades. The western wall of the piazza was moved in stages late in the fourteenth century by the removal or abbreviation of many medieval buildings. This allows visitors approaching today from the north to see the Piazza della Signoria first within a carefully calculated angle from its northwest corner. This, in turn, opens horizontally on each side of the central visual axis by 45 degrees, and vertically, by 45 degrees above horizontal to the top of the tower. (Among the many idealized proportions thought up by the giants of the Renaissance, this one makes some sense in terms of the cone of normal vision.)

It is hard to believe that such sophisticated visual/spatial demands were financed and carried out in war-torn fourteenth-century Florence. And whether there is such a thing as an ideal angle for first viewing architecture can be debated. But history does support the choice of approaching a monument or a space from one of its corners (the Parthenon in Athens, first seen through the Propylea, for example). The full frontal approach of the Renaissance, as with the Piazza della SS. Annunziata, is more usual, but there can be no denying the shock of pleasure when you first turn the corner at the end of Via dei Calzaiuoli.

1 Bandinelli's Hercules and Cacus and a very good copy of Michelangelo's David bracket the final placement of the entrance to the Palazzo Vecchio from the west. 2 From a terrace in the southwest corner of the square, the Duomo on the left and Florence's San Marco on the right suggest the dense urban fabric from which the Piazza della Signoria has been carved. 3 A bridge connects the Palazzo Vecchio to the Uffizi palace, and its arch echoes that of the Loggia beyond.

PIAZZA DELLA SIGNORIA

1 Il Biancone (the white giant) stands in the pool at the corner of the palazzo and forms a crisp corner to the space. 2 A grand collection of palazzi stretches along the north side of the square, and the space is contained by a bend in the Via de' Cerchi. 3 The equestrian statue of Cosimo I dei Medici stands at the joint between the two sides of the L- shaped piazza. 4 The corner view of the Palazzo Vecchio is considered to be its best and was carefully constructed by the planners of the Renaissance. 5 Palazzo and tower are framed in the approach from the west along the Via Vacchereccia.

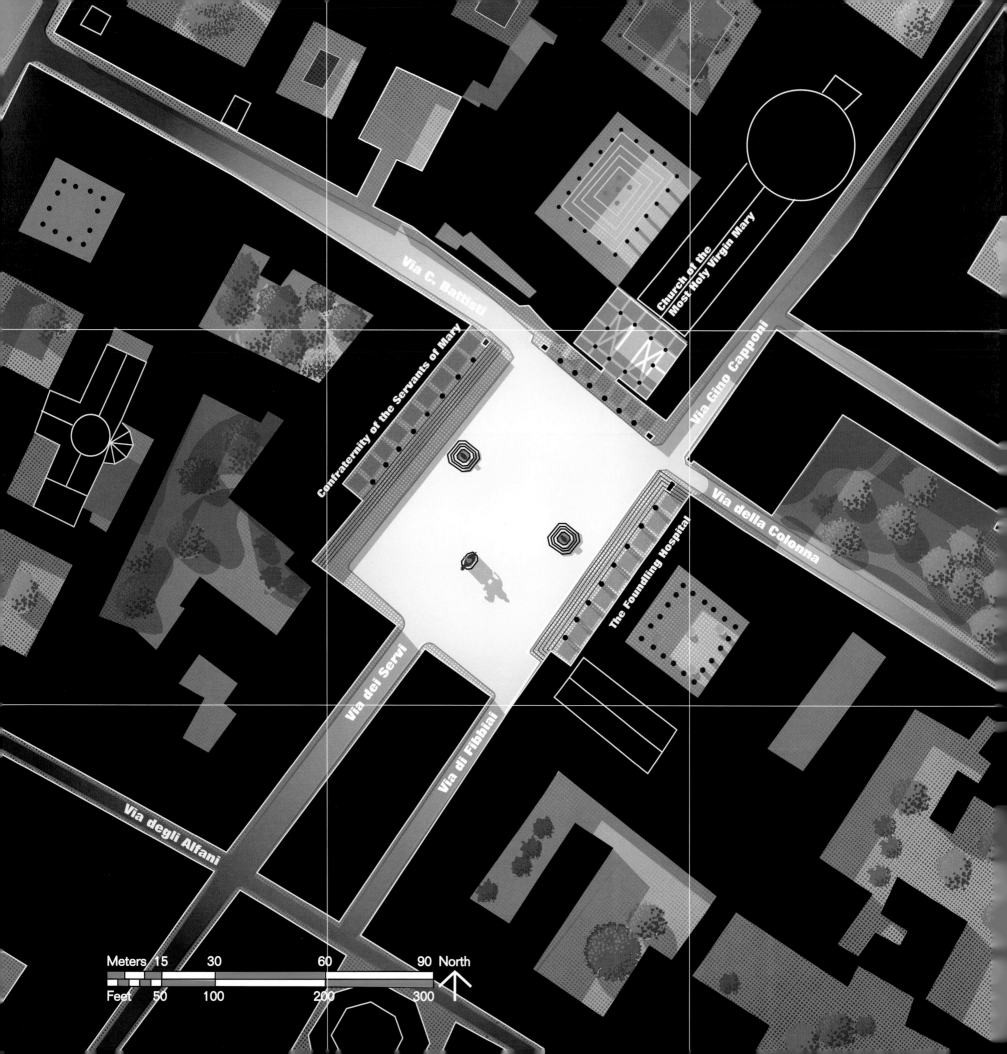

Via C. Battisti

Church of the
Most Holy Virgin Mary

Via Gino Capponi

Confraternity of the Servants of Mary

Via della Colonna

The Foundling Hospital

Via dei Servi

Via di Fibbiai

Via degli Alfani

Meters 15   30   60   90 North
Feet   50   100   200   300

PIAZZA DELLA SANTISSIMA ANNUNZIATA

Florence

PLAN DIMENSIONS	RATIO OF WIDTH TO LENGTH	AREA	TYPICAL HEIGHT TO SKYLINE	HIGHEST POINT	RATIO OF WIDTH TO SKYLINE HEIGHT	ANGLE OF VIEW FROM THE SHORT SIDE TO THE SKYLINE	KEY DATE
207 × 246 ft (63 × 75 m)	1 to 1 (approx. square)	1.2 acres (0.5 ha)	50 ft (15 m)	none	4 to 1	14°	1421, start of Brunelleschi's design for the Spedale degli Innocenti

Source of drawing data: Cadastral quadrants in Novelli, ed., *Atlante di Firenze*

This secluded space on the edge of downtown Florence seems trying to hide its importance as key to the development of Renaissance urban planning. The Piazza della Santissima Annunziata certainly does not trumpet its dignified beauty; the classical simplicity of its organization risks being considered obvious. The square is, however, the achievement of a rare handful of giants in spatial design, architecture, sculpture, and—when you look inside some of the buildings—painting.

The church that gives the square its name is dedicated to the most holy (Santissima, abbreviated SS.) Virgin Mary (the Annunziata, i.e., the recipient of the Angel Gabriel's annunciation) and considerably predates the square. Its oratory dates back to 1250 in the late Middle Ages, and it was reconstructed and expanded in the mid-fifteenth century as part of the creation of the piazza. For me, the church is altogether outclassed, and it is certainly dwarfed, by the children's home, the Ospedale degli Innocenti, the product of Florence's affluent silk merchants' guild's desire to make a major gift to their booming city. The guild's goldsmith member Filippo Brunelleschi (1377–1446), a pioneer of the Italian Renaissance, was asked in 1419 to design a home for orphans and the children of hard-pressed families; soon after, he won the competition to design the great dome of the Florence cathedral.

Though not trained as an architect, Brunelleschi had studied and probably visited the ruins of ancient Rome. Across the front of the beautiful ospedale, and virtually at right angles to the church, he stretched a magnificent arcaded porch—his version of a Roman portico—embodying the birth of the Italian Renaissance. A century later, in 1525, Antonio da Sangallo the Elder (1485–1546) duplicated the hospital's portico in front of his building opposite for the Confraternity of the Servants of Mary. Sangallo also is credited, along with other artists, with the design of a cloister and loggia in front of the church. And with this, ecco! three sides of a square.

As decoration for the piazza, Andrea della Robbia (1435–1525) added to the tympanum over each column in the ospedale's arcade a series of glazed terra-cotta relief roundels; his white swaddled babies on their blue disks have become the best-known feature of the space. The square was embellished in the early seventeenth century with a bronze equestrian statue of Grand Duke Ferdinand I. Twenty years later, a second Grand Duke Ferdinand had two fountains from the nearby port city of Livorno transported to the square; their Baroque effulgence is somewhat out of keeping with the rhythmic serenity of the piazza.

The plan of the space is close to a square. Minor dimensional variations undoubtedly arose from the imprecise placement of the children's home at a time when the square was not foreseen. But the irregularities are neither as pronounced as those that form Michelangelo's trapezoid on the Capitoline Hill, nor as subtly calculated as those to be seen across town at the carefully shaped medieval Piazza della Signoria (see page 68). Every square needs at least one grand entry, and here, from the duomo on the southwest, the Via dei Servi leads directly to the piazza. The axial view from this street may be naïve compared to the subtler sideways entry to the Piazza della Signoria, but it works.

Rarely does a series of superstars who work over a long span of time on a single space come up with a result that is simply beautiful—and beautifully simple. The Piazza della SS. Annunziata forms a convincing transition between two great eras in art and architecture: the dazzling close of the Middle Ages and the stately elegance of the Renaissance. Time spent slowly walking through and around this purist's piazza, with side trips to the courtyards that sprout off it, is both rewarding and memorable.

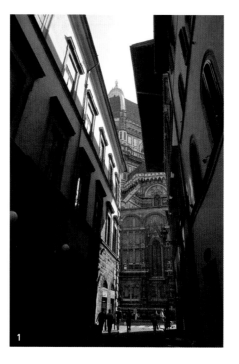

1 The Via dei Servi originates at the side of the Duomo, Brunelleschi's other great achievement. 2 San Gallo's Confraternity of the Servants of Mary is behind the equestrian statue of Fernando I dei Medici and to the left of the church. 3 The arcade of the church was added after that of the Ospedale degli Innocenti beyond. 4 Brunelleschi's arcade is virtually identical to Sangallo's reproduction on the opposite side of the square. 5 One of the colorfully weathered fountains stands in front of the church. 6 Andrea della Robbia's blue and white rondelles rest gently within the stone and plaster of Brunelleschi's arcade.

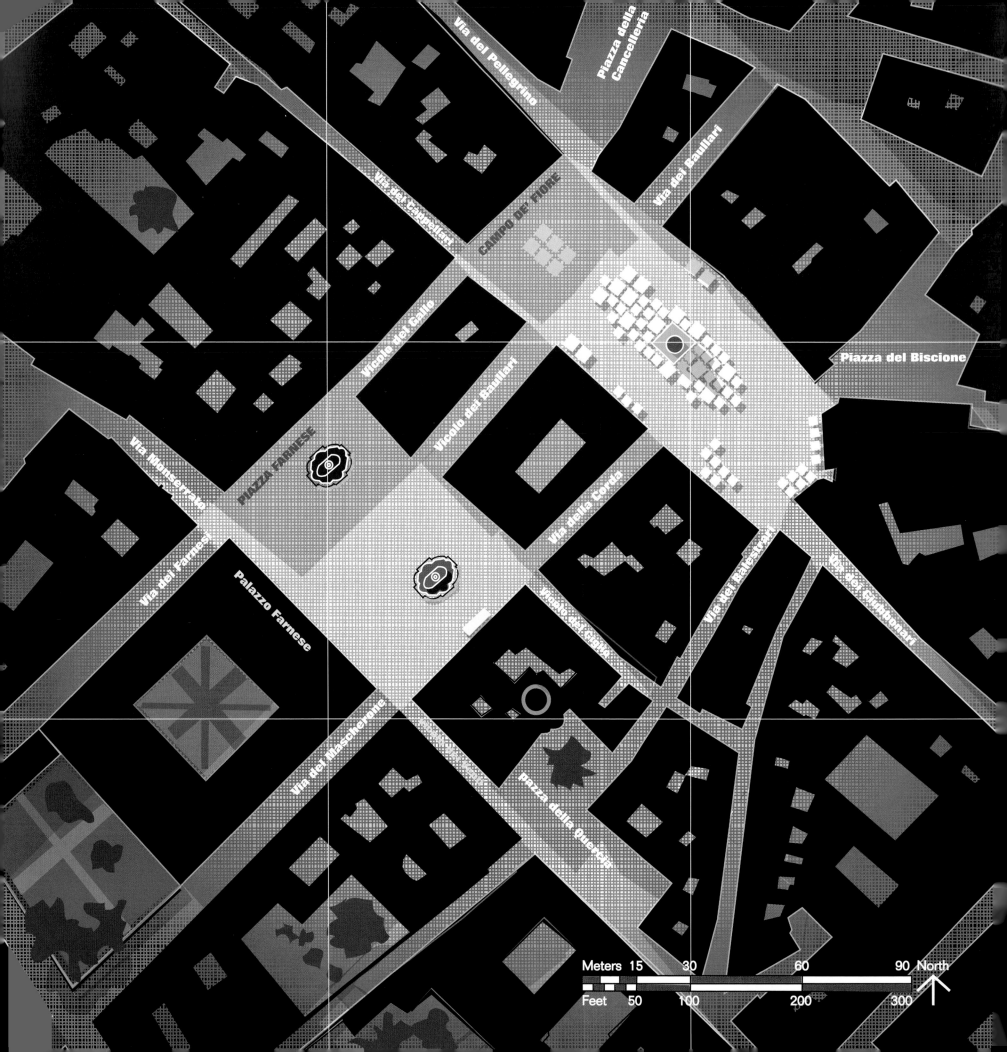

Via del Pellegrino

Piazza della
Cancelleria

Via dei Baullari

Via dei Cappellari

CAMPO DE' FIORE

Piazza del Biscione

Vicolo del Gallo

Vicolo dei Baullari

Via Monserrato

PIAZZA FARNESE

Via dei Farnesi

Via della Corda

Via dei Balestrari

Via dei Giubbonari

Palazzo Farnese

Vicolo del Gallo

Via dei Mascherone

PIAZZA della Quercia

Meters   15   30   60   90 North

Feet   50   100   200   300

CAMPO DE' FIORI AND PIAZZA FARNESE
Rome

PLAN DIMENSIONS	RATIO OF WIDTH TO LENGTH	AREA	TYPICAL HEIGHT TO SKYLINE	HIGHEST POINT	RATIO OF WIDTH TO SKYLINE HEIGHT	ANGLE OF VIEW FROM THE SHORT SIDE TO THE SKYLINE	KEY DATE
148 × 368 ft (45 × 112 m); 174 × 243 ft (53 × 74 m)	1 to 2; 1 to 1 (approx. square)	1.2 acres (0.5 ha), 1 acre (0.4 ha)	80 ft (25 m), old walk-ups; 95 ft (30 m)	90 ft (28 m), new buildings; 100 ft (30 m), cornice of palazzo	2 to 1; 2 to 1	29°; 30°	1514, start of construction of Palazzo Farnese

Note: Heights are calculated from photographs and are not exact.
Source of drawing data: Dimensional data from Novelli, ed., *Atlante di Roma*

I like to think of this interesting and successful pair of squares as a
mischievous girl and her stately dowager aunt. The raucousness of the
Campo de' Fiori and the noble serenity of the Piazza Farnese define
their relationship in sound and sight. Like most of the historic center
of Rome, the area around these squares distributes its space in various
combinations. These two were made for each other, although they
do make an unusual pair. I think it best to start with the saucy niece.

The Campo de' Fiori—meaning field of flowers—has a daily cycle all its own. In the morning it is a bustling marketplace for vegetables and fruit, meats, spices, and all manner of practical household objects. Sellers hawking their wares and shoppers competing for their attention—"Tocca me!" I'm next!—can make quite a racket. Tourists, meanwhile, come in droves to gawk at the hubbub. By 1:00 P.M. the square has fallen quiet, and the soundscape consists mostly of the whoosh of brooms and the rumble of garbage trucks scooping up the morning's mess. Almost the only merchants doing business at this hour are florists carrying on the Campo's original function, and the owners of surrounding restaurants and cafés. The afternoon is quiet; shops on the periphery—a bakery, several butchers, a pharmacy—do a sedate business between 4:00 and 7:30 P.M. In the evening, the noise level rises again. Native and tourist adults come to stroll and dine, and teenagers to hang out.

The Campo was paved in the fifteenth century, when the market was established. Like much of historic Rome, its floor consists of San Pietrini—little St. Peters—rough-cut, molar-shaped, black stones nicknamed for the rock on which, church legend has it, St. Peter built his church. Incongruously, the Campo has served as an execution site, most notably for the burning in 1600 of the priest-philosopher Giordano Bruno, deemed a heretic by the Inquisition. His gloomy, hooded statue near the center of the square is its only permanent fixture—unless you count the lone newsstand that does business throughout the day.

Three short, parallel streets connect the Campo with the Piazza Farnese. This space has served various uses—a horse market, a racecourse, a hiring hall, and various spectacles prepared for diplomats' families. After the coarse rhythm of the Campo de' Fiori, visitors welcome the stately calm that accompanies the first glimpse of the Palazzo Farnese and its noble square. In many respects the Piazza Farnese is simplicity itself. One great building forms the square's southwest wall, rising regally over a small church, aristocrats' houses, and several nice restaurants on the other sides. Surprisingly, the flag flying over the door to this quintessentially Italian palazzo is the French tricolor: France holds a renewable ninety-nine-year lease to the building for use as its embassy, but Italy can claim it as a masterwork of three of its best architects.

Cardinal Alessandro Farnese, eventually elevated to the papacy as Paul III, commissioned the palace that gives the piazza its name, and work on it began in 1514. The first architect on the job was Florence's Antonio da Sangallo the Younger (1483–1546). Another Florentine, Michelangelo Buonarroti

(1475–1564), took over the design after Sangallo's death in 1546, but even he did not live to see the building's completion. This was accomplished in 1589 by Giacomo della Porta (1541–1604). Michelangelo was responsible for the most remarkable features of the façade—notably, the raising of the height of the upper floors and the huge overhanging cornice. Michelangelo's ability to grab the stylistic language of the Renaissance and twist its elements to his own desires is a Mannerist trait—a practice that led to the Baroque.

When you stand in front of the palazzo, you see that, just where the upper floors might be expected to diminish in perspective, Michelangelo has stretched the building both upward and outward in his distinctive way. What lies behind the palazzo's looming windows can only be glimpsed at night, when the lights inside the French embassy allow a distant view of sumptuous interiors and, if you're especially lucky, its fine ceiling frescoes.

The piazza has almost no furniture. At either side stand two identical fountains that feature great tubs of Egyptian granite supposedly brought from the Baths of Caracalla; the water spouts from great, sculpted fleurs-de-lis symbolic of France. The tubs are said to have served as a sort of royal box for Roman aristocrats during horse races and other spectacles. The piazza is never crowded, but it is rarely empty. Day and night, it serves as one of Rome's great outdoor living rooms.

1 The Campo de' Fiore, during the day, is a popular fruit, vegetable, and flower market. 2 The statue of Giordano Bruno stands in the center of the Campo and, even on a sunny day, tends to cast a pall on the busy market set up around its base. 3 The eastern side of the Piazza Farnese is punctuated by the small church of Santa Brigida. 4 The French Embassy has occupied for several centuries the building designed by Michelangelo and inherited from the Farnese popes. 5 The Vicolo dei Baullari is one of the three short streets that connect the Campo to the Piazza Farnese, and the powerful palazzo swells in size as one walks toward it. 6 This is one of the two identical granite tubs supposedly brought from the Baths of Caracalla to form the fountains of the square.

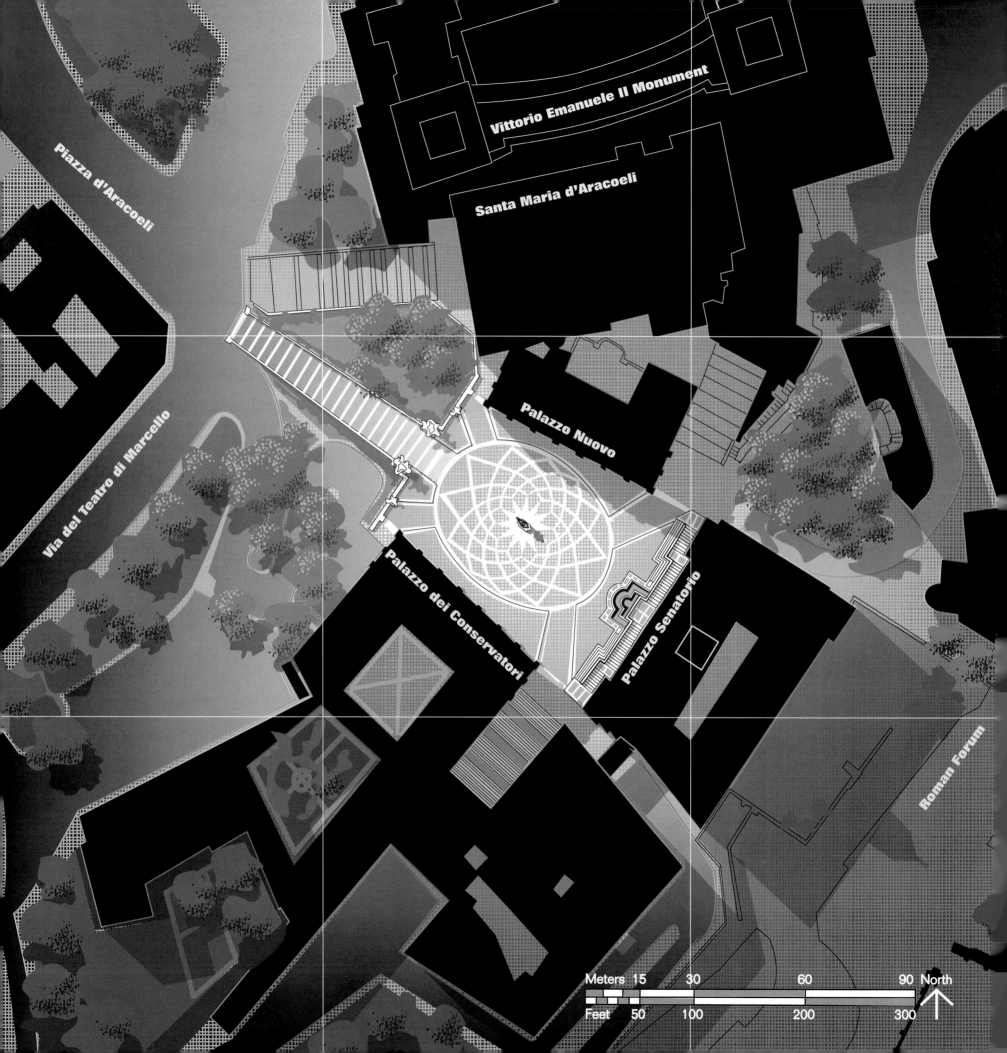

Piazza d'Aracoeli

Vittorio Emanuele II Monument

Santa Maria d'Aracoeli

Via del Teatro di Marcello

Palazzo Nuovo

Palazzo dei Conservatori

Palazzo Senatorio

Roman Forum

Meters 15 30 60 90 North
Feet 50 100 200 300

PIAZZA DEL CAMPIDOGLIO
Rome

PLAN DIMENSIONS	RATIO OF WIDTH TO LENGTH	AREA	TYPICAL HEIGHT TO SKYLINE	HIGHEST POINT	RATIO OF WIDTH TO SKYLINE HEIGHT	ANGLE OF VIEW FROM THE SHORT SIDE TO THE SKYLINE	KEY DATE
164 × 262 ft (50 × 80 m)	1 to 2	1 acre (0.4 ha)	70 ft (22 m)	200 ft (60 m), Senate building tower	2 to 1	24°	1534, start of Michelangelo's work on the square

Source of drawing data: Cadastral maps from Novelli, ed., *Atlante di Roma*

The square atop the Capitoline Hill, historically the most important of Rome's famous seven hills, is a satisfying and unique spatial experience. The Piazza del Campidoglio is one of the few squares in Europe designed all at one time, and by a great artist: the multitalented Michelangelo Buonarroti. The Campidoglio, meaning capitol and so called in Roman dialect since Michelangelo's time, shows the power of its designer's genius on a place that has been of supreme (if sporadic) importance for most of two millennia.

The position and height of the Capitoline Hill made it the ideal natural prominence for worshipping the king of the gods, Jupiter, and for ruling an empire (as well as for meting out justice). The Capitoline is still topped by the thirteenth-century Santa Maria in Aracoeli (Saint Mary of the Altar of Heaven), the latest of the churches erected on the site of a temple to Juno, queen of the gods.

A succession of governmental buildings occupied the site on the hilltop's east side, where Michelangelo would shape his Senate building. Its immediate predecessor faced the wrong way—that is, east looking over the Roman Forum toward the Palatine Hill, not west, toward the Vatican, the seat of power of the supreme ruler of the Papal States. The slope leading to the old Senate building's front was steep and scrubby. West of the Senate was the Conservatory Palace, but the rest of the hilltop was so small that it got twisted in relation to the Senate.

All in all, the famous hill was something of a mess when Pope Paul III decided it should be shaped up for a celebration of the reconciliation between the papacy and Charles V, Holy Roman Emperor and king of almost all of Europe. His Holiness wanted not only to solidify the peace but also to reassert his own political power. He dictated a new network of roads leading from the Vatican to the base of the Capitoline Hill.

Happily, just at this time—1534—Michelangelo had decided to leave Florence for Rome, and Pope Paul virtually greeted the artist with a commission to put his architectural talent to work on the Campidoglio. Although Michelangelo designed much of what we see today, he saw very little of it built before he died in 1564. But with this one achievement, the famous painter, sculptor, and architect proved to be one of history's greatest urban planners as well.

Michelangelo's gently stepped ramp, the cordonata, a stunning contrast to the adjacent 124-step flight to the Aracoeli, was far from completed in time for the arrival of Charles V and his retinue, who had to make their way across the old route through the Forum and up the Capitoline's inhospitable east side. They did find on the piazza at the top the splendid second-century bronze equestrian statue of Emperor Marcus Aurelius, which had been moved from the papal complex at S. Giovanni in Laterano (St. John Lateran) and placed on a pedestal of Michelangelo's own design. The strong symmetry he imposed on the space mandated that the equestrian be placed at the square's center, but there is some speculation that Michelangelo may have considered the central position less powerful than the asymmetrical placement of

1 This view of one Senate stairway includes all the materials and architectural details that Michelangelo chose to re-employ. 2 The Senate rises into view as one climbs the stepped ramp from below. 3 The Palazzo Nuovo is composed of architectural elements chosen from the façade of the Senate. 4 The Senate and Marcus Aurelius greet one on arrival.

1 A reasonable copy of the famous equestrian statue of Marcus Aurelius stands on a central pedestal designed by Michelangelo. 2 The Palazzo Nuovo forms the northern arm of the trapezoidal space that surrounds the equestrian statue. 3 A cross section through the Capitoline Hill from the piazza shows how the Senate towers over the Roman Forum on the left and the streets leading to the Piazza Venezia on the right. 4 The piazza, seen from the steps in front of the Senate, displays its famous floor pattern and the view of Rome as it is grasped by the two flanking arms of the Palazzo dei Conservatori and and the Palazzo Nuovo.

the equestrian statues by Donatello and Verrocchio in Padua and Venice (see pages 46 and 42). In any event, he made the best of it by setting the statue in a very effective paving pattern. (The original Marcus Aurelius statue recently was meticulously restored and today stands, protected, inside one of the Capitoline Museums. Many critics dislike the *falso*, the copy that replaces it, but it looks fine to me.)

The old Senate building, a sort of city hall, was an asymmetric combination of centuries-old add-ons. To start improving it, Michelangelo placed in front of it a fountain basin flanked by a heroic pair of stairways. His plans for a new façade with huge two-story Corinthian pilasters were executed shortly after his death. Two loyal architects, Carlo Rainaldi and Giacomo della Porta, took over the project, following Michelangelo's plan, with two façades that flank the Senate, enhancing the old Palazzo dei Conservatori and the Palazzo Nuovo—today's Capitoline Museums—and moved the tower of the Senate on axis with the composition.

We do not know Michelangelo's thinking when he shaped the dynamic space in front of the three buildings. Since the Palazzo dei Conservatori (to the south) already sat 8.5 degrees off the axis of the Senate, Michelangelo's love of symmetry is probably what led him to place the Palazzo Nuovo (on the north) at the same 8.5 degrees off the other side of the centerline. The resulting tense trapezoidal form has precedents and successors—for instance, the forecourt of St. Peter's (see page 92). Someone as sensitive and knowledgeable as Michelangelo was certainly aware of the spatial effect in Venice's Piazza San Marco, whose slanted, perspective-manipulating sides shrink your perception of the great Venetian basilica (see page 34). Here, similarly, the subtly angled sides make the Senate building look closer and smaller—more in scale with its neighbors. Once you reach the head of the stepped ramp, you see the square as a simple rectangle. Its tension is apparent in drawings but hardly discernable in reality.

Perhaps the most famous single element of the Piazza del Campidoglio is its floor. The paving consists of dark basalt setts, or cubes, and flush travertine slabs. The pattern makes a great oval that nearly touches the façades of the three buildings and accepts the angled sides of the trapezoid. Although the design was very specific to this special place, it has been copied and adapted often.

The piazza can be approached through narrow uphill passages on either side of the Senate, none of which allow space in the square to leak out. But almost everyone marches up the great stepped ramp. Near the top are

the gigantic, ancient Castor and Pollux statues that were placed here, along with their steeds, in 1583. But the visitor's gaze quickly moves across the square to the tower atop Michelangelo's Senate building. Marcus Aurelius, lower though closer, comes into full view only when you reach the top step. From there the welcoming arms of the two side buildings pull almost forcibly into the piazza.

After you have caught your breath, it is natural to turn back toward the cordonata you've just ascended. That's when you see this great square's illusory fourth wall: a sweeping panorama of Rome. Saint Peter's in the Vatican, miles away, is in plain view, just as Pope Paul would have liked Charles V to see it.

Proceeding farther within the enveloping walls, and particularly when you have reached the head of Michelangelo's Senate stairs, the angled sides of the tricky trapezoid, reinforced by the oval in the pavement, hold everything in place. From here it's quite clear that the two sides are identical in height, but that the Senate building behind is much taller. And the fourth side is not there at all. It sounds like a strange recipe, but the use of similar architectural detailing and a common Roman palette—creamy travertine, golden Roman brick, bronze, and basalt—work beautifully.

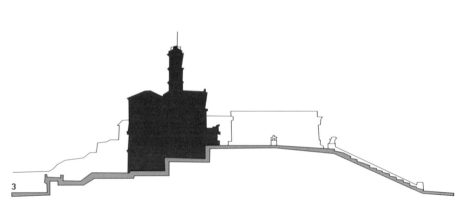

PIAZZA SAN PIETRO
Rome

PLAN DIMENSIONS	RATIO OF WIDTH TO LENGTH	AREA	HIGHEST POINT	RATIO OF WIDTH TO SKYLINE HEIGHT	ANGLE OF VIEW FROM THE COLONNADE TO THE SKYLINE	ANGLE OF VIEW FROM THE CENTER:	KEY DATE
690 × 790 ft (210 × 240 m)	1 to 1 (incl. trapezoid and ellipse)	12.5 acres (5 ha) TYPICAL HEIGHT TO SKYLINE 65 ft (20 m)	150 ft (46 m), façade of basilica	10 to 1	6°	11°	1656, Bernini begins work on the piazza

Sources of drawing data: Gromort, *Choix de Plans*; various Vatican guides; and aerial images from Google Earth

The square in front of Saint Peter's Basilica (plan overleaf) presents problems. On the one hand, thanks to television, it is probably the best-known urban space in the world, often in use for grand ceremonies such as canonizations and the huge crowds they draw. It is the parvis (forecourt) of a great basilica. And it was designed by Gian Lorenzo Bernini, a genius of the Renaissance. But on the other hand, it is too wide for the space it was meant to contain. Its main western wall is grossly out of scale with the basilica behind and the activities it was meant to display. And where its eastern end was meant to be closed, it opens onto a seemingly endless avenue. What remains, alas, is a set of monumental mistakes—but errors with lessons to teach.

St. Peter's Basilica

Sistine Chapel

Meters 15 30 60 90 North

Feet 50 100 200 300

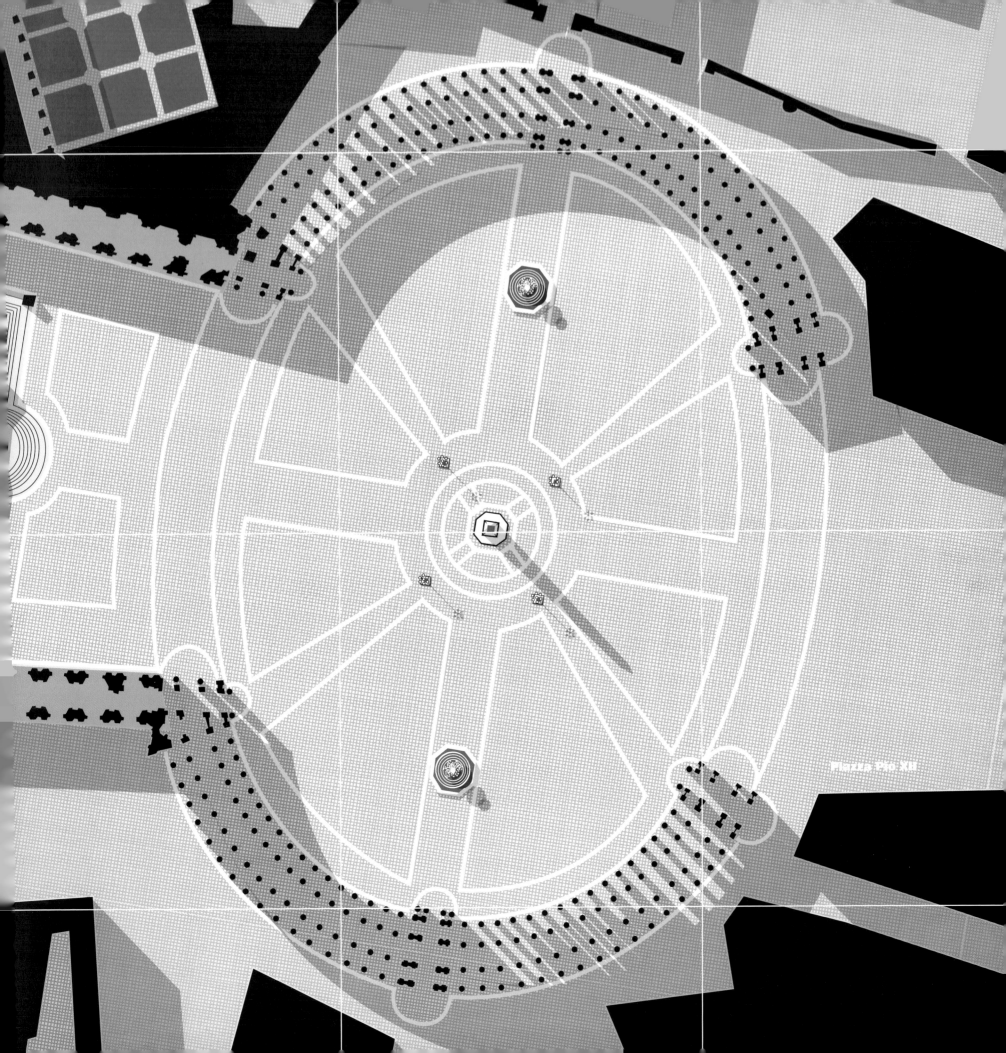

Piazza Pio XII

The Basilica di San Pietro—St. Peter's—has some 1,700 years of history, starting with Constantine, the emperor who Christianized Rome in the fourth century. Constantine erected an important church on the site, revered as the burial place of the first Bishop of Rome, Saint Peter. It stood here, periodically modified and enlarged, until the early sixteenth century, when Pope Julius II decided that the Church needed a brand-new, unprecedentedly grand basilica.

The planning and execution of the structure Julius imagined and its forecourt continued through the reigns of more than twenty more popes and engaged the talents of an all-star succession of architects and sculptors—Donato Bramante, three sons of the Sangallo family, Carlo Maderno, Giacomo della Porta, Domenico Fontana, Michelangelo, and finally Bernini. Designs came and went, as did designers. A first stone was actually laid in 1506 by Pope Julius for a church with a plan in the shape of an equal-armed Greek cross by Bramante, but pope, plan, and planner all passed from the scene. After more abortive tries and a decision to go with a Latin cross plan, Pope Paul III, undoubtedly tired of so many changes, essentially ordered Michelangelo, then seventy-two, to take over the design.

Michelangelo established the final form of the north, west, and south façades. He started construction of the famous ribbed dome, which, after he died, della Porta completed. A building that had begun with a sense of horizontality under Bramante acquired a complex vertical thrust culminating in its dome, which is visible from practically any rise or rooftop in Rome. As for the church itself, Heinrich Wölfflin, the great Swiss art historian, summed it up: "There is no instance in Western architecture of a building so flagrantly, so hideously discordant, achieving such a rousing success" (quoted in Lees-Milne, *Saint Peter's*).

Bernini, who worked extensively on the interior, was hired by Pope Alexander VII to lay out the church's parvis, the Piazza di San Pietro. Bernini may have realized that the space's width would be too great and its height too shallow to enclose people in the comfort of an ideal square. For whatever reason, he brought the arms of the galleries extending east from the portico in toward each other. The slanted sides of the trapezoid that resulted have exactly the reverse effect of the sides of Piazza San Marco. As at the Campidoglio (see page 86), slanted sides seem actually to decrease the dimensions of a church that is already huge. (The paving patterns of the basilica and piazza in my drawing are not accurate and are intended only to convey scale and complexity.)

This is what the composition might have looked like if the sides of the forecourt were parallel:

and this is how Bernini's trapezoidal parvis actually looks:

Bernini also tried to have the colonnade raised in height to two stories with Palladian openings, which would at least have added to its sense of enclosure. But instead—perhaps for reason of cost—he was left with what may be the world's tallest single-level colonnade. He also wanted to close the piazza at its eastern end with a gatehouse but was overruled. No gatehouse was built, but a hodgepodge of houses just beyond the piazza to the east effectively closed the square. This residential area was bulldozed in the 1930s to create the Via della Conciliazione, a broad, stick-straight boulevard into which the piazza now spills freely. A Mussolini-era addition, it was, and remains, a dreadful example of naïve urban planning.

The piazza is furnished with a few, excellent sculptural pieces, including the great southern fountain by Maderno. This is the splashiest piece of statuary in a city with many such. Paired with its copy by Bernini, the two provide brilliant brackets for the great Egyptian obelisk placed at the center of the square in 1586. Including its base, the obelisk rises to 131 feet (40 meters). Fine though they are, these three pieces look lonely when the piazza is not filled with most or all of the sixty thousand people it reportedly was designed to hold, and their human scale is quickly lost.

Squares are supposed to lift the spirits of the people they enclose. Windows and doors are meant to give the people who see and use them a familiar sense of scale. Here, the misleading effect of 20-foot (6-meter) doors is to shrink the observer to half size before the majesty of the Church. Even the pope, blessing his flock from a window of his apartments, looks tiny. The enormous flat space, surrounded by its distant colonnade, defines nothing so much as an arena or a playing field—which I suppose makes a certain kind of sense, since a Roman imperial hippodrome lay here long before it occurred to Constantine to honor St. Peter with a basilica.

1 The fountains alternatively dominate the sky and nestle within the arms of the colonnade. 2 Inside Bernini's colonnade, the visual jumble of the Vatican palaces to the north is largely hidden.

1 Framed by a pair of Bernini's columns, the basilica seems almost in scale.
2 The majestic sweep of the colonnade stops short of closing the piazza, leaving the Piazza Pio XII and the Via della Conciliazione as an open wound at its eastern end.
3 St. Peter's, its colonnade, and the obelisk as seen from the east are enormous and the visitors are minuscule. 4 Viviano Codazzi rendered the square in 1630, showing the portico by Maderno and the construction under way at each side for Bernini's extensions. One of the towers is credited to Bernini, but opinions differ as to whether both were built. In any case, they are gone today.

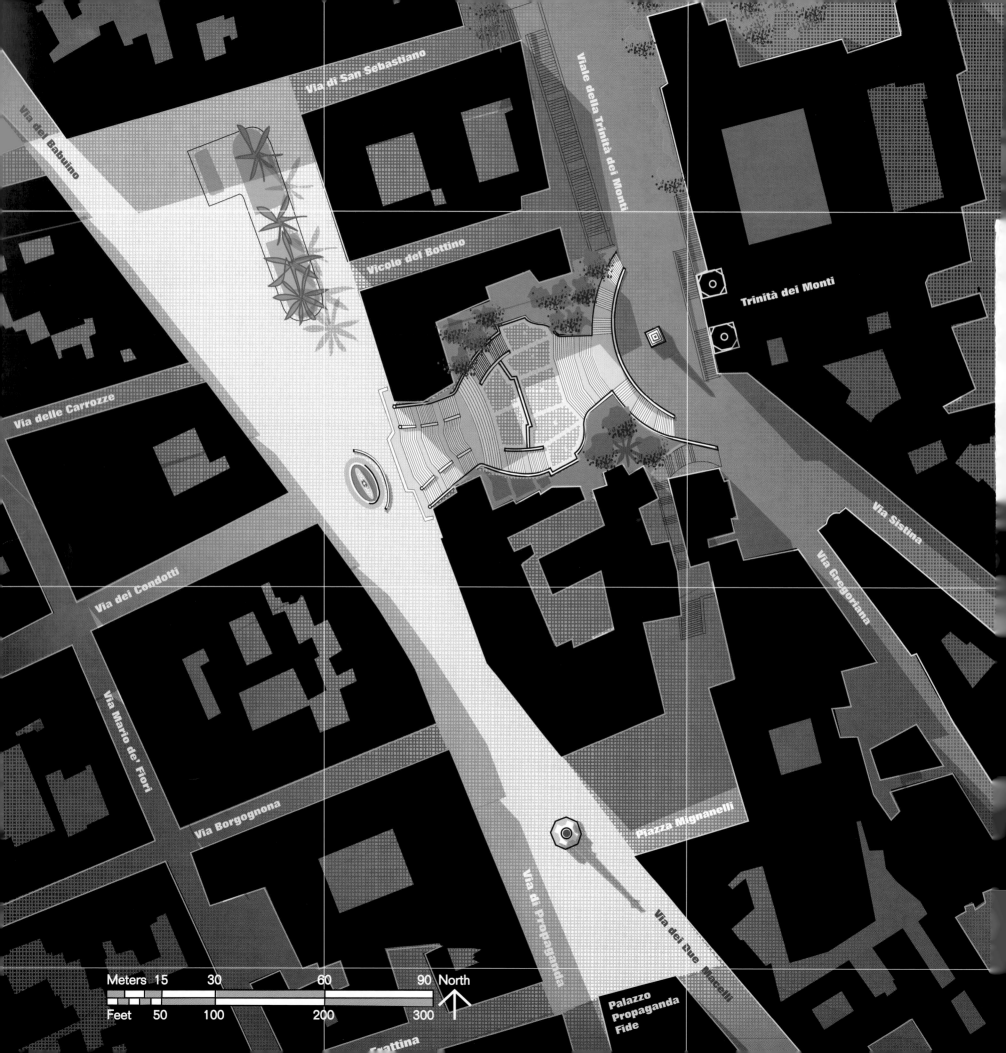

Via del Babuino

Via di San Sebastiano

Viale della Trinità dei Monti

Vicolo del Bottino

Trinità dei Monti

Via delle Carrozze

Via Sistina

Via dei Condotti

Via Gregoriana

Via Mario de' Fiori

Via Borgognona

Piazza Mignanelli

Via di Propaganda

Via dei Due Macelli

Palazzo
Propaganda
Fide

Frattina

Meters 15   30   60   90   North

Feet   50   100   200   300

PIAZZA DI SPAGNA
Rome

PLAN DIMENSIONS	RATIO OF WIDTH TO LENGTH	AREA	TYPICAL HEIGHT TO SKYLINE	HIGHEST POINT	RATIO OF WIDTH TO SKYLINE HEIGHT	ANGLE OF VIEW FROM THE SHORT SIDE TO THE SKYLINE	KEY DATE
variably 65, 230, and 330 × 850 ft (20, 70, and 100 x 260 m)	1 to 3	2.5 acres (1.0 ha), including the steps	65 ft (20 m)	210 ft (65 m), tip of church spire above the square	4 to 1 on average	16° on average	1623, completion of the Barcaccia fountain

Source of drawing data: Novelli, ed., *Atlante di Roma*

What may be the world's most popular square, the Piazza di Spagna in Rome, is certainly delightful and pretty—also strange and by no means square. A pair of spatial triangles is formed by the acute intersection of three streets: the Via del Babuino streaking southward from the Piazza del Popolo; the Via dei Due Macelli shooting north from a tunnel under the Quirinale Palace; and the modest Via di Propaganda, doing little more than closing the area on the south. The junction results in the shape of a lopsided bow tie. The most interesting east–west street, which enters the northern triangle, is the Via dei Condotti, the shopping street in a town that knows how to shop.

The main event of the piazza is the Spanish Steps—the Scalinata della Trinità dei Monti—named for the two-towered church erected at the top of what may be the most dramatic flight of stairs in the world. The ensemble was built for the French by Italian designers and ended up named for the former Spanish Embassy at its base.

The Scalinata, with its one hundred thirty-seven steps rising between twelve landings, forms a Baroque, almost symmetrical shape. Anyone who walks up or down, or just sits there in the sun, feels like royalty. Banks of flowers, particularly azaleas, add brilliant color to the soft beige travertine and basalt pavers. The French wanted to place a statue of King Louis XIV at the top of the steps, but an Egyptian obelisk, erected in 1788 by Pope Pius VI, stands there instead. The church and the ancient obelisk in front of it would be of no particular interest if they didn't crown the Spanish Steps; but the steps would look silly if they didn't lead somewhere. The elements definitely work together.

At the base of the steps a crowd always surrounds and often wades right into a fountain in the shape of a half-sunken boat, the Barcaccia. The fountain, by Pietro Bernini, father of the great Gian Lorenzo, was placed here in 1629 to commemorate the 1598 flood of the Tiber River. It was purposely given its inactive, sunken form to accommodate the low water pressure in this part of the city.

From here you can look across the piazza's southern triangle toward the Jesuits' Palazzo di Propaganda Fide, which still serves its centuries-old purpose as a training school for Jesuit missionaries. The palazzo forms the southern wall of the Piazza di Spagna. In 1644 Gian Lorenzo Bernini, who lived nearby, gave its plain façade the more decorative appearance it has today. A Roman Corinthian column found under a monastery in 1777 was erected in this part of the piazza in 1854. A sculpture of the Virgin Mary stands atop the column, and Old Testament figures appear on the base. Every year on December 8 the pope celebrates the dogma of the Immaculate Conception here.

Looking at the Piazza di Spagna as a whole, especially considering the effect that similarly slanted sides give to the squares of the Campidoglio, St. Peter's, and San Marco, you might predict that a twosome of such planar spaces would be twice as interesting. Instead, they crash into each other and erupt into what may be considered the world's first great spatial take off— right up the Spanish Steps.

High Street

Apollo Street

Ermou Street

Marine Gate

Chadrevan Mosque

Socrates Street

Castellania

Euripides Street

Pythagoras Street

Aristotle Street

Ibrahim Pasha Mosque

Meters 15   30   60   90 North
Feet   50   100   200   800

FOUNTAIN SQUARE OF HIPPOCRATES

Rhodes

PLAN DIMENSIONS	RATIO OF WIDTH TO LENGTH	AREA	TYPICAL HEIGHT TO SKYLINE	HIGHEST POINT	RATIO OF WIDTH TO SKYLINE HEIGHT	ANGLE OF VIEW FROM THE SHORT SIDE TO THE SKYLINE	KEY DATE
100 × 120 ft (30 × 36 m)	1 to 1 (approx. square)	0.3 acres (0.1 ha)	30 ft (10 m)	50 ft (15 m), rooftop gardens	4 to 1	18°	1507, completion of the Castellania

Source of drawing data: Cadastral maps from the Greek Ministry of Culture, Foundation for the Financial Administration and Realization of Archeological Works

The Fountain Square of Hippocrates in the Old Town on the island of Rhodes is one of the smallest of the great spaces in this book and, if you discount the ancient underpinnings of many Italian squares, one of the oldest. It has given joy to Rhodians and foreigners for more than five centuries. It is not unique, but it is an excellent example of a medieval marketplace that has maintained its identity and usefulness through the centuries while adapting to changing uses and rulers.

The name of the space comes not from the great Greek physician but from Hippocrates of Chios, a mathematician of the fifth century B.C. Eudemus of Rhodes (370–300 B.C.), an important student of Aristotle and the first historian of science, was his chief promoter, and many nearby streets are named for other famous mathematicians.

The square lies at the junction of several important commercial streets, all quite narrow and heavily used day and evening by pedestrians. Its tension and influence extend deep into the surrounding area along each of the streets anchored at its center. The approach to the square is especially strong if you come at it from the west on High Street (later, Socrates Street), the main tourist drag of the Old Town. Its path roughly follows one of the original orthogonal roadways of the ancient Hellenic city that preceded the medieval town of the Greeks and the Turks.

The square is confidently contained by two-story structures, both levels of which are accessible to the public. Signage is varied but restrained, and incandescent lights add a uniform sparkle at night, with no neon intrusions. Since 1992, the town has prohibited motor traffic between April and October.

Since prehistoric times, practically every people ever to set sail in the Mediterranean (except, curiously, the Egyptians) established a foothold on Rhodes, many laying claim to this advantageously located island. The Phoenicians, Minoans, Achaeans, Dorians, and Persians all coveted Rhodes. The steady traffic of actual or would-be conquerors didn't slow down until 1309, after which for two centuries the Byzantine Christian Knights of Saint John ruled Rhodes. In 1522, Turkish Muslims took charge and held Rhodes until 1912, when the Italians took over after a long and bitter war. Britain eventually returned Rhodes to Greece after World War II.

The Rhodes we encounter today in Hippocrates Square mostly reflects the domination of the Byzantines and Turks. Before surrendering to Suleiman the Magnificent in 1522 and taking flight, the Knights of St. John erected a strange building that came to be called the Castellania after the castellan, or ruler. The year 1507, after a massive earthquake, seems to be the likeliest date of its construction. Sited by the waterfront just inside the expanded city walls, it has served many purposes. Originally a courthouse for settling maritime disputes, then variously a Muslim house of prayer and a British health department, today it houses the city's main library.

The Castellania is a foursquare block of nicely detailed Venetian Gothic stonework. Its ground floor consists of four bays of protective vaulting under the hall above, with wrought iron normally barring entry.

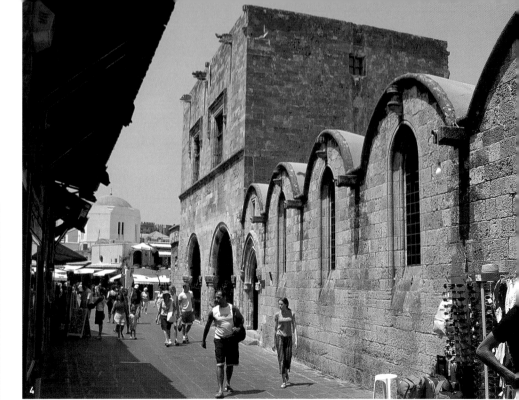

1 The fountain of the square is decorated with delicate blue and gold tile work, bas-relief panels around its base, a bronze owl at its top, and ever-present pigeons. 2 Entry from Ermou Street to the north passes under a vine-laden trellis. 3 The square spreads out below the terrace at the top of the Castellania stairway, and the white canvas used for awnings and parasols provides a visual unity. 4 The approach along Aristotle Street announces the Castellania with its red-tiled vaults. 5 An overhead relieving arch frames the square and the Marine Gate beyond at the entry from Pythagoras Street. 6 The square revolves around its fountain. Traffic continues east to the right toward a smaller fountain in Hebrew Martyrs Square. The pink dome of a former mosque in the northeast corner of the square is next to the stair of the Castellania, and shops rebuilt after the 1924 fire are behind the arcade on the left.

Four red-roofed barrel vaults cover the eastern wing as it stretches down Aristotle Street toward the old Jewish quarter. The building's jewel is a noble stairway with elegant stone detailing that is purely Italian in character and may in fact have been transported from Verona. It gives access to an open landing above, from which a grand panorama of the modest square can be seen; the library is also accessible from here. The stair's principal role, however, is as part of the stage set from which everyone can see and be seen.

To the left of the Castellania sits an old pink-domed, abandoned mosque. An elaborate stone party wall in the fashionable Venetian Gothic style of the day creates a visual separation between the Castellania's noble stair and the humble painted plaster of its neighbor. Exactly when the wall was built is a matter of controversy and conjecture. What we see today dates from a beautification program undertaken in the early 1920s. Whether the Italian architects on the job were restoring something of which they had records is simply unknown.

A pretty little fountain of unknown date was placed in front of the mosque and the Castellania and anchors the space surrounded by the informal enclosure of buildings that define today's Fountain Square of Hippocrates.

Four streets radiate from the square: Ermou goes north and Aristotle goes east along the sea wall; Pythagoras and Euripedes head south. Each bends subtly on leaving so that, from within the square, you really can't see out along them. Only the looming towers of the Marine Gate, the drum and dome of the Chadrevan Mosque, and the more distant minaret of the Ibrahim Pasha Mosque suggest that there is a town beyond the square. Each of the streets, which used to house artisans and craftsmen, is now lined with shops selling tourist paraphernalia. But a market is a market, and it would be unfair to look down on today's trade just because it is so popular. As a busy public room, Hippocrates Square feels right and works beautifully.

Residents and tourists of the Old Town manage to detour through its pleasant envelope at least once or twice a day, whether shopping or hoping to meet someone for a chat and perhaps a drink or a meal. When dogs and cats, balloon sellers, and an organ grinder join the square's swirling mix of humanity in the evening, the scene from restaurant terraces above is both natural and theatrical.

The only concern for planners is not to spoil it. The town has passed laws against neon signage, and many shops that were rebuilt after a disastrous fire in 1924 have been designed to copy the original styles. The prospects for this delightful nucleus of Mediterranean life under the sun are good; in 1988 UNESCO declared medieval Rhodes a World Heritage Site.

1 The Chadrevan Mosque on the left follows a widening in Socrates Street and marks the approach to the Castellania beyond. 2 The cafés swing into action as dark descends, and each has its hawker shouting its virtues and those of the open-air restaurant above. 3 Just about everyone in town manages to gather around the fountain at some point in the evening. 4 The stair and a wall that covers the old mosque next door were beautifully detailed by the Italians, who knew how to build for the sharp sunshine. 5 The Castellania and its stair tie the square back to its history of five centuries during which it served many functions—most recently as a municipal library.

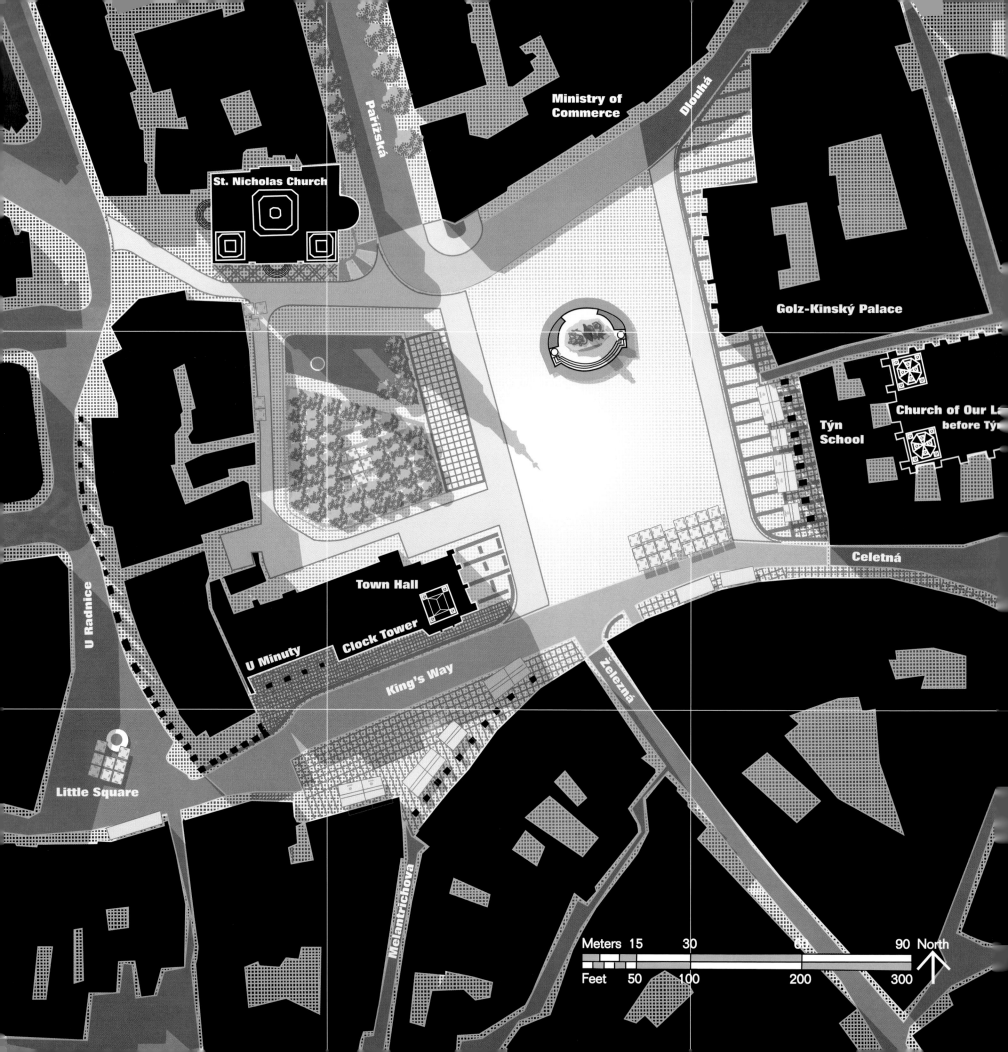

St. Nicholas Church

Ministry of
Commerce

Pařížská

Dlouhá

Golz-Kinský Palace

Church of Our La
before Tý

Týn
School

Celetná

Town Hall

U Radnice

Clock Tower

U Minuty

King's Way

Železná

Little Square

Melantrichova

Meters 15   30   60   90 North

Feet   50   100   200   300

OLD TOWN SQUARE

Prague

PLAN DIMENSIONS	RATIO OF WIDTH TO LENGTH	AREA	TYPICAL HEIGHT TO SKYLINE	HIGHEST POINT	RATIO OF WIDTH TO SKYLINE HEIGHT	ANGLE OF VIEW FROM THE SHORT SIDE TO THE SKYLINE	KEY DATE
395 × 460 ft (120 × 140 m)	1 to 1 (approx. square)	4.2 acres (1.7 ha)	65 ft (20 m)	approx. 200 ft (60 m), tops of various towers	6 to 1	10°	1338, work begun on town hall tower

Source of drawing data: Cadastral information from the city of Prague

A venerable city with a market square at its center is something so typical of Western Europe that it rarely deserves mention—except when it is one of the best. Now seven hundred years old, Prague's Old Town Square (Staroměstské náměstí) is unique in that it still stands at the heart of what has become an important modern city. The many eras through which it has passed are brilliantly represented by a host of beautiful buildings. Some have barely changed, while others show tasteful transitions from one great era to the next. Prague has accepted and embellished the best architecture to be found, reproducing it in distinctively Czech visual language and detail. The silhouette of the city, with its chisel-shaped rooftops and spiky towers, is as recognizably Czech as the music of Dvořák, Janáček, and Smetana. It was born here and still echoes in almost every church and lane.

Long ago, at a ford in the Vltava River, wooden houses and stone churches belonging to the princes of Bohemia had to be surrounded by a protective wall against Slavic tribes. The imprint of that wall, which defined Prague's Old Town, is obvious on maps but hard to find in place because it has been embedded in the city as it grew. The roads and lanes that led through the Old Town's thirteen gates still converge, however, in a star not unlike those imposed on Paris by Baron Haussmann. The square itself is carefully composed, dominated by three sets of towers and one spooky monument.

Pedestrians usually arrive by way of Celetná, Prague's principal shopping street. It starts at the Powder Tower and passes along the southern edge of the square as the King's Way en route to the Charles Bridge and the castle beyond. Dlouhá comes in from the northeast, and the Pařížká (Paris Boulevard) leaves, heading north through the now-renovated Jewish quarter. Both ends of the arcaded U Radnice fan open in triangles that provide a good look back at the church towers of St. Nicholas and Our Lady before Týn.

The ominous Jan Hus Memorial means a lot to any Czech, because Hus was a significant pre-Protestant writer who was burned at the stake in 1415 by the Council of Constance, where he had gone to plead his case against excommunication. Installed in 1915, the monument functions like a Roman fountain—as the pivot point of the swirling square. The pale patina of its bronze is a good foil to the green of its shrubbery and the western trees.

The town hall (Obecní dům) is made up of an interesting set of houses. The houses were bought up over the centuries to provide municipal office space. They stretch westward along the widening of the King's Way (or Royal Way) and end with an arcaded house called At the Minute (U minuty) with spectacular sgraffiti murals on the walls of its upper floors. The town hall's tower was begun around 1340 and has always had a clock—in fact, three clocks. The most recent collection of timepiece-and-whirligigs was assembled between the 1760s and 1860 and always attracts a crowd as the hourly bell-ringing approaches.

The tower is topped by what may have been the first of Prague's distinctive chisel- or wedge-shaped roofs that rise toward a flat ridge, with pinnacles at either end, surrounded by spiky finials at the four corners. Similar—but never identical—tower tops appear all around town: on the Týn church, on Charles Bridge, and on the Powder Tower. The town hall turns a corner northward and ends abruptly in pink masonry. The very welcome park of trees to the north replaces the rest of the town hall. It is maintained as a

memorial to the Prague Uprising, the departure of the Nazis, and the arrival of Russian tanks toward the end of World War II.

The Týn church, in a uniquely Czech version of Gothic, does not sit on the square but rises behind a school and looms over the space in dark silhouette. Partly obscured by the school, the church is also surrounded by houses of the same period, which were later renovated in the more fashionable Baroque. One of them, the White Unicorn, has been restored in the previous Gothic style and predates both the Týn church and the Renaissance Golz-Kinský Palace, which bites into the church's northern corner. The palace, by Prague's best-known architect, Kilian I. Dientzenhofer, was given its late-Baroque cladding by Ignatz F. Platzer.

This history of architectural preemption has only gradually come to light in the process of detailed restoration by the government, defining a square that has always been in an ambitious state of flux. The other force for change in the square has been the raising of the ground on the east bank of the nearby Vltava River to prevent flooding. As a result, medieval ground floors have been buried, becoming cellars, and Gothic entries open into an upper level that has become the ground floor.

The great Church of St. Nicholas, a brilliant assembly of architectural parts, anchors the northwest corner of the square. It is punctuated by its Baroque articulation of curves and notches. Rather than bracketing the front of the church, its dramatic towers face the square, and its rounded apse has great sculptural effect at the head of the Pařížká. Along the south wall of the square, houses with the welcome shelter of arcades were largely rebuilt after the fires of 1945.

The floor of the Old Town Square has been decorated with brilliant black and white masonry, some of it marking historic events. It serves to ground the square's many and various buildings on a plane that graphically adopts their scale.

Chance has played an important role in the development of many squares, but few have taken advantage of new opportunities as well as Prague. Generations of less than sensitive leaders might have allowed Old Town Square's historic abuses and terrible accidents to leave it a wounded ruin. But today's buildings overlap their neighbors and eat each other's corners in a charming way, while some do an about-face and enhance a space for which they weren't designed. All this can be seen and savored in a careful walk around this unusually complex and well-contained space.

1

2

3

4

5

1 At the base of the clock tower is an elaborate astronomical clock. 2 The grand entry to the Ministry of Commerce is Art Nouveau at its best. 3 St. Nicholas Church dominates the northwest corner of the square at the head of the Pařížská Street. 4 The church also closes the shopping street along the square's western side. 5 Spendid sgrafitti cover the upper floors of the "At the Minute" building. 6 The monument to Jan Hus lends a sober note to an otherwise joyous square.

OLD TOWN SQUARE

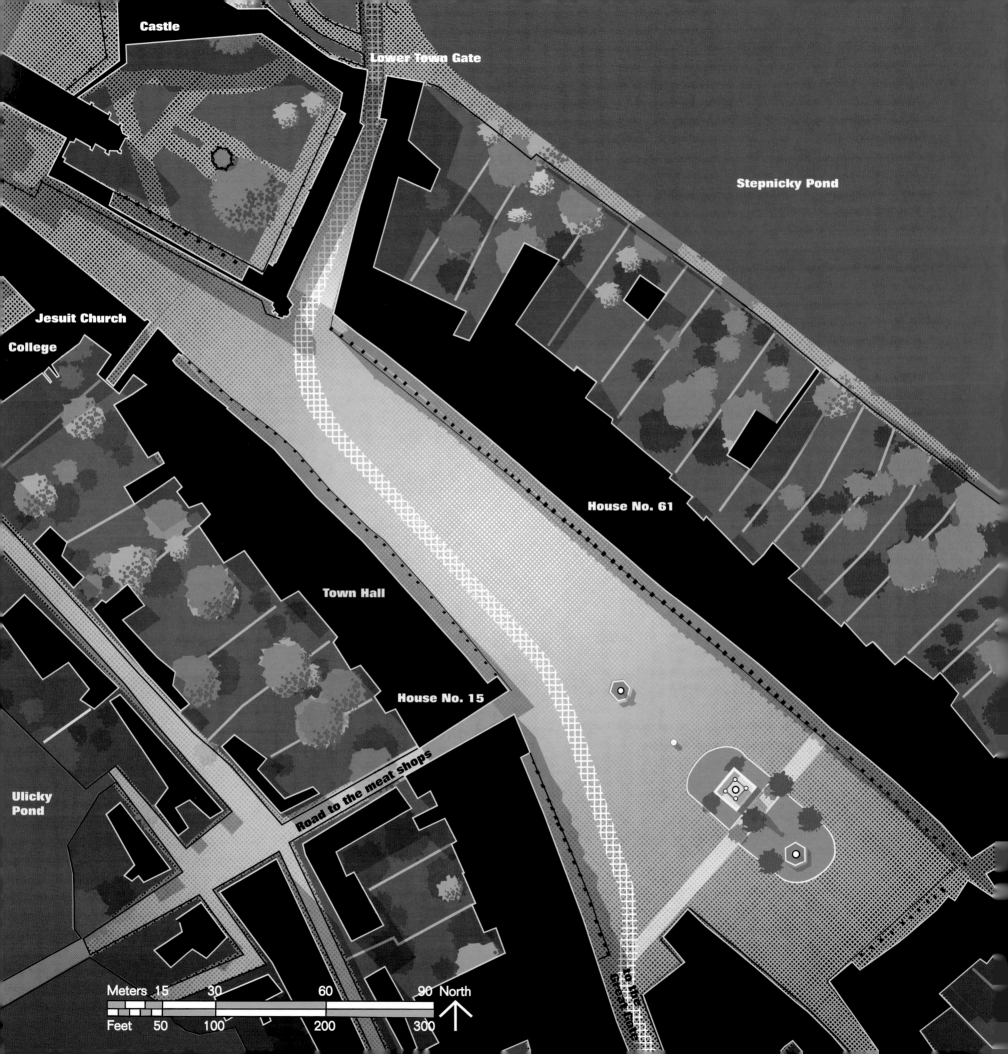

Castle

Lower Town Gate

Stepnicky Pond

Jesuit Church

College

House No. 61

Town Hall

House No. 15

Ulicky
Pond

Road to the meat shops

Meters 15   30   60   90 North

Feet   50   100   200   300

OLD TOWN SQUARE

Telč

PLAN DIMENSIONS	RATIO OF WIDTH TO LENGTH	AREA	TYPICAL HEIGHT TO SKYLINE	HIGHEST POINT	RATIO OF WIDTH TO SKYLINE HEIGHT	ANGLE OF VIEW FROM THE SHORT SIDE TO THE SKYLINE	KEY DATE
approx. 165 × 985 ft (50 × 300 m)	1 to 6 (in an irregular, bent shape)	1.8 acres (0.8 ha)	65 ft (20 m)	approx. 180 ft (55 m), towers of Jesuit church	3 to 1	22°	1354, the founding of Telč

Source of drawing data: Cadastral data from Miloš Drdácký and J. Buzek of the Institute of Theoretical and Applied Mechanics at the Czech Academy of Sciences, Telč

The small town of Telč (population 6,000), in Moravia near the southern Czech border with Austria, is little more than a group of suburbs around a narrow town square—but what a square! Old Town Square (Náměstí Zachariáše z Hradce) has a bent triangular shape that leads up to a Renaissance-era castle, and the space is surrounded by row houses with spectacular façades. It seems right out of a storybook, and this is the story.

The noble Hradec family, headed by Zacharias who had inherited the Moravian domain, founded Telč in 1354 on the mound of a Romanesque farmstead where two paths crossed in dense woods. Wooden one-story houses on masonry cellars soon enclosed the market square, and a Romanesque church was dedicated to the Holy Ghost; its towers are still the most prominent symbols at the southern end of the town. A wall was built to protect the town during the many wars among the area's landowning families. Although most of the wall has been taken down or incorporated into buildings, its two gates still give ceremonious access to the north and south ends of the Old Town Square's axis.

Within two decades of Telč's founding, ponds were built on either side of the community, giving the medieval town the appearance of a water fortress. The ponds served both to stock fish and to supply water for fighting fires—at least as great a menace as the region's frequent wars. The town suffered two disastrous fires, in 1386 and 1530; the rebuilding that followed helped establish Telč's architectural character.

The blaze of 1530 destroyed many houses, and a fury of construction followed. Some of the demolished houses were eventually replaced by the Jesuit church, and the rest were rebuilt. Stone arcades were added to support two upper levels and an inventive gable for each house. Construction was so coordinated that many of the houses shared party walls, each supported by a single stone column. These were all lined up about 10 feet (3 meters) in front of the existing cellar walls. The stuccoed façades of most of the houses were and still are decorated in a venerable sgraffito technique, the color of an underlying layer of plaster exposed by scratches through the top layer or layers. Many of the houses have trompe l'oeil bossage that resembles shadowed, three-dimensional rustication.

In 1553, Zacharias was betrothed to Katerina of Valdstejn, an engagement that combined his wealth with hers, which came from silver mines. The accumulated riches helped Zacharias to complete the restoration of his palace, an old Gothic fortress, in High Renaissance style. Everyone in Telč watched the updating of the old building, which greatly influenced the redesign of their own houses.

One of the handsomest houses is number 15, where a small street leading to the old meat shops interrupts the southern side of the square. This break gives visitors a three-dimensional view of two sides of the building; an elegant oriel enhances the corner. The brilliant bossage decoration, lost under replastering, was discovered and restored in 1952.

1 Close to typical houses on the north side of the square, the deep details of the applied façades and arcade are impressive. 2 The south side of the square turns subtly west past Lipart's reconstruction of St. Margaret toward the Jesuit church. The tall crenelations top the Town Hall. 3 House No. 61 is known as the Baker's House and was bought in 1532 by baker Michael and redecorated with sgraffiti in 1555. His profession is marked by a pretzel on one of the columns, and this egocentric façade is one of the best known on the square. 4 The entrance to the Jesuit college is elegantly detailed. 5 The town of Telč is seen first across one of the ponds that surround it. 6 Approaching the lower town gate, one passes alongside a tower of the castle's Renaissance courtyard. 7 Continuing toward another tower of the castle, the first houses on the square are seen.

After Zacharias died in 1589, the town passed into the control of absentee landlords, and little new was built for a century. The Jesuits arrived in 1651, and the continued decoration of gables on the square took on a distinctly Baroque flavor. Another attempt to enhance the space in Baroque style came in 1718, when the area's best-known sculptor, David Lipart, was commissioned to design the Column to the Virgin in the center of the square.

If you enter the square from the northwest by passing through the Upper Gate you might easily dismiss Telč as a kind of false-fronted Potemkin village. The remarkable gables are unmasked from every side, and the houses that sit behind them with long gardens sloping down to the ponds are modest in comparison. The situation isn't that different from the "backs" of the Circus at Bath (see page 179) or the houses that extend behind Henri IV's façades at the Place des Vosges. But once you've accepted the stage-set character, you can enjoy it. The palette of wild colors, competing gable profiles, and dazzling trompe l'oeil details create a truly unique urban space. The push-pull war between Gothic and Renaissance that characterizes so much of Czech architecture creates a visual tension that works well in shaping the square.

The proper entrance is from the Lower Gate on the south. From here the castle is seen to crest the top of a long, ramped space, the narrowing of which exaggerates the apparent height of the towers and walls at its far end.

Recent restoration and care on the part of both Telč itself and the Czech Republic's government have led to a remarkable revitalization of the square. UNESCO added the entire town to its list of World Heritage Sites in 1992.

1 House No. 15, at the corner of the street leading to the meat shops, is the most beautiful house on the square, with its oriel and painted rustication. 2 New cobblestones are being laid to respect the old pathways and edges of the square. 3 The strong southeast corner of the square is just past David Lipart's Column to the Virgin. 4 This section of the south arcade features the original vaults and polygonal columns on high stone bases. 5 The arcade on the north, designed to support the new façades, was built by local masons familiar with similar work in nearby Slavonice. 6 The Virgin column sits on an island of green in the middle of the square.

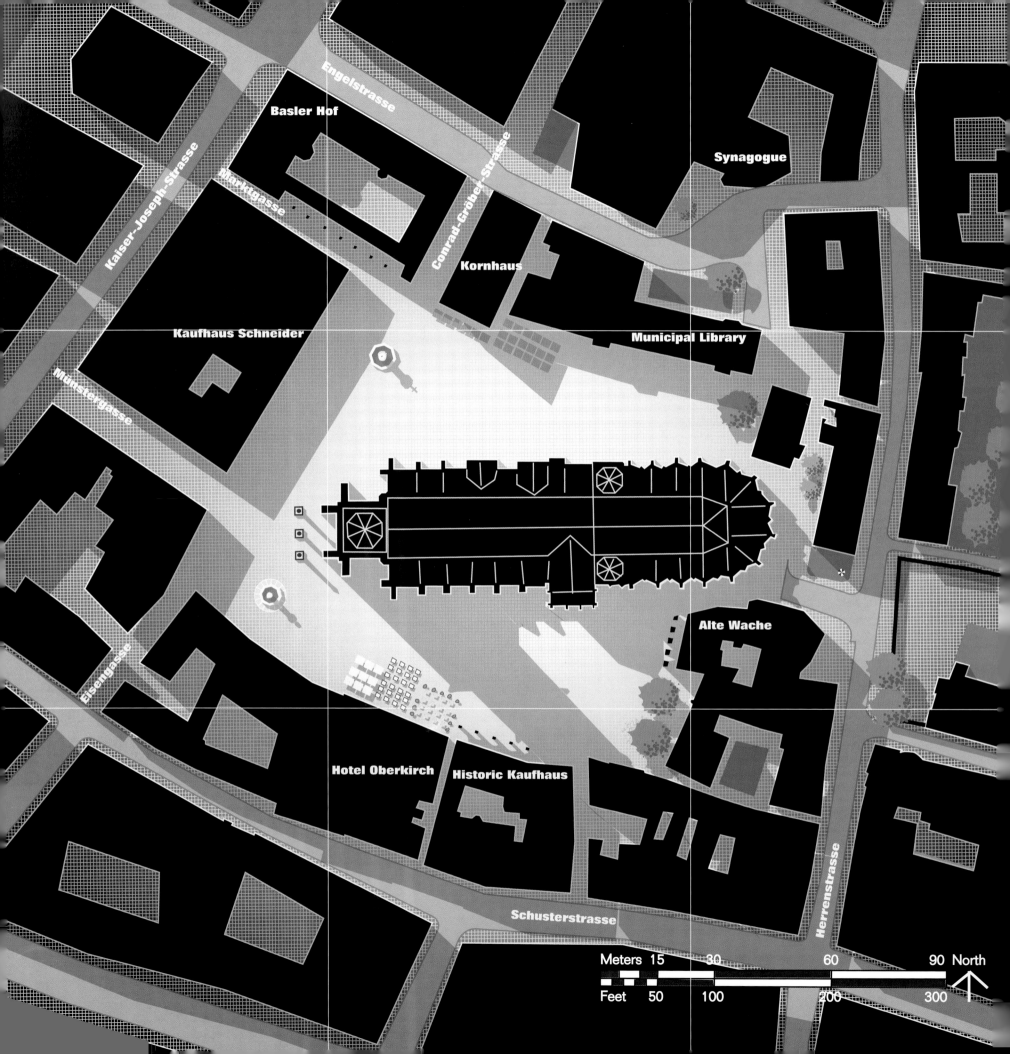

Basler Hof

Engelstrasse

Synagogue

Kaiser-Joseph-Strasse

Marktgasse

Conrad-Gröber-Strasse

Kornhaus

Kaufhaus Schneider

Municipal Library

Münstergasse

Eisengasse

Alte Wache

Hotel Oberkirch

Historic Kaufhaus

Schusterstrasse

Herrenstrasse

Meters 15   30   60   90 North

Feet   50   100   200   300

MÜNSTERPLATZ

Freiburg

PLAN DIMENSIONS	RATIO OF WIDTH TO LENGTH	AREA	TYPICAL HEIGHT TO SKYLINE	HIGHEST POINT	RATIO OF WIDTH TO SKYLINE HEIGHT	ANGLE OF VIEW FROM THE SHORT SIDE TO THE SKYLINE	KEY DATE
368 × 410 ft (112 × 125 m)	1 to 1 (approx. square)	3.4 acres (1.4 ha)	50 ft (15 m)	380 ft (116 m), top of the spire	7 to 1	8°	1360, completion of the cathedral tower

Source of drawing data: Cadastral map from the city of Freiburg

Few countries faced as difficult a reconstruction challenge after World War II as Germany, and few dealt with it as well. Every bomb-damaged city managed its reconstruction in its own way, and the approaches taken ranged from piece-by-piece restoration to complete replacement. The neighboring cities of Freiburg and Ulm were both hit very hard in air raids of November 27, 1944, but the cathedral (Münster) of each city remained essentially intact. The surrounding buildings that formed their squares (Plätze), however, were badly damaged. Freiburg and Ulm took different approaches to rebuilding their squares, and the two can be usefully compared (for Ulm, see pages 124–29).

On the edge of the Black Forest, Freiburg is one of Germany's most beautiful university towns and, appropriately, has one of the country's best medieval cathedral squares. Freiburg draws life and vigor from students and tourists from all over the world. Wherever possible the town took great, costly pains to rebuild its old buildings exactly as they had been. Ulm, in contrast, gave itself great freedom in the restoration.

Throughout Western Europe, the relationship of major structures such as cathedrals and their squares varies. Often, the cathedral façade forms part of one wall of the square; in other cases, the cathedral stands amid its surroundings, thus looking somewhat like the proverbial elephant in the room. In Freiburg, there it is—right in the middle of a space that completely surrounds it. You can hardly help noticing it all the time.

Freiburg's Münsterplatz is crowded with history, architecture, and commercial activity. The northern European sun is rarely bright and generally undependable. The shadows on the cathedral façade are further darkened by the heavy color of its red sandstone. Some historians regard Freiburg's as the only Gothic church tower in Germany, and the cathedral is almost overwhelmed by what the Swiss historian Jacob Burckhardt regarded as the most beautiful tower in all Christian architecture. At 380 feet (116 meters), it certainly is tall, and its laciness contrasts strikingly with its square base. But, along with the rest of the cathedral's dark red sandstone, the tower can seem more oppressive than beautiful.

A market existed before the first church on the site, the construction of which began in 1120. A chancel, transept, and tower were completed by 1230. During two politically unstable centuries, construction on what was still just a parish church continued eastward until 1513, when the new chancel with its eleven chapels was consecrated. Finally, in 1827, the church assumed its cathedral role. A large masonry shop has always stood next door, and some part of the building is always enshrouded in scaffolding for restoration.

The Münsterplatz is defined by an assembly of buildings of various colors, details, and uses, the forms of which represent commercial history from the twelfth century to the twenty-first. They are of nearly uniform height, and the closeness of the buildings makes for a unified square. You can enter it by any number of streets and alleyways, but the Münstergasse points right at the tower and the statues in front of it. Just to the right is Saint George's Fountain, which pairs with the Fish Fountain in the northern corner. Both are gilded and pretty and have fine benches all around the water for visitors to rest.

1 The town against the Black Forest is seen looking east from the cathedral tower. 2 The cathedral tower establishes its somber presence at the end of Münsterstrasse. 3 The south portal of the cathedral overlooks that half of the square dominated by the Kaufhaus. 4 Many shop signs are set into the cobbles. 5 A garden just east of the apse seems to capture the spirit of the square. 6 There is a fine little nook behind the white gables of the Kornhaus (Granary).

After the cathedral, three buildings dominate the space with their shape, color, and history. The Kornhaus on the north turns its stepped gable to the square; its elegant stone window surrounds are set off against its bright white stucco façade. Originally the town's granary, it has since been an abattoir, theater, ballroom, butcher shop, and fruit market. Opposite, south of the cathedral, is the gaudy historic Kaufhaus (Merchants' Hall), resplendent in red stucco, with gilded detail and coats of arms representing the noble families that controlled Freiburg for more than four centuries. Its corner oriels, multicolored roof tiles, and stepped gables seem straight out of a fairy tale and conceal their rather prosaic function as an enclosure for a customs house and a municipal finance office. The east end of the square is closed by the yellow gable and arcade of the Alte Wache (Old Guard), which was the Austrian guard post built for the watch garrison stationed in Freiburg in 1733. The building has since been used for choir practice, as an art club, as a wine museum, and for public restrooms (according to the town's Web site, "Germany's only outhouse that is classified as a national monument").

The rest of the houses surrounding the cathedral serve to support the more important structures by the use of their elegant, small-scale detail and modest background character. Of special note is a modern department store, the Kaufhaus Schneider (now Breuninger). It wraps around a white, medieval-style building on the corner of Münstergasse. Heinz Moll, an architect from Karlsruhe, won a competition in 1979 to insert this very large store into the postwar void. He did so with a modern vocabulary that sympathetically mirrors the scale, color, and texture of its neighbors, and closes the square gracefully. Several streets entering the square provide routes for the narrow channels of water that flow through the town. They also enable café setups with portable greenery.

Compared with the dramatically creative approach that the neighboring city of Ulm took in renovating its Münsterplatz, Freiburg's planners proceeded with extreme caution. The picture-book reconstruction of Freiburg's old town conveys a strong fidelity to the city's past and a reluctance to take risks. To be sure, the planners started with a bit of a handicap: the square surrounding Freiburg's Münster is hardly big enough for its job. It barely has room for its sparse furnishings, which are limited to a few old trees and two fountains. On weekday mornings, when market stands cluster around the cathedral, you can hardly move around, let alone appreciate the relationship between what seem to be old buildings and the great structure they are meant to enhance. Even on Sunday mornings,

when there are no market stalls, a walk around the cathedral is a procession through bottlenecks.

But despite the crowds and the lack of light, the Freiburg Münsterplatz has a grandeur that lifts the spirit. It encourages examination of the complex shapes within it and serves as a beacon. The tight network of space around the Münster probably resembles squares as they were in a medieval town, where the top of the cathedral tower could often barely be seen. If the mind says, "It's nothing but a stage set," the heart says, "So what? It's a delightful place to be."

1 Red and gold oriels of the Kaufhaus echo colors found throughout Freiburg. 2 Entry to the square from the northwest is along Marktgasse, which has one of the town's drainage canals at its center. 3 The south portal of the cathedral lends dignity to the market before it. 4 Café tables next to the Kaufhaus are a good place to view the square. 5 The eastern end of the south side is enhanced by the recently restored Alte Wache, which served as the main guard post for the Austrian watch garrison in the eighteenth century. 6 An alleyway next to the Hotel Oberkirch provides access to the square from the south.

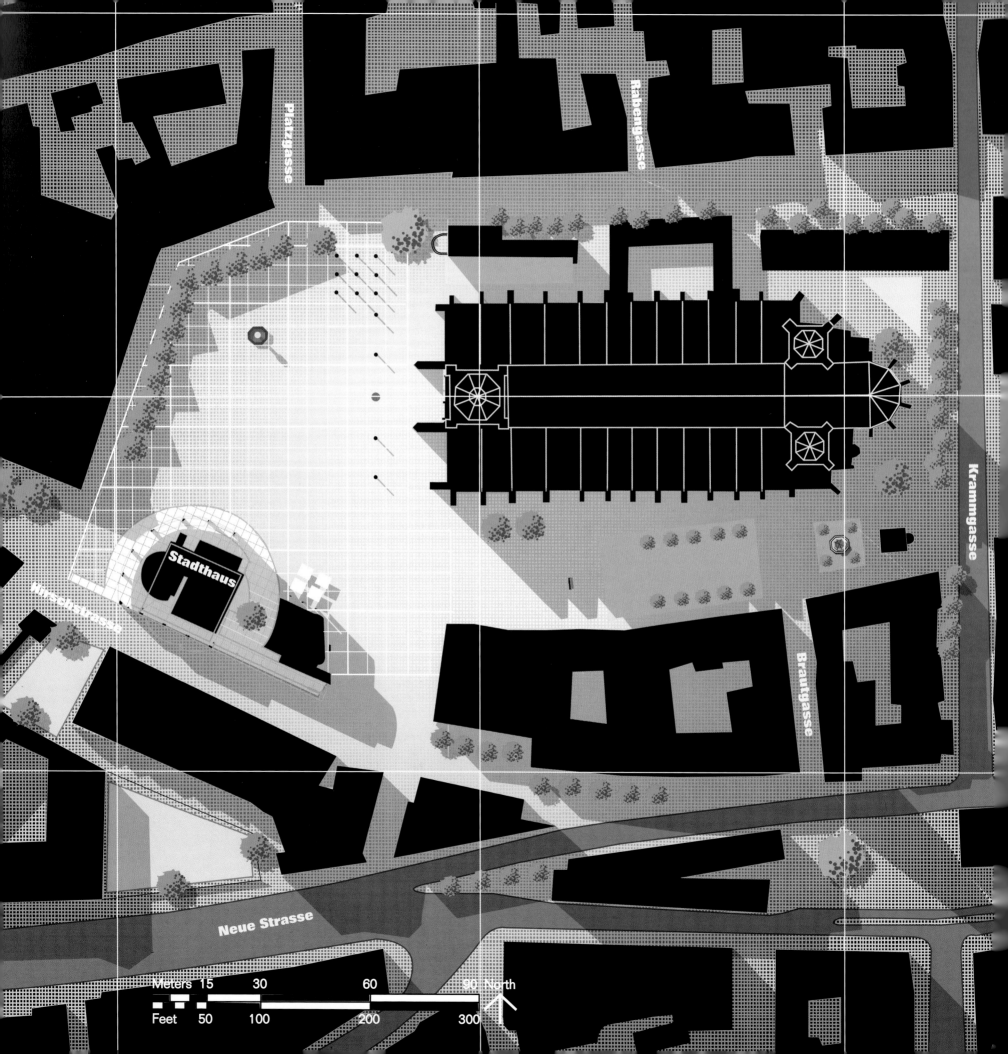

Platzgasse

Babengasse

Krammgasse

Stadthaus

Brautgasse

Neue Strasse

Meters 15   30   60   90 North
Feet   50 100   200   300

MÜNSTERPLATZ

Ulm

PLAN DIMENSIONS	RATIO OF WIDTH TO LENGTH	AREA	TYPICAL HEIGHT TO SKYLINE	HIGHEST POINT	RATIO OF WIDTH TO SKYLINE HEIGHT	ANGLE OF VIEW FROM THE FOOT OF THE CHURCH TO THE SKYLINE	KEY DATE
295 × 395 ft (90 × 120 m), cathedral parvis	1 to 1 (approx. square)	2.6 acres (1.1 ha)	65 ft (20 m)	530 ft (161.5 m), top of the spire	4 to 1	12°	1377, start of cathedral construction

Sources of drawing data: Cadastral map from the city of Ulm

Just over 100 miles (170 kilometers) from Freiburg, Ulm straddles the banks of the Danube River, and although the two cities' cathedral squares— Münsterplätze—have slightly different birthdates, they are virtual twins. They grew up over the same five and a half centuries, only to be laid low in the same bombing raids of 1944. As noted in the discussion of Freiburg, the two cities took different approaches to postwar revitalization. Neither had to rebuild the square around its cathedral entirely, but major repairs were needed in both Münsterplätze. While Freiburg pretty nearly restored its square to its original form, Ulm seized the opportunity to give its cathedral square a fresh face with venturesome modern features.

Freiburg's cathedral tower may or may not be the world's most beautiful, but Ulm's, at 530 feet (161.5 meters), is indisputably the tallest. Construction of the Ulm cathedral and the space around it have been going on since the foundation stones were laid in 1377. The steeple was topped out only in 1890. The town's population has waxed and waned over the centuries, but a market has always been held on the parvis in front of the cathedral. As the church grew in size and importance, its spatial setting was found inadequate for such a huge building. In particular, a medieval monastery just south and west of the cathedral crowded it; the monastery was torn down in the late nineteenth century. But no one had planned what was to replace the monastery, and the town argued over the issue throughout most of one hundred years. Several architectural competitions were held, but were inconclusive. World War II put a halt to the discussion, and after the war a rather banal group of three- and four-story buildings was erected in line with the previous western façades, topped by roofs with gables similar to those that had been destroyed. No attention was given to the footprint of the old monastery.

After more fruitless competitions, ten internationally recognized architects were invited to submit plans for Ulm's Stadthaus, an information center. The commission went to Richard Meier, an American architect whose designs have often been distinguished by the purity of their whiteness. (The citizens of Ulm may have been comfortable with white, since most of the town's half-timber buildings have white stucco infill.) While the brilliant white building that Meier designed for the gap in Ulm's Münsterplatz is complex and beautiful, it neither aims to evoke the original monastery nor blends inconspicuously into its context. Rather, the architect took on the problem and created the right solution. Meier's Stadthaus contains a tourist information facility, a gallery, meeting places, and a pleasant café.

Freiburg

Ulm

126

GERMANY

1 The world's tallest cathedral spire and the new Stadthaus make unusual neighbors. 2 The Münsterplatz and its market are not that different from their medieval heyday, although most is new construction. 3 Platzgasse leads to this authentic half-timbered house. 4 Trees and shops prevent the square from extending along the north side of the cathedral. 5 The granite paving pattern is extended to control each of the objects in the ground plane of the square. 6 The Stadthaus is faced by the extension of Hirschstrasse. 7 A geographic rosette is set in the stones in front of the cathedral. 8 On the south side a Russian orthodox chapel closes the space. 9 An extension of the Münsterbauhütte (cathedral construction shed) serves further to concentrate attention on the parvis in front of the cathedral.

One must admire the crisp clarity of most of the cathedral square's recent furnishings and fittings. The pattern of the paving, in Meier's hallmark Cartesian arrangement of gray granite, was inspired by features of the cathedral's façade. It determines the placement of newly planted trees, which to some extent screen the uninteresting postwar buildings. Even the access plates for the electrical and plumbing services required for the daily market fit into the pattern, although the market wagons that roll in each morning don't seem to be governed by the architect's grid.

Also worth noting is Ulm's decision to abandon the model of its old gabled buildings for the continued reconstruction of the area around the Münsterplatz. The city selected instead a group of architects, including a former associate of Meier, Wolfram Wöhr, to design of a set of related white, flat-roofed buildings that continue the line of Hirschstrasse as it joins Neue Strasse toward the east.

In comparison with Freiburg, Ulm had ample space around its cathedral. After creating a surrounding set of new façades where its old buildings had been, Ulm chose to fill the space like a park with trees and minor structures that heighten the drama of the parvis in front of the cathedral. Meier's civic structure and the cathedral's tower clasp the rounded space while gentle trees and friendly shops encompass the flanks of the church. The market activity is thereby controlled within the resulting space.

This use of exterior enclosure is neither better nor worse than Freiburg's; it's just different, although Ulm's is undeniably more venturesome. Ulm has come to love its brilliant white Stadthaus, and the buildings that redefine the north side of the Neue Strasse form a most successful extension.

(In the interest of full disclosure: the author joined Richard Meier as partner several years after the design of the Ulm Stadthaus.)

1 The gabled silhouette of the Stadthaus resembles those of its neighbors. 2 The Lion Fountain was moved at Richard Meier's suggestion as punctuation of the parvis. 3 The same fountain is engulfed on market days. 4 The materials of the cathedral are as varied as the time periods in which it was built. 5 A stone sundial has been set into the brickwork of the southwest corner of the cathedral. 6 The accessible terrace of the Stadthaus provides a good view of the square. 7 The vast sweep of the parvis can be seen only on marketless Sundays.

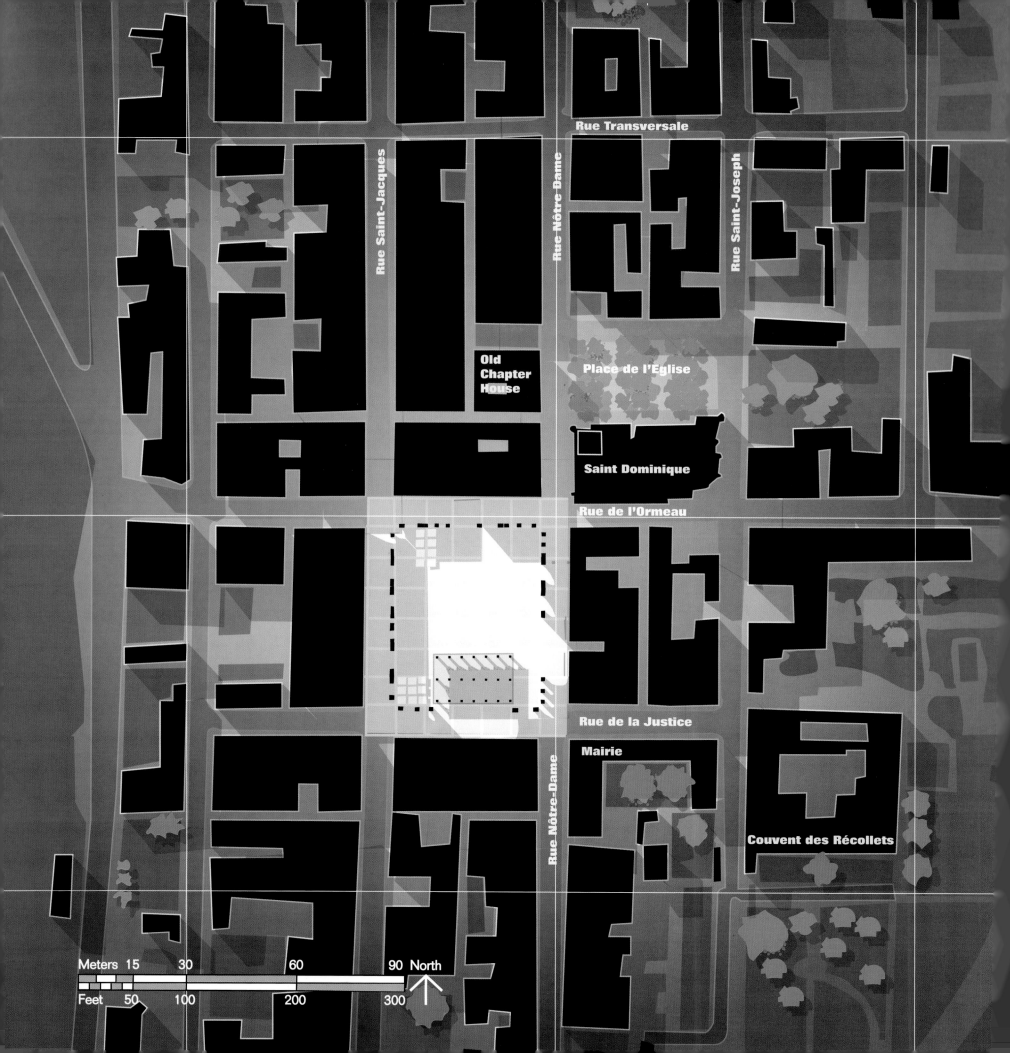

Rue Transversale

Rue Saint-Jacques

Rue Nôtre Dame

Rue Saint-Joseph

Old
Chapter
House

Place de l'Eglise

Saint Dominique

Rue de l'Ormeau

Rue de la Justice

Rue Nôtre-Dame

Mairie

Couvent des Récollets

Meters 15   30   60   90 North

Feet   50   100   200   300

PLACE DES CORNIÈRES
Monpazier

PLAN DIMENSIONS	RATIO OF WIDTH TO LENGTH	AREA	TYPICAL HEIGHT TO SKYLINE	HIGHEST POINT	RATIO OF WIDTH TO SKYLINE HEIGHT	ANGLE OF VIEW FROM ANY SIDE TO THE SKYLINE	KEY DATE
135 × 154 ft (41 × 47 m)	1 to 1 (approx. square)	0.5 acres (0.2 ha)	35 ft (10 m)	35 ft (11 m), the average ridge	4 to 1	14°	1285, establishment of the bastide

Sources of drawing data: Cadastral map from the town of Monpazier; and Google Earth

With a population well below one thousand, the tiny town of Monpazier in the Dordogne department of southwest France has a fittingly small square: the Place des Cornières. But the dignity of its proportions, the quality of its stonework, and the care with which its materials have been maintained make this a grand place. Its scale is entirely consistent with the little roads and narrow alleys leading to and from it.

Monpazier was founded in 1285 during the reign of Edward I, when the Plantagenet kings of England ruled half of France. Edward gave permission to the Baron of Biron (whose castle a few kilometers away still looms above the town) to build a bastide, a Provençal word with no English counterpart meaning a new town built expressly to settle and defend an area. The site was the flat top of a hill high above the River Dropt, at the crossing of two main roads. The north–south Rue Notre-Dame passes in front of the Church of Saint Dominique (begun in 1289 but finished only in 1506) and its former chapter house. Thereafter it forms one of the arcades alongside the Place des Cornières, which serves as Monpazier's marketplace. The east–west Rue de l'Ormeau goes past land reserved for Saint Dominique and its cemetery.

Some four hundred bastides were built in England and France, in the thirteenth and fourteenth centuries. Most have a fortress-like aspect, whether or not they are actually walled. The world in which the bastides came into being was fraught with conflict, especially between France and England; the period of the bastides encompasses the Hundred Years War (1337–1453). In this bellicose environment, construction of Monpazier (the name means, roughly, "hill of the peacemakers")—reflected at least a desire to quell the constant battling.

The main feature of a bastide is a regular grid plan, a heavily arcaded market square at the center, and a church nearby. Once you've been in the square of one bastide, you will recognize others. The bastide is a most logical and beautiful way to plan a new town and resembles the colonial plazas that Spain built in the New World four centuries later (see page 197). What looks at first to be continuous row houses above an arcade are actually a very carefully designed set of individual houses separated by slots about one foot wide called andrones. These were required by bastide construction code to prevent fire from spreading from one building to another. Roofs, eaves, arches, and a range of common materials, all resembling one another although not following an exact pattern, subtly join the houses of Monpazier. On each of three sides, a space interrupts the arcade. What might look like mistakes have in fact become welcome little courtyards.

In most bastides, the corners of the squares are open to allow the passage of vehicles, thus causing major leakage of the space. At each of the four corners that give the Place des Cornières its name, the corner columns are pulled apart but the buildings above are then cantilevered (or corbelled—it's hard to tell which) to create a visual closing of the square. The overhangs don't quite touch—again, to prevent fire from spreading—and the slot of light that passes between them is small but distinct. These clever corners crisply define the space enclosed, particularly overhead.

Along the south side of the square is the bastide's characteristic freestanding wooden market hall, which provides shelter for merchants, particularly at festival times; it used to protect enormous metal drums containing grain. The exposed structure of the hall is a matter of pride for any bastide that has one. The large wooden members can span up to 20 feet (6 meters). Monpazier's hall isn't the grandest or most complex, but it is a fine one that plays its unusual role of a space within a space with elegance.

Bollards now prevent free vehicular passage through some of the Place des Cornières's arcades, but the visual continuity of the streets leading up to them is clear and unobstructed.

Considering that the bastides are known for the consistency with which their squares were formed, Monpazier has encompassed its space with dignified clarity and maintained its unique detailing with pride. The resultant enclosure provides a spatial experience of unusual satisfaction.

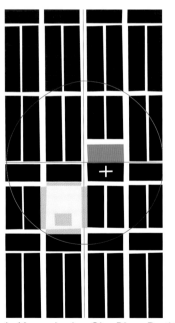 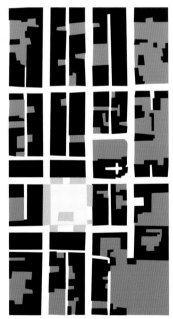

In *Monpazier, Les Cles D'une Bastide* Michel Coste has proposed a grid for the ideal city that might have been the basis for Monpazier. Large and small passageways, church, cemetery, and marketplace, following ancient units of measurement and even the "golden mean," appear in his symmetrical study.

A drawing at the same scale as his proposal shows how close the original architect and his successors were able to follow his (or their) ideal grid.

1 The north side of the square faces the hall on the left. 2 The southeast corner is seen through the silhouette of the hall. 3 Backing up, these parts of the square can be glimpsed through the southeast extended corner. 4 The north and east sides show their architectural variety with the tower of the Saint Dominique church behind. 5 Approaching the square along Rue Nôtre-Dame from the south, a slot of light can be seen between the two corner buildings.

1 The east side arcade is interrupted by a courtyard with an alley at its base. 2 The north side is also interrupted for a court that shelters a vine-covered dining area. 3 The northwest corner is a popular dining spot. 4 The hall seems to have been slid out of the courtyard behind it like a drawer. 5 The square seen from the east side courtyard illustrates its spatial complexity. 6 The hall as seen from the east side arcade shows the power and clarity of its exposed wooden structure. 7 The northwest corner shows how Monpazier has opened its ground level for the passage of horses and trucks while corbeling out the upper levels to close all but a small slot of space between the two sides.

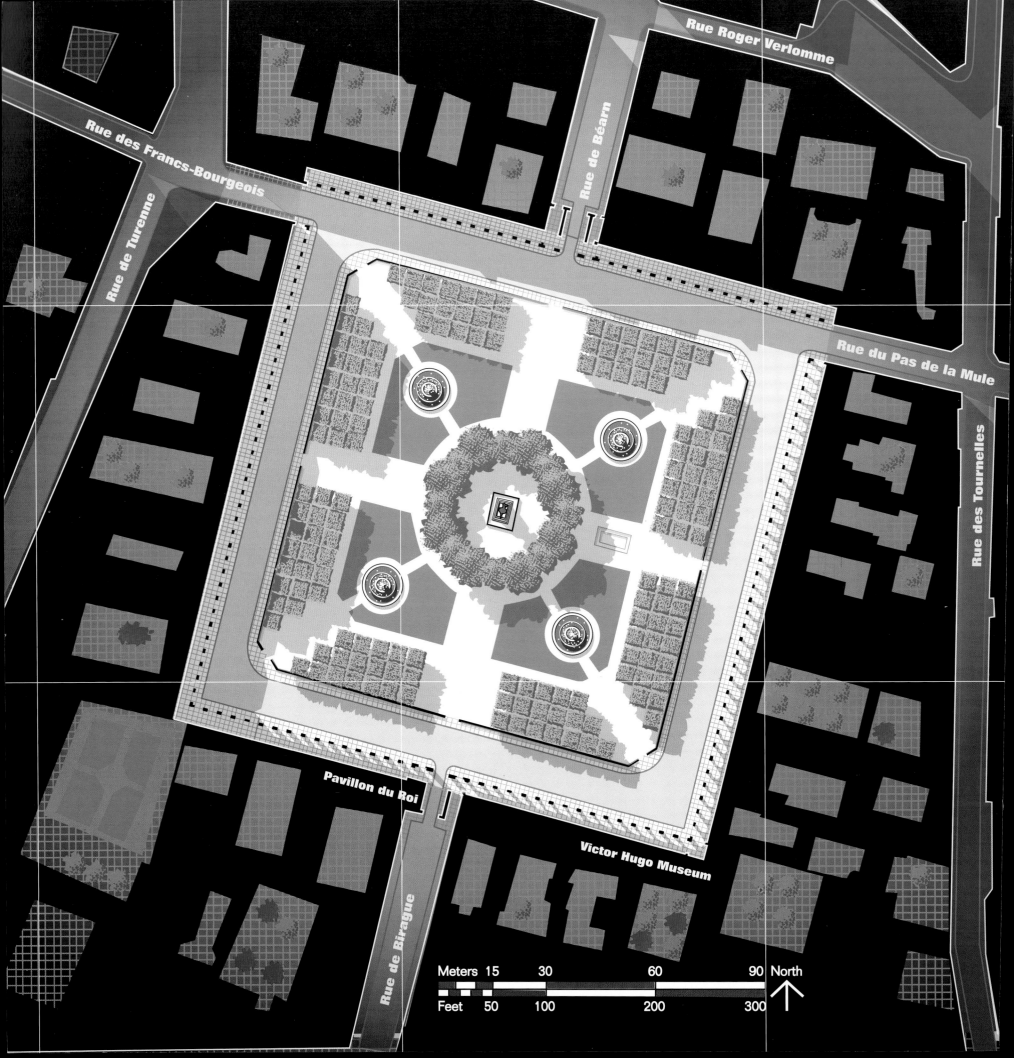

Rue Roger Verlomme

Rue des Francs-Bourgeois

Rue de Béarn

Rue de Turenne

Rue du Pas de la Mule

Rue des Tournelles

Pavillon du Roi

Victor Hugo Museum

Rue de Birague

Meters 15   30   60   90   North

Feet   50   100   200   300

PLACE DES VOSGES
Paris

PLAN DIMENSIONS	RATIO OF WIDTH TO LENGTH	AREA	TYPICAL HEIGHT TO SKYLINE	HIGHEST POINT	RATIO OF WIDTH TO SKYLINE HEIGHT	ANGLE OF VIEW	KEY DATE
468 × 468 ft (143 × 143 m)	1 to 1 (square)	5 acres (2 ha)	65 ft (20 m)	85 ft (26 m), roofs of the royal pavilions	7 to 1	FROM THE SIDE: 8° FROM THE CENTER: 15°	1612, completion of construction

Source of drawing data: Cadastral material from the city of Paris, adjusted to update tree patterns on the basis of onsite measurements and photos

The oldest formal square in Paris is certainly its best. One of the few successful square squares, the Place des Vosges meets just about every standard of greatness for an urban space. The art and architecture historian Paul Zucker declared it to be "certainly the perfect realization of this form, in its Platonic purity." (Such enthusiasm is not universal. Camillo Sitte dismissed the form of the square square as unattractive.) While the Place des Vosges may be a bit wide for its height, its carefully placed trees and fountains effectively screen distant façades until they can be examined up close.

Vehicles do enter the *place*, but so slowly that you can disregard them, and the openings that serve them do not impinge on the square's unity or allow the space to leak into the neighborhood. The square still serves its original design as a commercial and residential site, and the harmony of its composition attracts people to it as a calm eddy space in an otherwise noisy and somewhat disorderly part of town.

Most squares are formed by various buildings, each with its own shape and history; every square's spatial quality is defined by the surface made up of adjacent or close-by façades, and its integrity is determined by the tightness of its buildings' placement. Together, the façades form the inner surface or membrane of a vessel that contains the space. When the gaps between buildings are too large, the membrane "breaks," and the space leaks visually into the city beyond. When a square is conceived like the Place des Vosges and the nearby Place Vendôme (see page 145) as a unity, the containing façades not only define the form of the buildings but also create the uniquely integral surface of an inner space. Theater offers a parallel, except that a stage set extends to contain the audience perceptually, while a square's façades do so actually. The buildings behind the façades relate to the square no more than the braces supporting stage flats relate to the stage's scenery.

King Henri IV ordered the design and construction of the Place des Vosges in 1605. According to art historian Hilary Ballon, the young king was looking for a new, profitable industry for France and hoped to emulate Italy's success in the silk business. Just outside Paris he found a silk mill the dimensions of which were to determine those of his new place. The mill faced a little-used horse market on the site of several deadly duels, and it was decided to enhance its real estate value by enclosing it with ground-floor shops and living quarters above for Italian artisans producing the prized fabric. Sites for buildings laid out in a U shape facing the silk mill were offered to buyers willing to build behind the royal architects' uniform façades.

However great the initial commercial idea, it didn't work. Before the U was complete, the silk factory was torn down, and the square was completed with another collection of identical façade units. The result was the uniform four-sided composition of red brick, white limestone, and blue slate roofs that we find today. It's no wonder that, when it was new and still known by its original name as the Place du Roi (King's Square), the square became an attractive location to live in, and there was no trouble selling units to friends of the court.

1 The dense canopy of the trees that surround the square provides a sharp contrast to the sunny fountains and greensward. 2 Arches that once closed the Rue des Francs-Bourgeois at the northeast corner were removed for modern traffic. 3 Louis XIII is surrounded by fine old trees but still dominates his Place Royal. 4 Turgot's famous plans of Paris included this view of the place in 1739. 5 This engraving by Israel Silvestre was published in 1652. Artistic license has removed the eastern houses so as to provide this grand view westward with king to the left and queen to the right. The same artist seems to have forgotten the Rue des Francs-Bourgeois along the right-hand side.

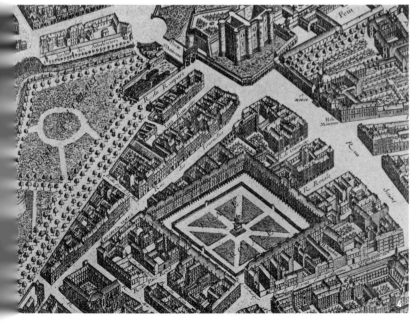

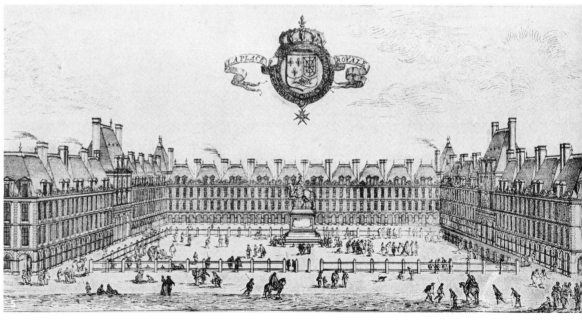

The east and west sides are made up of separately roofed houses, nine to a side and each 52 feet (16 meters) wide. Each house rises above four strong arches 13 feet (4 meters) on center, which create deep arcades giving protected access to ground-level commerce, now reopened as elegant shops and restaurants. The vaulted overhang tastefully shields the commercial signage. Taller, grand pavilions built by King Henri and named for him and his queen occupy the central bays of the square's north and south sides. The pavilions are supported by three extra-wide arches and are regally detailed. The royal architects planned a closed square approached only from the south via the Rue de Birague, which explains the care lavished on the southern back of the Pavillon du Roi (King's Pavilion).

Each house has four tall windows, with two upper floors and two attic levels. The houses appear to be faced in red brick; King Henri asked for the brick, but some accounts say there were too few bricklayers in Paris, and some builders made do with painted stucco. Others say that the houses were basically brick with some later stucco patches. Viewed from the ground, the walls certainly look like brick and are trimmed with white limestone. The houses are topped by steep, 50-degree slate roofs that are quite blue: the ensemble is consummately French. (The colors are exactly those used in the Place Dauphine at the tip of the Île de la Cité—also commissioned by Henri IV.)

The Place des Vosges façades are notable not only for their handsome surfaces but also for their voids—the shadows within the arcades and the pattern of window openings. Minor variations on basic themes—irregularly spaced tall chimneys, differently detailed dormers, an odd wrought-iron balcony here and there, and even a few cupolas—confer vitality.

When the square was completed, all this was in place, but the center was an empty field of sand. No one seems to know exactly when the square began to be filled with all its urban furniture, but the presence of fountains, fixed benches, and, most important, the meticulously placed and manicured clusters of trees, or bosks, gives the square a quality quite unlike its original bare form. The present arrangement is relatively recent. A photo from the early twentieth century shows small trees lining the periphery in a rectilinear pattern; this plan, now superseded, still appears in the city's official survey.

The comfortable proportions we perceive in the Place des Vosges result from some optical trickery, either intentional or accidental, by those who laid out the trees. The roof ridge of the square is rather low, making the space seven times wider than its skyline is high. For an "ideal" outdoor living room, seven to one is much too wide in the opinion of many students of urban design. In adding the square's screens of trees, however, the twentieth-century renovators seem instinctively to have been pushing the observer toward the center, where the surrounding buildings' "human details" can be recognized at a comfortable distance of three and one-half times their height. The effect is to raise the skyline against the ceiling of the Parisian sky. As in the Jardin du Palais-Royal (see pages 152–53), branches are trimmed with typical French precision to 10 feet (3 meters) above the ground. Further, the canopy of each tree is trimmed to a cubic shape, in contrast to the older, taller trees in the square's center, which make a romantic explosion. Trees are placed on a strict grid 16½ feet (5 meters) square, reinforcing the Cartesian regularity of the square. Like their cousins in other French parks, the trees line up in perfect rows from any viewing angle.

The central circle of trees surrounds and engulfs the heroic statue of King Louis XIII, which is best seen in winter when the trees have lost their leaves. Cardinal Richelieu installed the statue in 1639, but the original was torn down during the Revolution and replaced with a copy in 1829. The place got its present name shortly before that: Napoleon named it after the département Vosges for its speedy payment of taxes.

Although King Henri intended his square to be open for public use, the aristocratic owners of the first residential sites took control after his death and erected a fence with gates locked to all but the square's residents. Today the gates are no longer locked, and visitors leaving the shade of the arcade need only cross a sleepy one-way street to gain access to the central green. The attractive and pleasant walking surface within the fence is bank-run gravel, a sandy material much used in France not only for its appeal to the eye and the foot but also because it absorbs rainwater quickly without the need to slope the pavement toward drains.

On a sunny spring or summer day, you may be tempted to join the sunbathers who cover the lawns, or take shelter on benches under the leaves. And it's always a pleasure to pause at the public sandbox near the eastern entrance, which is usually filled with children under the watchful gaze of nannies.

1 Le Pavillon de la Reine faces that of the King from the north side of the square where its three arches lead to the Rue de Béarn. 2 At the north end of the west arcade, a popular bistro puts its tables out under the arches. 3 The south end of the same arcade has potted pines to mark the entry to one of Paris's most famous restaurants.

1

1 The *place* as used today is great for sunbathing, walking, and simpler games than the jousting matches of yore. 2 View of the square in 1961, when assorted shutters covered much of the discolored red façades. 3 The original role of the *place* was for spectacle, such as the engagement of Louis XIII and his sister, shown in this tinted engraving of 1677 by Claude Chastillon. Note the great variety in depth and development behind the uniform façade of the square. 4 The south façade of the Pavillon du Roi was fully detailed to announce the square from outside along the Rue de Birague. 5 The northeast corner, viewed from the south, appears fully closed.

2

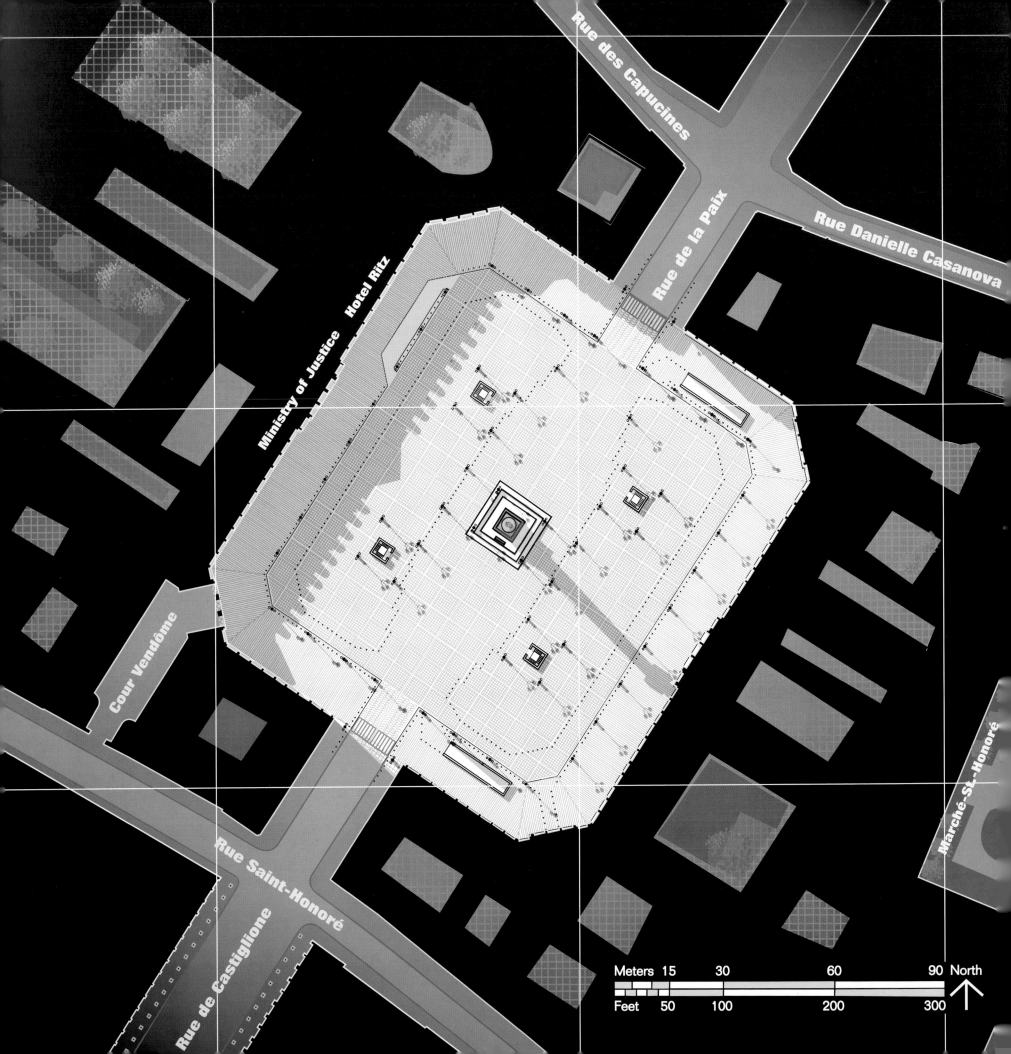

Rue des Capucines

Rue Danielle Casanova

Rue de la Paix

Ministry of Justice   Hotel Ritz

Cour Vendôme

Rue Saint-Honoré

Rue de Castiglione

Marché-St-Honoré

| Meters | 15 | 30 | 60 | 90 | North |
| Feet | 50 | 100 | 200 | 300 | |

PLACE VENDÔME

Paris

PLAN DIMENSIONS	RATIO OF WIDTH TO LENGTH	AREA	TYPICAL HEIGHT TO SKYLINE	HIGHEST POINT	RATIO OF WIDTH TO SKYLINE HEIGHT	ANGLE OF VIEW FROM ANY SIDE TO THE SKYLINE OPPOSITE	KEY DATE
410 × 453 ft (124 × 140 m)	1 to 1 (approx. square)	4.2 acres (1.7 ha)	65 ft (20 m)	145 ft (44 m), top of the column	6 to 1	9°	1699, completion of design and start of construction

Source of drawing data: Cadastral printout provided by the city of Paris; and measured drawings made on site by Mario Jossa

As famous for its shopping as for its history, the Place Vendôme is one of the best-known squares in Paris. It connects two of the principal thoroughfares in the heart of the city: the Rue de la Paix and the Rue de Castiglione. One seems always to be driving through it—which, in fact, is the cause of most of its problems as a public square: it was not designed to be driven through.

One of the grand schemes of Cardinal Richelieu, King Louis XIII's prime minister, was to glorify the monarch with a statue surrounded by a large square. First called the Place des Conquêtes, then the Place Louis le Grand (Louis the Great), it was to include the royal library, the academies, the mint, and a hotel for visiting ambassadors. Richelieu selected Jules Hardouin-Mansart (1646–1708), the king's favorite architect, to design the *place*, and a statue of His Highness was commissioned. The design work began in 1680 and went on for nearly twenty years. A triumphal arch was to frame the façade of the Chapel of the Capucines behind it to the north; and its north, east, and west sides were to border a space left open on the south side to the Rue Saint-Honoré, old Paris's main east–west thoroughfare. But this scheme was judged too grandiose and expensive—the king was short of funds, partly because of another Mansart project under way at Versailles. So the architect was sent back to the drawing board to come up with something smaller. Taking a further money-saving step, Louis turned the square and the responsibility for building it over to the city.

Construction of the square began in earnest in 1699, with the façades—now on all four sides—propped up from behind, mostly with no actual buildings: a true stage set. The monumental statue was erected at the center, and the angled, cut-off corners that appeared in the original design took shape; they still give the Place Vendôme its unique octagonal form. When the rest of the backup buildings were completed in 1720, the Place Vendôme stood on its own, linked to the thoroughfares that bypassed it to the north and the south by short connectors.

In 1792—from the balcony of the Chancellery (now the Ministry of Justice building) that still dominates the western side of the square, Georges Jacques Danton proclaimed France's first republic. The French Revolution got under way, and the statue of the king came crashing down. The *place* became known as "Pikes' Square," for all the aristocratic heads displayed on poles and, after seven years, it was renamed after César de Vendôme, whose hotel had occupied the site originally.

The connector roads to thoroughfares were eventually swept up in the late nineteenth century, when Georges-Eugène Haussmann (1809–1891) reconfigured Paris. Haussmann's plan plowed one great thoroughfare through the middle of the square, which acquired a new honoree: Napoleon. The Little Chapel of the Capucines gave way to construction of the Rue de la Paix. The great column in the center of the square became its most prominent feature and, with its green patina, almost the sole source of color. Modeled after

Trajan's column in Rome, the column was a tribute to Napoleon's victory over the Austrians at Austerlitz in 1895. Its bronze came from 1,250 captured enemy cannons. Statues of a succession of national heroes have since crowned the column's top.

The Place Vendôme has attracted many wealthy residents and elegant commercial establishments, becoming the most upscale shopping district in the world—and a virtual parking lot until in 1972 a multilevel car park was built underneath. Traffic now moves quite easily around the column and through the square: the standing taxis and town cars in front of the Hotel Ritz are grace notes. It no longer takes special courage to walk across the slow-moving line of vehicles that circle the square and descend into the car park. But there isn't much reason to do so, and few pedestrians are to be seen. There are no benches, no trees, no protective arcade, no reason to linger. However, following construction of the car park came the installation, as its roof, of a beautiful paving pattern designed by the late Pierre Prunet, one of Paris's chief architects in charge of historic monuments. The conception and redesign of the square's surface in 1991 was no easy task. To reestablish the floor as one gently ramped surface, sidewalks were eliminated to meld with the roof of the garage below. Granite stripes mark the six-meter grid that derives from the dimensions of the square and the 12-foot (4-meter) façade interval. The spaces in between are filled with granite cobblestones or setts in a rectilinear pattern.

The traditional fanlike pattern used in the older parts of Paris paves the streets entering the square. The arrangement of setts that make up this design, called *posé en arceaux* or *posé en queue de paon* ("placed in arcs" or "peacock-tail placement"), used to be set in sand, but rioters could easily lift them out to use as missiles and to build barricades, so the pavers are now anchored in cement. Prunet had specified ochre-colored granite for the setts to recall the original sand—a nicety with special appeal to an architect—but the gray used was less costly.

With its fame as a shopping mecca, its place in history, and the beauty of its walls and floor, the Place Vendôme stands ready for its former greatness. It started out as a noble conception. Without the through traffic, and with some pedestrian amenities, the space could reassume its theatrical role in history.

1 The roof of the garage below is the floor of the square articulated in several patterns of granite that replace Mansart's original sand. Traffic is guided by an ingenious system of bollards in stone and stainless steel, some of which can be lowered to the surface to allow for the passage of emergency vehicles. 2 Napoleon as emperor crowns the tower wearing the imperial toga of Rome. 3 The square as seen from its northwest corner at a moment between passages of traffic still looks as grand as it should. 4 The square is an octagon formed by Mansart as he blunted the corners of the two U-shaped parts of his original royal space. The ground floor is faced with shallow arches that look better as an arcade when the gates are opened. 5 The column base depicts many of Napoleon's victories in bas-relief. 6 The merchants who guard their prized addresses work hard to maintain their façades and to impose strict signage standards—black, white, wood, and gold—that establish a strong sense of place.

148

Veüe et Perspective de la Place de Louis le Grand

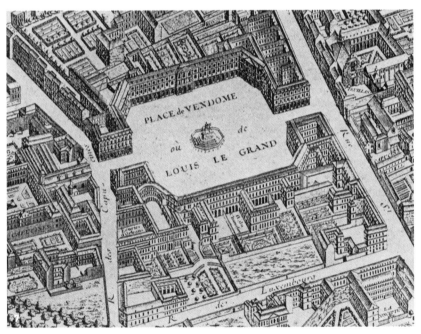

1 Looking toward its column from afar, one can wish that the real arcades that originate at the Rue de Rivoli and continue here along the Rue de Castiglione had been used in the *place* itself. 2 At the point of entry from the Rue de Castiglione, there is a fine collection of building detail and street furniture that gives the square its class. 3 This pedestrian approach from the Cour Vendôme in the southwest corner frames the essentials of the place nicely. 4 The view to the north was straight to the Chapel of the Capucines when it was the Place de Louis le Grand in this drawing of 1720. 5 The damage done to the *place*'s sense of enclosure by Haussmann's radical surgery in creating the Rue de la Paix straight ahead is nothing compared to destructive lanes of traffic that bypass the column in rhythmic bursts of noise. 6 Granite comes in three sizes: 16-inch (40 cm) squares define stripes laid on a grid of 20 feet (6 meters) that is filled with smaller squares of 6 inches (15 cm) on a side. Outside the *place*, streets take over with traditional 4-inch (10 cm) "setts" laid in the pattern of an armstroke. 7 Turgot's plan of 1739 shows the bracketing of a square between two busy east-west thoroughfares and a statue of the king that was fully in scale with a quiet eddy-space. 8 Automobiles had taken over the square by the 1950s and the *place* had become a parking lot.

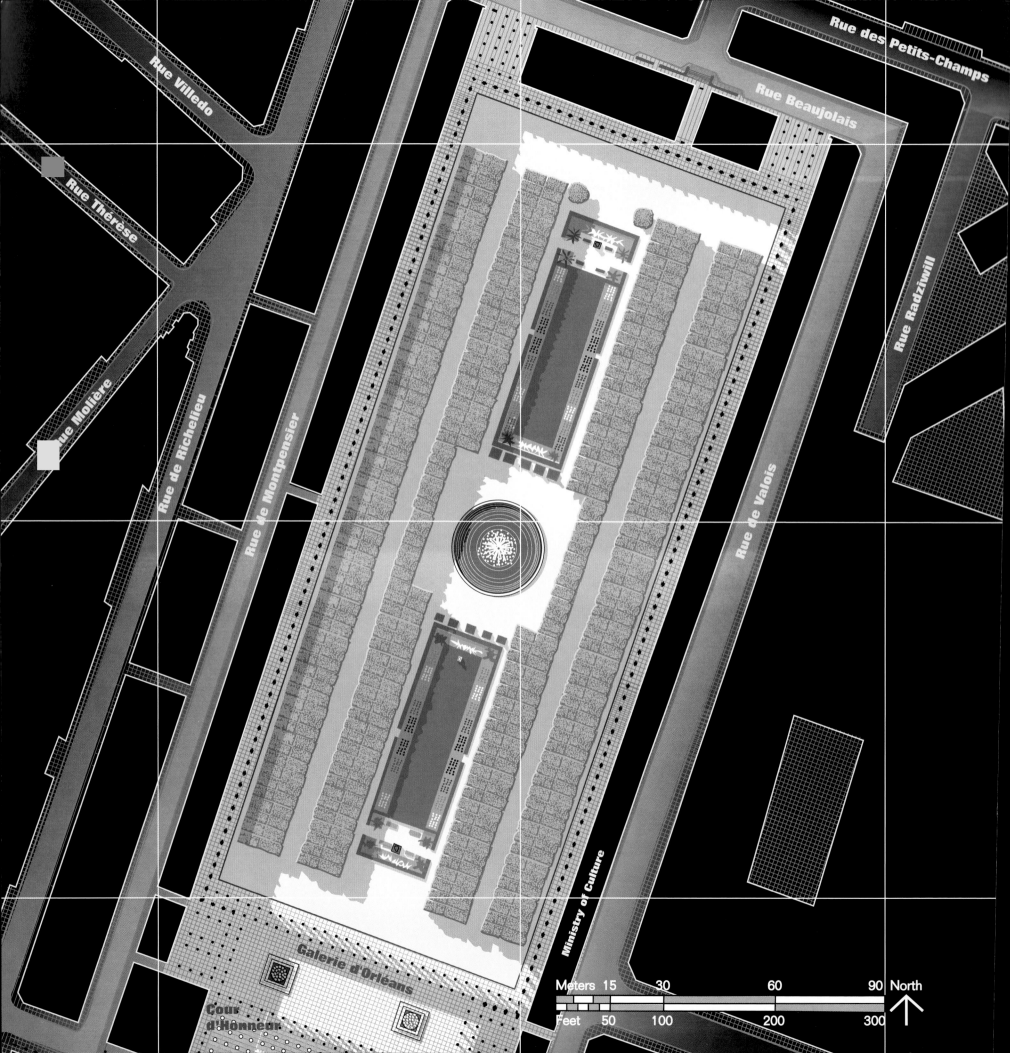

Rue des Petits-Champs

Rue Beaujolais

Rue Villedo

Rue Thérèse

Rue Molière

Rue de Richelieu

Rue de Montpensier

Rue Radziwill

Rue de Valois

Ministry of Culture

Galerie d'Orléans

Cour d'Honneur

Meters 15   30   60   90   North

Feet   50   100   200   300

JARDIN DU PALAIS-ROYAL

Paris

PLAN DIMENSIONS	RATIO OF WIDTH TO LENGTH	AREA	TYPICAL HEIGHT TO SKYLINE	HIGHEST POINT	RATIO OF WIDTH TO SKYLINE HEIGHT	ANGLE OF VIEW FROM SHORT SIDE:	KEY DATE
304 × 738 ft (93 × 225 m)	1 to 2	5 acres (2 ha)	50 ft (15 m)	60 ft (18 m) to the ridgeline	6 to 1	9°	1782, final Victor Louis design
						FROM LONG SIDE: 5°	

Source of drawing data: Cadastral printout from the city of Paris building department

Although it is right in the center of the First Arrondissement in Paris, the incredible Jardin du Palais-Royal is little known to most of the world. Entrances to the huge *jardin* (garden) are hidden along the narrow streets surrounding it. Two wings of buildings behind the Palais-Royal define a space of somewhat serious mien, discouraging crowds of visitors. The Jardin du Palais-Royal is not a short cut to anywhere else. It is a destination for people who search out quiet and calm.

The feel is of a long rectangular space: the jardin is double the length of an American football or British rugby field and much wider than either. The only wheeled vehicles allowed are scooters, bicycles, and baby strollers: so much for the automobile! The plantings include relatively insignificant lawns edged with low hedges around beds of flowering perennials. The trees are splendid—long, double rows of deciduous trees trimmed with mathematical precision to a clearance of 10 feet (3 meters). They provide welcome shade in summer and practically disappear in winter. In the middle of the jardin, a round pool 82 feet (25 meters) in diameter with a splashing fountain at the center is usually full of sailboats directed by very young captains. The sandy floor of the square is furnished with fixed benches and Parisian park chairs peopled year-round by young and old.

The façades that make up the square's north, east, and west sides give a monumental dignity to six stories of the most sought-after residential and office space in Paris. Grand arcades with one hundred eighty arches shelter an assortment of antiquarian specialty shops and fine restaurants. Two floors of grand parlors, where famous artists and writers once entertained, now enhance life for the well-to-do and the ministry of culture, whose presence in the southeast corner probably accounts in part for the excellent upkeep of the square. Two additional levels are tucked under gray-blue zinc roofs. The three-story-high pilaster-columns are of typical Parisian limestone, and a uniform use of gray and white striped awnings at most openings is nearly as decoratively important as the elegant masonry detailing. Wrought-iron fencing topped with recently regilded finials fills the arches: it was once meant to keep the rabble out, but the gates stand open today.

The southern wall is formed by a handsome colonnade that separates it from the Galerie d'Orléans and beyond that, the Cour d'Honneur—two courtyards that recall a turbulent period of architectural variety. Recent sculptural additions by Pol Bury and Daniel Buren have sparked controversy, which seems fitting for a space that has endured many changes of ownership and centuries of serenity interrupted by political wrangling and more than a little violence.

Cardinal Richelieu had just been named prime minister to King Louis XIII in 1624 when he bought a group of buildings to transform into his principal residence. They had the advantage of fronting on the main east–west route through Paris, the Rue Saint-Honoré, and were just a block from the royal family's sometime residence at the Palais du Louvre. The property already had small gardens that ran down to the city ramparts, which,

1 The central fountain is the most popular part of the garden for sailing boats, playing ball, reading, and lounging. Real Parisians know this to be one of the hidden treasures of their city, and the surrounding apartments are among the most sought after in town. 2 The quiet northeast corner shelters a fine restaurant at its base. 3 Victor Louis's noble colonnade disguises the six stories behind it. 4 The arcades serve today as shelter for visitors and shoppers. 5 Victor Louis's original drawing is lost, but this lithograph was made for the King shortly after construction.

JARDIN DU PALAIS-ROYAL

Richelieu knew, would soon be demolished, permitting a desired extension of his garden. For eighteen years Richelieu's grand plans, good taste, and great wealth went toward the redesign and enlargement of what came to be called the Palais-Cardinal. When the ramparts were gone, Richelieu sold development rights for the construction of a series of houses that would completely encircle the garden. This potentially profitable real estate venture had a few restrictions: the developer had to build all the houses within four years, and no windows could face the garden lest the cardinal-prime minister be disturbed. The house sites were quite large, varying in width from 46 to 52 feet (14 to 16 meters), and were oriented outward toward the streets that ringed the garden. Several lots that were reserved for passageways from the garden to the surrounding streets remain open to this day.

Before his death in 1642, Richelieu deeded both palace and garden to the crown, and Queen Anne of Austria, consort of Louis XIII, moved into the renamed Palais-Royal with her two young sons: the future Louis XIV and Philippe, Duke of Orléans. The beginnings of political trouble soon led to much coming and going of the royal family, and when they ended up back in the Louvre in 1660, the Palais-Royal passed ultimately to Philippe. To redesign the gardens, Philippe chose André Le Nôtre (1613–1700), the great landscape architect of Versailles.

On Philippe's death, his son—another Philippe—assumed title to the Palais-Royal, eventually ushering in its golden age. Using his great power and good taste, he amassed a brilliant collection of art, while further transforming the interior of the palace. During his regency, which lasted until 1723, the Palais-Royal was truly the center of government. But the place fell into scandalous disrepair after his death in 1742. In the following decades the great philosopher-writer Denis Diderot (1713–1784) wrote of young libertines in the palace garden, following the "stale air of prostitutes," whom the duke protected from the police. The houses surrounding the garden had apparently become so seedy that a tall trellis had to be built in front of them to hide the mess and foul smell of their occupants.

During the centuries that followed, the palace was owned and occupied by notables of all kinds: royalty, nobility, theater people including Molière and his troupe, the Paris Opéra, the Comédie-Française, and then revolutionary governments. Fires, both accidental and planned, together with changes in use, kept the palace and ground a virtual building site for much of the time.

During the chaos of the French Revolution, the Palais-Royal figured prominently as a place of assembly and riot. Yet another Philippe, the Duke of

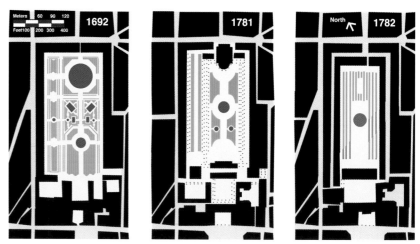

DEVELOPMENT OF THE JARDIN DU PALAIS-ROYAL
Drawings based on three plans from the collection of the Musée Carnavalet appear here at the same scale (about 1:5000). Le Nôtre's original 1692 plan for the garden (left) shows the problematic asymmetry of centering everything on the old Cour d'Honneur. Victor Louis's 1781 scheme (center) shows his proposed new auditorium at the north end of the garden, with the Cour d'Honneur expanded along its north–south axis. In 1782, Victor Louis widened the Cour d'Honneur along its east–west axis. The proposed symmetrical garden (right) is similar to what was eventually built, including today's inner line of buildings (the structure shown at the south end burned down). This final version shows the rigorous lines of trees rather than floral garden shapes—the preference of an architect over that of a landscape designer.

Orléans—the great-great-great grandson of King Louis XIII and a sympathizer with the revolution—inherited most of the palace and its collections. Using his adopted moniker of Philippe-Egalité, the Citizen King, he abided by two stipulations: the gardens had to remain open to the public, and no construction could be undertaken without advance financing. Despite these egalitarian restrictions, Philippe-Egalité hatched a very grand and daring project that would also produce income: construction of a new line of buildings within the boundary of the garden, with shops on the ground floor and residences above. The east and west wings had to be a very thin 43 feet (13 meters) in width to avoid making an already narrow garden too cramped. Predictably, all the residents of the old buildings that had previously fronted on the garden were furious, including the archbishop of Paris, but they were unable to stop the plan from proceeding. The better commercial spaces were quickly bought up, particularly at the north, where the buildings were deeper.

Happily for the eventual form and design of this real estate development, two things happened in 1781. The opera burned for a second time, allowing the Cour d'Honneur to be widened (see diagram), and the duke took on a new architect, the very talented Victor Louis (1731–1800). After another fire and several false starts, Victor Louis persuaded his patron that the reconstruction of the palace was so extensive that it should enclose a larger,

1 Approaching from the south, the first view of the garden is through the colonnade of the Galerie d'Orléans. 2 Jules David showed this reconstruction of a steel-and-glass Galerie d'Orléans after its wooden predecessor burned down in 1827. Once the most fashionable shopping arcade in Paris, today it is open to the air. 3 The first garden designed by Le Nôtre for Cardinal Richelieu can be seen beyond the palace refurbished by Le Mercier. 4 One of Paris's oldest and finest restaurants—Le Grand Vefour—hides within the arcade of the northwest corner. 5 Hand-painted metal soldiers are sold by one of the most honored of the old shops.

JARDIN DU PALAIS-ROYAL

open court facing north. This space and the garden beyond could reflect the palace's width and symmetry, growing from 200 to 300 feet (60 to 90 meters) between the new wings that defined it.

Victor Louis certainly knew the Place des Vosges nearby (see page 137). Both squares have four residential levels above shopping arcades, and the arches are almost exactly the same in width. The two are very different spaces, however. The Place des Vosges appears as a row of identical houses in which the horizontal lines dominate, and its regular, square shape has a neutral sense of repose. At the Jardin du Palais-Royal, in contrast, vertical lines dominate, and its long, rectangular shape gives it tension and thrust. While both spaces lie within the Renaissance, Baroque, and Neoclassical stylistic spectrum, the Place des Vosges grew from the rustic architectural tradition of France, while the Jardin du Palais-Royal uses the Italian vocabulary of High Baroque with all its stagecraft—more successfully than does another of its neighbors, the Place Vendôme (see page 145).

After post-Revolutionary France settled down, the newly renamed Palais-Egalité and its garden remained very much the center of Parisian life, continuing to endure ups and downs. The period of Napoleon's domination saw harsh battles within the jardin and damage to the palace. With Napoleon crowned emperor in 1852, it became again the Palais-Royal, though never Palais-Impérial. After that, all Paris agonized through the Franco-Prussian War of 1870–71, the Siege of Paris, and then the Commune, which included a failed attempt to incinerate the Palais-Royal. Toward the end of the nineteenth century, it was a seedy slum with circus acts, brothels, gambling, and a wax museum. Once again, after oscillating between corruption and slumber, it revived in the 1930s. Two resident artists, the writer Colette and the multitalented Jean Cocteau, spearheaded a successful movement that restored the majesty of the Jardin du Palais-Royal.

Some two centuries after Victor Louis's grand design was carried out and about eighty years after Colette and Cocteau made their mark, many old establishments remain loyal to the jardin—three medal merchants, six stamp sellers, the world's most famous source for toy soldiers, the square's first and finest restaurant, and more. The gambling dens and brothels are long gone, and upscale new enterprises seem to be arriving at a steady rate. Philippe-Egalité's vision of a people's palace garden—a city's great outdoor living room—is a thriving reality.

1 The trees of Paris are a sculptural wonder, and these allées are descended from Le Nôtre's original vision. 2 The gardens are subtle compared to many more spectacular flower shows in Paris, but they add welcome color in the summer. 3 The success of the 1788 Circus in the middle of the garden was short-lived; foundation failure and fire destroyed it after eleven years. 4 Lunchtime breaks from the surrounding commercial and government offices are a short walk away. 5 The attics used to serve as servants' quarters but are now much-prized apartments. The gray-and-white striped awnings are a great unifying factor in this beautiful space.

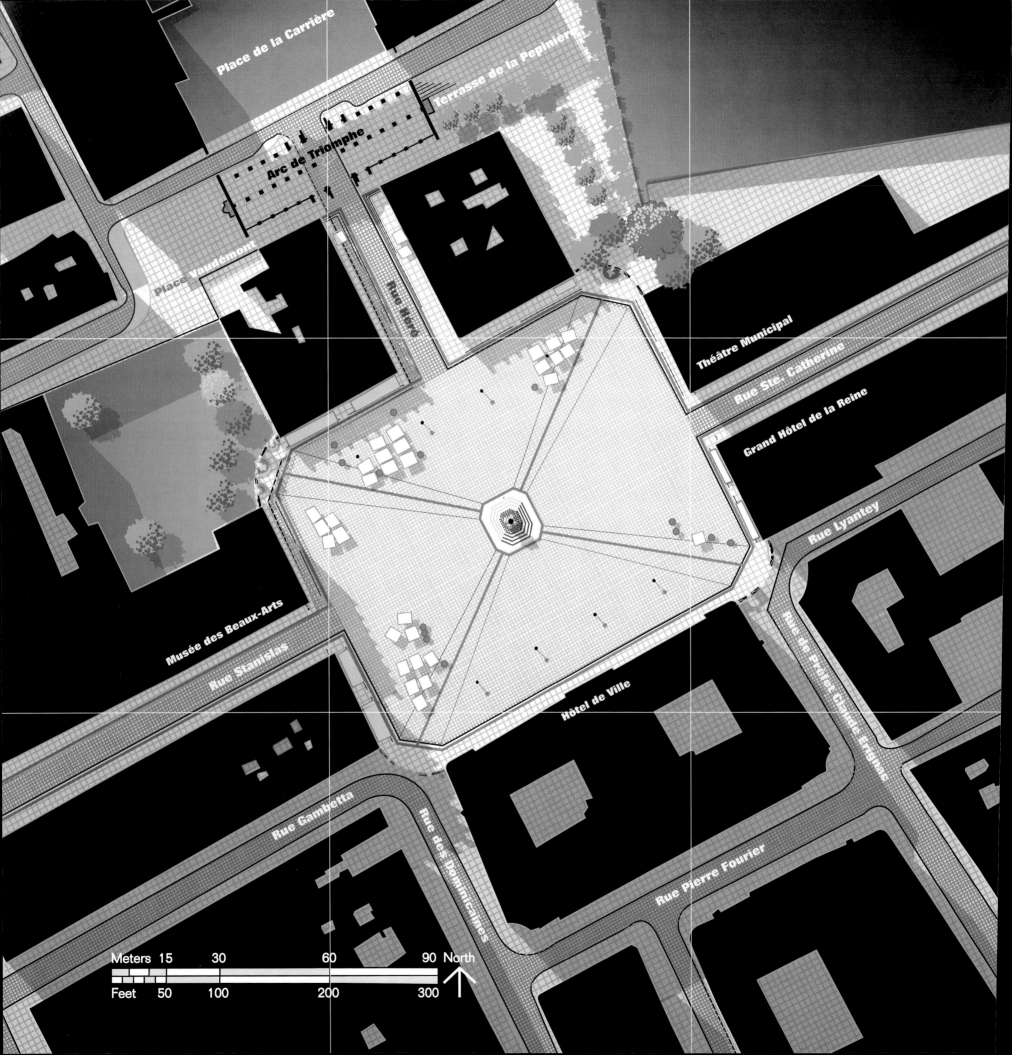

Place de la Carrière

Terrasse de la Pepinière

Arc de Triomphe

Place Vaudémont

Rue Héré

Théâtre Municipal

Rue Ste. Catherine

Grand Hôtel de la Reine

Rue Lyantey

Musée des Beaux-Arts

Rue Stanislas

Hôtel de Ville

Rue de Préfet Chanzie Brignie

Rue Gambetta

Rue des Dominicaines

Rue Pierre Fourier

Meters 15   30   60   90 North

Feet 50 100   200   300

PLACE STANISLAS

Nancy

PLAN DIMENSIONS	RATIO OF WIDTH TO LENGTH	AREA	TYPICAL HEIGHT TO SKYLINE	HIGHEST POINT	RATIO OF WIDTH TO SKYLINE HEIGHT	ANGLE OF VIEW FROM THE SHORT SIDE TO THE SKYLINE	KEY DATE
333 × 393 ft (102 × 120 m)	1 to 1 (approx. square)	3 acres (1.3 ha)	65 ft (20 m)	78 ft (25 m), top of city hall clock tower	5 to 1	11°	1755, completion of construction

Source of drawing data: Cadastral map from the city of Nancy

Place Stanislas is, while one of Europe's grandest urban spaces, almost unknown. Every Frenchman seems to have heard of it; few have seen it. Most architects know its fame, but none seem able to describe it. The obscurity of Place Stanislas may be in part a result of its being in a relatively out-of-the-way city in northeast France. Perhaps it has been overlooked because it was built during a frivolous time in architecture. Compared to the rational solidity of the late Renaissance and the turgid emotionality of the Baroque, the gilt floral work of the subsequent Rococo seems trivial. Commissioned by Stanislas Leszczyński, the sometime king of Poland who was also duke of France's Lorraine département, Place Stanislas has hardly changed since it was completed in an incredibly short four years. The taste of a strong ruler with refined and educated sensibilities shaped this square with great integrity.

When Prince Stanislas took over Nancy, the town was already rich in beautiful buildings, many arranged with considerable urban sensitivity. As court architect, Emmanuel Héré (1704–1763), collaborating with Richard Mique, designed a new royal quarter made up of several buildings and two splendid squares that connected to the city's Old Town. From Héré's smaller Hemicycle de la Carrière at the north, the main space—though not an uninterrupted sightline—runs down a promenade of trees and identical façades, through his triumphal arch, and across Place Stanislas to the city hall.

Héré's plan for Place Stanislas followed the pattern for royal squares already taking shape elsewhere in France: Bordeaux, Montpellier, Rennes, and eventually Paris—all had their place royale, a powerful, symmetrical space with a statue (usually equestrian) of the king at the center. Stanislas chose to honor his son-in-law, King Louis XV; after the French Revolution, Louis was replaced with a statue by Georges Jacquot of Stanislas himself. Héré was designing his royal square just fifty years after Jules Hardouin-Mansart laid out the façades of Paris's Place Vendôme (see page 144), and Héré was surely aware of that precedent. Take away the mansard roofs from the Place Vendôme and the two squares are very similar, although Nancy's is about one-third smaller. Each uses a monumental, two-story order of pilasters above a flat arcade, which one wishes were three-dimensional.

Place Stanislas is bordered by seven buildings that are tightly organized in a way that effectively contains the space. Although streets entering from the east and west might be feared to cut the square in two much as the Place Vendôme is severed by its thoroughfare, they have never served much cross traffic and today are closed to vehicles. More important, the Nancy streets are so narrow that a view along the east–west axis is only briefly visible. The northbound road passing through the triumphal arch is visually obscured by the arch's deep reveal and heavy shadow, and you must peer through its central vault to glimpse the space beyond. The floor of the square is paved with light-colored stone setts and dark stripes that draw your attention to the statue that is Place Stanislas's focal point.

The four corners of Place Stanislas present a risk of spatial leakage, which can undermine the integrity of an urban square. The brilliant solution to this potential problem is the wrought ironwork designed by Jean Lamour. The grilles, painted a very dark brown, might have been too open but for the extraordinary gilding of their floral embellishment. Made up of broad curving forms that refer to the arches of the neighboring buildings, the grilles allow the square to wrap itself around the visitor. (It was beautifully restored,

at great cost, in 2005 for the two-hundred-fiftieth anniversary of the square's completion.) If in photographs the gold looks excessive, in place it succeeds visually to minimize the outflow of space, particularly around the dull gray sculptures by Barthélemy Guibal in the two northern corners.

Standing in front of the Hôtel de Ville, you will notice that the pavilions opposite are a low two stories high rather than the tall three stories of buildings on either side and the city hall's even taller pediment behind you. Were these pavilions kept low for military reasons, as is often claimed? Or are they meant to create a horizon against which Héré's triumphal arch appears especially imposing? In either case, they determine a subtly rising roofline as you walk southward from the older quarter, through the arch, toward Place Stanislas and the Hôtel de Ville's gigantic classical columns and rhythmic archways.

Place Stanislas was named a UNESCO World Heritage Site in 1983.

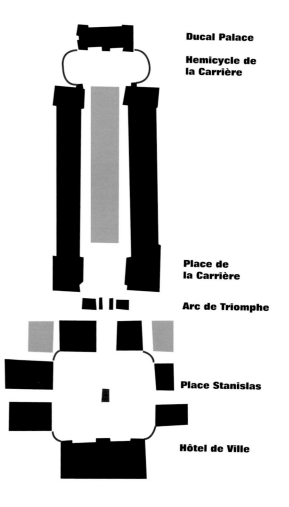

Ducal Palace

Hemicycle de la Carrière

Place de la Carrière

Arc de Triomphe

Place Stanislas

Hôtel de Ville

FRANCE

1 A procession of scholars passes in front of Neptune. 2 The Fountain of Neptune under its gilded arch in the northwest corner of the square resembles Bernini's work on the Piazza Navona in Rome. 3 Parasols offer protection from the summer sun in a square without arcades. 4 In this view of the Place Stanislas from its northwest corner, the Hôtel de Ville is to the right of the central statue of Stanislas. 5 Amphitrite stands in a basin of lead surrounded by the gilded wrought iron of Jean Lamour.

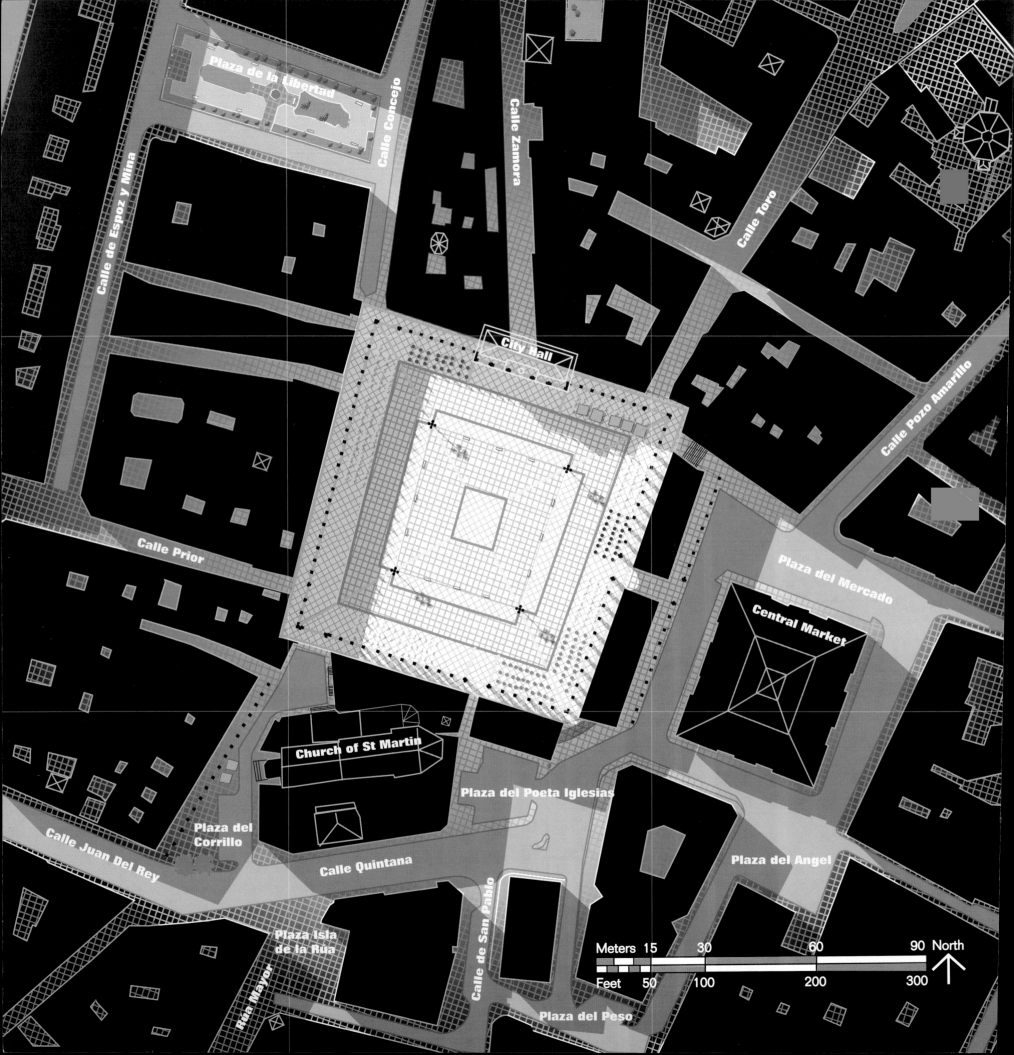

Plaza de la Libertad

Calle de Espoz y Mina

Calle Concejo

Calle Zamora

Calle Toro

City Hall

Calle Pozo Amarillo

Calle Prior

Plaza del Mercado

Central Market

Church of St Martin

Plaza del Poeta Iglesias

Plaza del Corrillo

Calle Juan Del Rey

Calle Quintana

Calle de San Pablo

Plaza del Angel

Plaza Isla de la Rúa

Rúa Mayor

Plaza del Peso

Meters 15   30   60   90   North

Feet   50 100   200   300

PLAZA MAYOR

Salamanca

PLAN DIMENSIONS	RATIO OF WIDTH TO LENGTH	AREA	TYPICAL HEIGHT TO SKYLINE	HIGHEST POINT	RATIO OF WIDTH TO SKYLINE HEIGHT	ANGLE OF VIEW FROM THE SHORT SIDE TO THE SKYLINE	KEY DATE
approx. 265 × 265 ft (80 x 80 m)	1 to 1 (a slightly skewed square)	1.5 acres (0.6 ha)	50 ft (15 m)	87 ft (26.5 m), top of city hall clock tower	6 to 1	11°	1755, completion of construction

Source of drawing data: Cadastral maps from the city of Salamanca

Salamanca's Plaza Mayor (great square) is, in a word, completely right. The space contained within this solid-cornered Spanish plaza has an ideal dignity and balance. Without its shallow Baroque relief, the box of negative space would be too plain; more complex ornamentation might need fanciful paving. The uniform arcade at the base of the plaza's perimeter provides the needed shade; trees, such as those filling Paris's Place des Vosges and Boston's Louisburg Square (see pages 137 and 203), would rob the Plaza Mayor of its unique purity of conception and execution. Salamanca's sandstone, from nearby Villamayor, offers a texture dense enough, despite weathering, to sustain elaborate carving, and its uniform creamy color turns a flaming red in the late afternoon sun of central Spain.

Similarities between the Plaza Mayor and other squares of the mid-eighteenth century suggest that its designers were well trained and widely traveled. The Plaza Mayor's construction was finished in the same year as Nancy's Place Stanislas and, although neither copies the other, they have many features in common.

Commissioned by Spain's first Bourbon ruler, French-born King Philip V, the Plaza Mayor was built to relieve market congestion around the city's cathedral and to provide a stage for bullfights and other spectacles. A dispute with the Salamanca town council drove the plaza's architect, Alberto Churriguera (1676–1750), to leave town quickly during its construction, but his loyal successor, Andrés Garcia de Quiñones, saw it faithfully completed to his design. One of three famous Spanish architect brothers, Alberto Churriguera worked at the time when the discipline of classic Renaissance gave way to the exuberance of the Baroque. The work of all three was so spectacular that their name was given to the style known as Churrigueresque, found throughout Spain and Latin America.

Carving the square out of the middle of a very busy city that was home to Spain's oldest university (founded in 1218) required expropriation of many important houses—an effort that, though earlier and smaller in scale,

resembles that of Baron Haussmann in Paris. Placement of the plaza at the core of a Gothic town required improvising connections to the existing urban fabric. Each of the plaza's four sides has different dimensions, and the corners are not right angles. The main streets, most now restricted to pedestrian traffic, crash into the back of the arcades at irregular points, most marked by archways of double width. This description suggests that the resulting space might be visually chaotic, but in fact the Plaza Mayor is one of the most elegant squares in the world. Its discipline and composure are a credit to fine architects working during a time dominated by a strong, accepted style and the use of a uniform material.

Churriguera concentrated his attention on a large archway, in the center of the square's eastern façade, that was to mark the Royal Pavilion, although the king is said never to have visited. When Quiñones took over, he brought with him a commission for a new town hall, which he placed in the center of the northern façade. The larger scale of the town hall, with three projecting levels within the same four-story height of the rest of the plaza, was no doubt intended to make it outshine the royals—who owed the city money for its support in the War of Succession—and it does. Compared to the visual complexity that characterized most of his family's work, Churriguera chose for

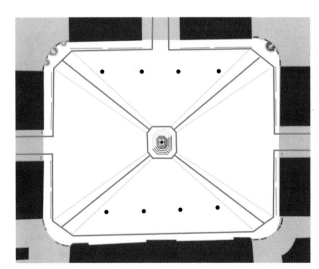

Place Stanislas, Nancy 1755

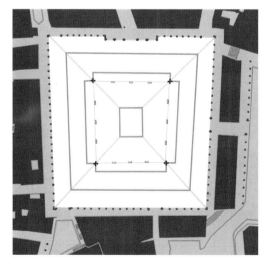

Plaza Mayor, Salamanca 1755

1 The Royal Pavilion dominates the eastern side of the square. 2 The city hall is just off axis of the near-central entry from the south. 3 The work of local artists, like this figure by Victor Ochoa, is frequently displayed to good effect since the only other freestanding objects in the plaza are benches and lampposts. 4 The red sandstone of the city hall seems almost on fire in the late afternoon sun. 5 The easiest entry for people and vehicles is through this grand arch from the Plaza del Corrillo in front of the Church of St. Martin. 6 The city hall is seen over a morning breakfast.

the Plaza Mayor a relatively calm vocabulary of repetitive arches, tall windows with shutters, and wrought iron balconies handed down from the Moors, with decorative medallions and balustrades.

With great care lavished on the plaza's walls, the square itself is otherwise so empty that it might be considered too bare; its one-time use as a bullring may explain the emptiness. Four lampposts, twelve benches, and the occasional, temporary placement of a sculpture are the square's only three-dimensional furniture. The stone pavement has a subtle pattern of gray granite highlighted by stripes of red stone. The space is locked in place by hard corners that link the four arcaded buildings forming the square.

If this monumental void were empty of people it would look barren, but it's not. All day, every day, all year long, Salamancans and visitors find reasons to pass through their great parlor, have a drink, eat a meal, do some shopping, or just soak up the pleasure of being in one of the world's great urban spaces.

Since 1988 Plaza Mayor has been recognized as a UNESCO World Heritage site.

1 A first glimpse of the plaza is from the Corillo in front of the church of St. Martin. 2 The entry from the Calle Prior is at the end of a busy shopping street. 3 The soft gray color of the stone pavers is articulated by red granite stripes. 4 The intersection of the three-story city hall with the four stories of the rest of the enclosure provides a point of architectural tension. 5 Arcades surround the plaza and are vaulted in masonry under the city hall. 6 The Royal Pavilion dominates the eastern side of the square. 7 The approach along the Calle Zamora from the north is seen through the wide arches of the city hall. 8 The royal archway leads directly in from the Central Market and passes under the Royal Pavilion. 9 A broad fan of steps is needed in descending from the Plaza Mayor to the Plaza del Poeta Iglesias.

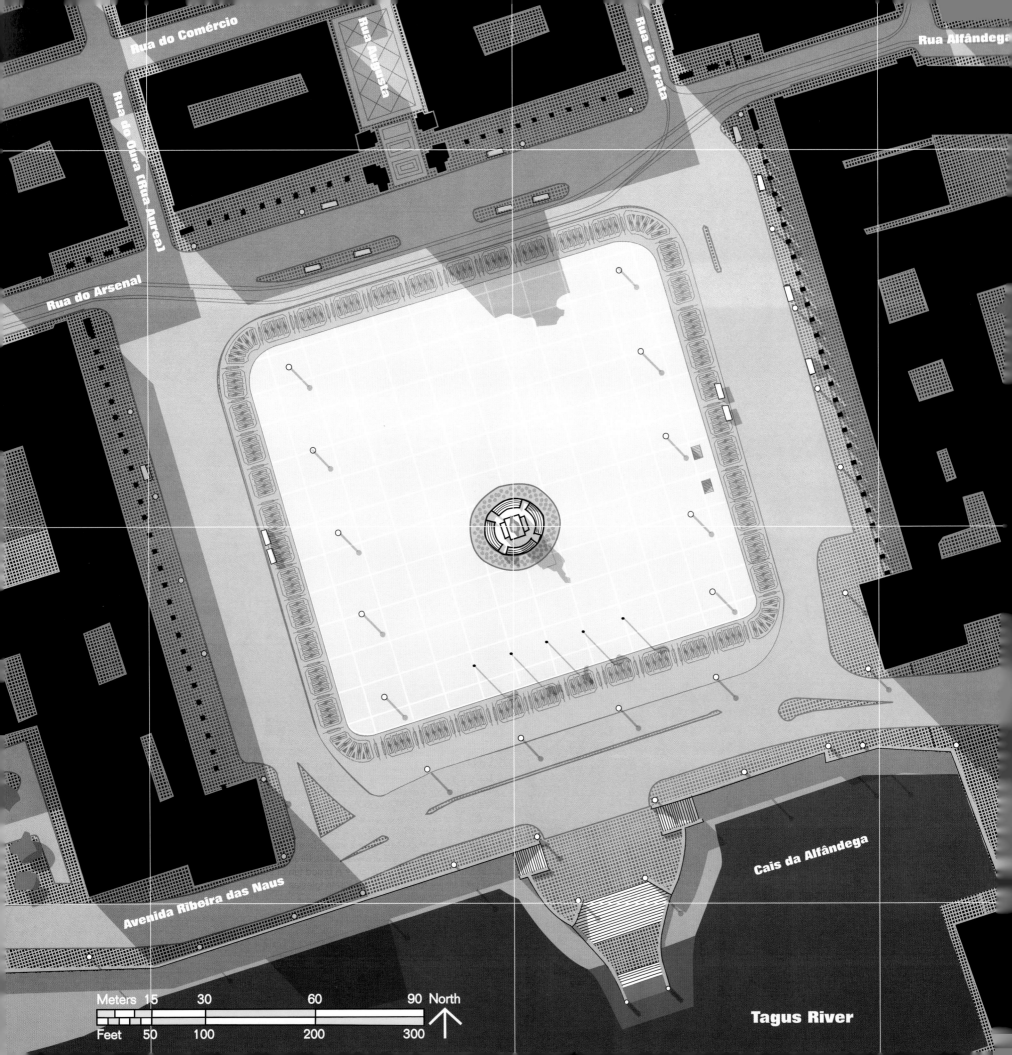

Rua do Comércio

Rua Augusta

Rua Alfândega

Rua da Prata

Rua do Oura (Rua Aurea)

Rua do Arsenal

Cais da Alfândega

Avenida Ribeira das Naus

Tagus River

Meters 15   30   60   90   North
Feet   50   100   200   300

PRAÇA DO COMÉRCIO

Lisbon

PLAN DIMENSIONS	RATIO OF WIDTH TO LENGTH	AREA	TYPICAL HEIGHT TO SKYLINE	HIGHEST POINT	RATIO OF WIDTH TO SKYLINE HEIGHT	ANGLE OF VIEW FROM THE SHORT SIDE TO THE SKYLINE	KEY DATE
575 × 605 ft (175 × 185 m)	1 to 1 (approx. square)	8 acres (3.2 ha)	65 ft (20 m)	145 ft (45 m), top of the triumphal sculpture	9 to 1	6°	1755, the great earthquake

Source of drawing data: Drawings from the city of Lisbon

Lisbon's Praça do Comércio (Commercial Square) is active, big, and bold. Its west, north, and east sides surround an open gateway to the wide mouth of the Tagus River, which forms the city's harbor. The square is not a pretty place. Residents of Lisbon don't walk through with shopping baskets. If they stop, it's to visit the central post office or one of the government offices that occupy the buildings on the square's periphery. Like most financial districts, the square closes up shop when the stock exchange shuts down.

No one even walks beside the river these days, since its banks are torn up with the construction of a new branch of the Metro (which ominously flooded and collapsed a few years ago). Most people come here to change trams: virtually every surface vehicle in the Lisbon transit system stops in the Praça do Comércio. Railroad buffs love Lisbon's trolleys, but their overhead wires form distracting webs in the sky. When I first visited the city in 1972, the square was one huge parking lot, and its prevailing color was a bilious green.

So why does this square end up on a list of fine spaces? In the eighteenth century, when Portugal was one of the wealthiest nations in Europe, its merchant ships sailed to all corners of the world from the quays on the Rio Tejo and returned with riches for King José I in his riverside palace. Noble guests arrived directly at the Cais das Colunas that served as the pier of the royal palace: gangplanks dropped to meet grand stairways that rose from the tidal waters to the square before the royal palace.

But at 9:45 a.m. on Sunday, November 1, 1755—All Saints Day—an earthquake rocked the entire Iberian Peninsula and much of North Africa. The temblor rolled on for six minutes; had there been a Richter scale, the quake would have registered 8.7. People who sought safety on the riverbank as buildings fell around them saw the water race out to sea, only to return with floods that wiped out the low-lying center of the city: a tsunami. Some one hundred thousand people died. In some ways Lisbon has never really recovered.

At the time, the remarkable Sebastião José de Carvalho e Melo, later named Marquis of Pombal, was Portugal's prime minister. When asked by the king what should be done, the prime minister's legendary reply was, "Bury the dead and feed the living." Pombal assembled the best scientists to be found, and they began to build a new Lisbon. He sent planners to London to study what had been done after that city's great fire, and they returned to advise the prime minister's chief engineer, Manuel da Maia, to create the grid of wide streets that still forms Lisbon's low-lying Baixa district. He had the foundations of broken masonry laced with shipbuilders' wooden pilings and virtually invented seismology.

Because the king had removed his court from Lisbon, Pombal decided to create a square where the palace had stood to serve the city's commercial interests. It was completed sometime after 1782. The triumphal arch that dominates its northern edge was added almost a century later.

Residents of today's Lisbon are proud of their square on the river, and the city has been doing marvelous things to improve its appearance.

The car park I remember is gone, and the yellow stucco is a vast improvement over the old green. The grand staircase down to the ferry landing will be reconstructed once the subway line has been completed. Even the overhead trolley wires seem less intrusive in the grandeur of the space.

The approach from the north along the Rua Augusta is one of the best in Europe. This pedestrian street is beautifully paved in the same wild mosaic patterns of white limestone and black basalt that continue in and around the square. Tented tables welcome your arrival. As you approach the square, the view through the arch's silhouette places the equestrian statue of José I against the river beyond in a grand way. And the east and west arms stretch out toward the ghostly river, creating an enveloping space as fine as Rome's Campidoglio (see page 82).

In a city that enjoys its raucous maritime façades and Baroque excesses, the square's classic rigor, which Pombal apparently demanded of its designer, Eugénio dos Santos, represents governmental dignity at its best. The statue of the king on his horse—of dark brown bronze that has suggested its popular name, Black Horse Square—stands slightly to the south of the square's center, facing the river, urging you to move toward the quay. Looking back, you see that the flags and the equestrian are framed in the arch, the focus of a whirligig of trolleys that are always en route to somewhere. And soon, a view of ferryboats on the cleaned-up harbor will justify a few moments at the water's edge.

The square is big, but its buildings are tall enough to contain its space. The arcades are deep and dark, and they extend into most of the nearby streets, where they finally pick up some shops and cafés. The dusty yellow stucco and patinaed stone read as serious rather than contrived. And the entire assembly is properly moored on the bank of a powerful river with challenging ambiguity. Pombal's genius was his choice of a disciplined classic style of his time that has since accepted some fine Baroque sculpture. The result is a melding of human intelligence and verve that deserves the admiration of all who come upon it.

1 In 1972, the square was painted green and was used principally as a car park. 2 It still looks pretty much the same today, except that its plaster is painted yellow. 3 This arcade starts from within the arch. 4 The square is well known to railway buffs all over the world for its network of trolleys. 5 This is the arch as seen from Alfândega on the east.

1 The great arch dominates the square. 2 Baroque finials lend emphasis to every corner. 3 The entire square opens its arms to those approaching from the riverside on the south. The sense of enclosure is one of shape rather than height. 4 The approach from the north along the Rua Prata provides the most dramatic spatial experience: street, arch, statue, and the river beyond. 5 Statue and arch support each other.
6 The square and its surrounding streets are known for their variety of stone mosaics.
7 This romantic vision of the square as it met the river in olden times was drawn by Franz J. Herding for a book by his friend Werner Hegemann.

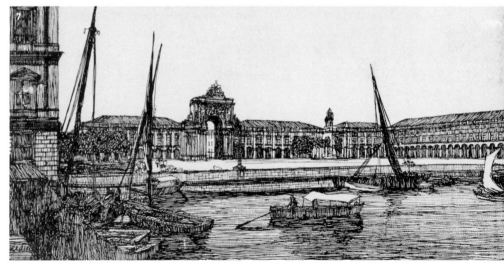

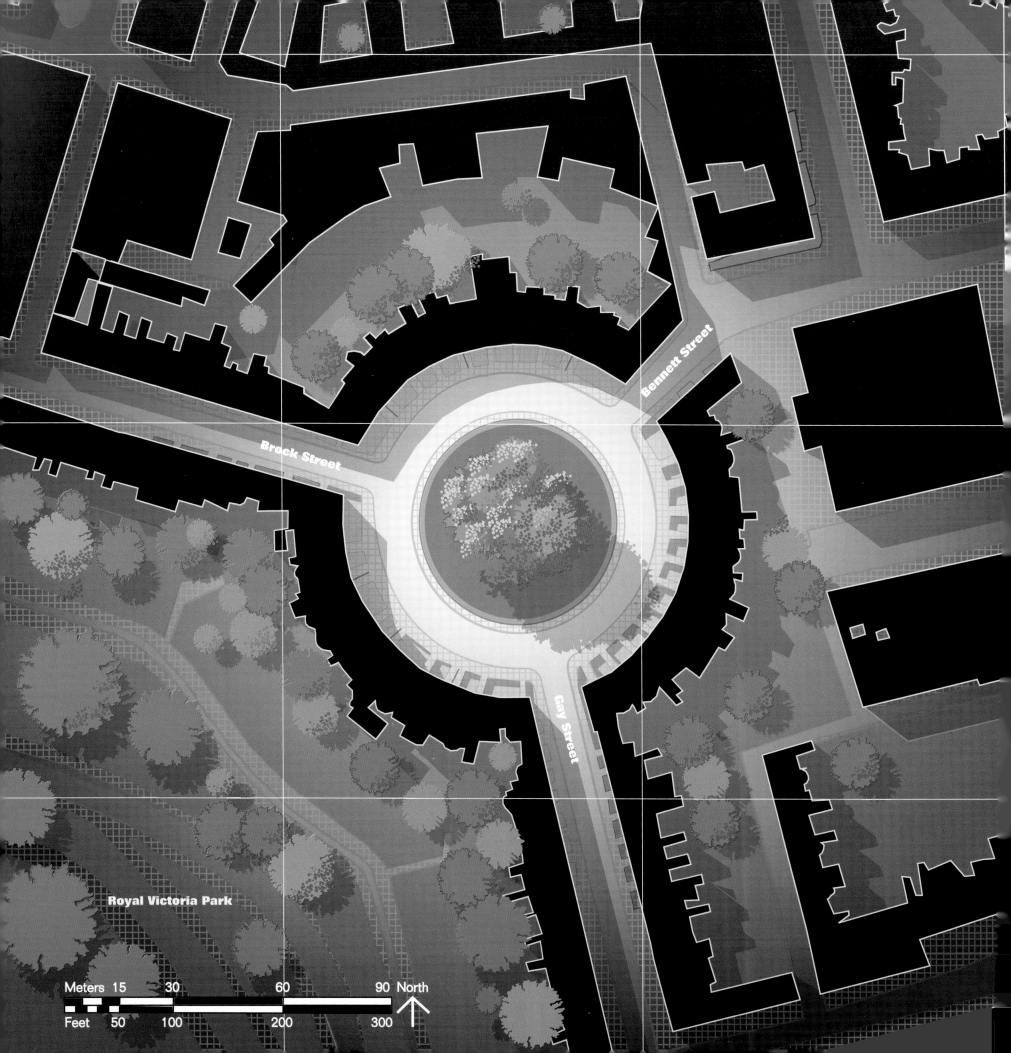

Bennett Street

Brock Street

Gay Street

Royal Victoria Park

Meters 15   30   60   90   North

Feet   50   100   200   300

THE CIRCUS

Bath

PLAN DIMENSIONS	RATIO OF WIDTH TO LENGTH	AREA	TYPICAL HEIGHT TO SKYLINE	HIGHEST POINT	RATIO OF WIDTH TO SKYLINE HEIGHT	ANGLE OF VIEW FROM ANY POINT ON THE SIDE TO THE SKYLINE OPPOSITE	KEY DATE
318 ft (97 m) diameter	circular	1.8 acres (0.7 ha)	50 ft (15 m)	50 ft (15 m), top of the ridge line of the buildings	6 to 1	9°	1754, start of construction

Source of drawing data: Cadastral information from the British ordnance survey

I think of the Circus in Bath in musical terms: it has a disciplined, classical form. At first glance, the circus's calm beauty is almost hidden behind a mass of huge trees, and the space develops only in a pedestrian's slow passage within its great enveloping composition. Details emerge throughout the day with the stately movement of sun and shadow across the concave drum. The crisp rhythm of sharp corners blends into the huge sweep of its whirling theme. The grand, unresolved chord of the nearby Royal Crescent and the staccato streets leading to and from discordant parts of Bath itself come to a restful resolution at the Circus.

Hot springs first developed for use by the ancient Romans, a fine local limestone used consistently for the city's buildings since the Middle Ages, and a tradition of architect-developer cooperation have combined to make Bath one of the most attractive cities in the United Kingdom. The city has extended its dedication to good design with excellent, modern, university buildings on the outskirts. It feels almost presumptuous to praise only the Circus, since it sits athwart a chain of inspired, famous urban spaces that starts at Queen Square and reaches a pinnacle at the great Royal Crescent. But the Circus at Bath is the Circus at Bath, and no list of great squares would be complete without it.

Credit for rebuilding Bath's famous spa and making the city Britain's premier out-of-London destination goes to three men: Richard "Beau" Nash (1674–1761), a Welsh-born man-about-town who became Bath's social arbiter, democratized use of the waters, and spread their popularity; Ralph Allen (1693–1764), a politician, tycoon, and investor who promoted the universal use in Bath of the beige stone from his own quarries; and architect John Wood the Elder (1704–1754), who gave Bath much of the gracious Georgian appearance it still has today.

In 1725 Wood proposed a large square to revive the Roman grandeur of Bath. His plan included a great place of assembly, a royal forum (later Queen Square), an imperial gymnasium, and other signature features of Bath. For the Circus, Wood not only drew inspiration from the grand spaces of London and ancient Rome (in 1771, Tobias Smollett has a character in one of his novels describe the Circus as Rome's Colosseum turned inside out), but he also thought he was creating a union of ancient Rome with Britain's legendary builders of nearby Stonehenge, the Druids. The diameters of the Circus and Stonehenge are very close. Wood wanted the Circus to be pure geometry, and arranged to knock off the top of a hillside to create a disk-shaped site, and on it to build a total of twenty-three houses in three crescent-shaped groups of ten, eleven, and twelve.

Wood purchased the land for the Circus in 1753, almost thirty years after his proposal, and he died a year later just as construction was about to begin. His equally gifted son, John Wood the Younger, finished his father's work by overseeing the construction of the Circus, which was completed in 1768. The younger Wood went on to connect it to Queen Square with Gay Street and then through Brock Street to his own great creation, the Royal Crescent.

The segmented façades looking onto the Circus are essentially identical: each consists of three floors starting at an entry stair over a light-well.

Columns grouped in pairs of the three classical orders—Doric, Ionic, and Corinthian—frame large, deep windows and rise to a strong, decorative parapet. Together, these features form one continuous façade with rich sculptural texture. Three streets interrupt the façade clusters but don't let much space leak out. From within the space you look outward through balanced, blocked gateways that are visible only from inside the drum.

The form of the repetitive façade has been credited to Andrea Palladio (1508–1589), whose work and writings were known to the Woods. Each segment covers a house, some quite different from their neighbors as can be seen by wandering behind the houses and looking at their greatly varied backs. Small details of ironwork and window muntins provide delicate variations. But the composition is a classic case of façades that look in, not out, and belong more to the negative space than to the positive parts that define it.

Originally the Circus had neither trees nor grass, just stone paving and a central, covered reservoir. Its lawn and plantings were added in 1829; whether they are an improvement is questionable. The trees are now so enormous that they compromise the architect's original conception. But they do establish the residential character of the space by bringing the observer closer to the highly detailed façades in much the same way as the central group of trees in the Place des Vosges (see p. 136).

UNESCO added Bath to its World Heritage Site list in 1987.

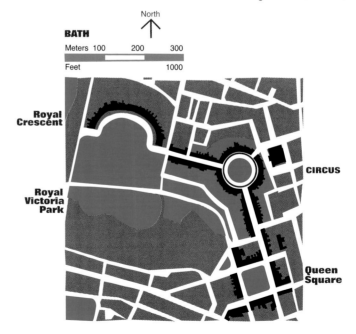

1 Each road explodes in whirling space and greenery upon entering the Circus.
2 Alleys behind the Backs give access to storage and service facilities. 3 The Circus trees veil the continuous façades that surround them. 4 The Backs give light to many more floors than are seen on the Circus and there is considererably more invention than can be imagined from the front.

1 At the corner of Brock Street, shadows sculpt the concave façade of the northern pavilion. 2 From the same point and at the same time, the eastern pavilion is in full sun while the southwest is lost in shadow. 3 The cornice is a powerful crown made up of column caps and frieze, railing and urns, not to speak of knife-like supports for the chimney pots. 4 All doors and window trim around the Circus are white; this is essential in maintaining the unity of the buildings and the space they define. 5 The staccato columns articulate the Circus chorus.

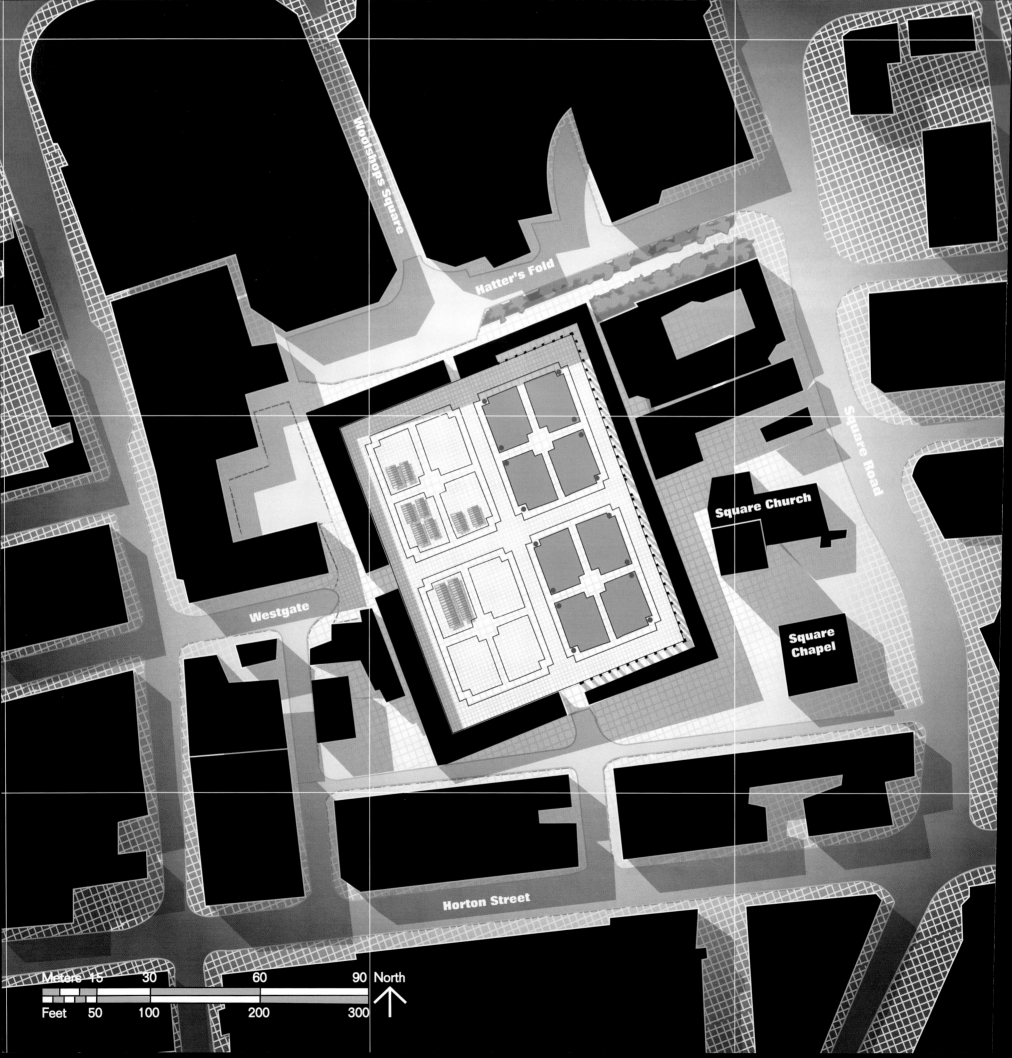

Woolshops Square

Hatter's Fold

Square Road

Square Church

Westgate

Square Chapel

Horton Street

Meters 15   30   60   90   North

Feet   50   100   200   300

PIECE HALL

Halifax

PLAN DIMENSIONS	RATIO OF WIDTH TO LENGTH	AREA	TYPICAL HEIGHT TO SKYLINE	HIGHEST POINT	RATIO OF WIDTH TO SKYLINE HEIGHT	ANGLE OF VIEW FROM THE SHORT SIDE TO THE SKYLINE	KEY DATE
230 × 288 ft (70 × 88 m)	1 to 1 (approx. square)	1.5 acres (0.6 ha)	35 ft (10 m)	40 ft (12 m) to the ridge	7 to 1	8°	1775, start of construction

Source of drawing data: Cadastral information from the ordnance survey as edited by Philip Smithies in *The Architecture of the Halifax Piece Hall, 1775–1779*

Is Piece Hall, one of the least-known sites in this book, a square?
A courtyard? Is it public or private? Should it still be valued long after its
original purpose has been lost? These are all good questions. Without
the enthusiastic recommendation of a Scottish architect friend, I doubt that
I would have visited Halifax, an industrial town in northeast England.
But Piece Hall is a surprise and delight. It has a sense of place that is all
its own, with a friendly atmosphere and a casual approach to commerce.
Despite an up-and-down history, Piece Hall wears its noble architectural
heritage with dignity and modesty.

1 The middle gallery runs behind rusticated piers and provides a glimpse of the arrangement below. 2 The north entry to Piece Hall is from Woolshops Square, which connects to the rest of the town's fine outdoor markets. 3 The green lawns match the sloping stone patterns used as a marketplace. 4 The upper colonnade uses Tuscan columns to crown a textbook collection of architectural detailing. 5 The cupola of Westgate marks the most important of the entries to Piece Hall. 6 The north side, like the south, is adapted to the fall in the land.

In the mid-eighteenth century, wool weaving was a major cottage industry in northern Britain. Pieces of fabric—hence, Piece Hall's name—produced on individual weavers' looms were sold at tightly controlled weekend markets that required shelter in large spaces. Many of these cloth halls were created in England and Scotland, and with the growth of the weaving trade, they became increasingly elaborate. Replacing a rundown seventeenth-century cloth hall, Halifax's Piece Hall was built in four years and opened in 1779. Its plan was based on—and competed with—similar halls in nearby Bradford, Leeds, and Wakefield, but it surpassed them in grandeur. Halifax chose to protect its textiles from sun damage by using deep façades, making Piece Hall immensely more attractive and versatile than the buildings of its neighbors.

Not long after Piece Hall opened, however, such halls fell into disuse. The Industrial Revolution, which brought machine manufacturing to the textile industry, gradually put northern Britain's home weavers out of business. As a result, most cloth halls were torn down. Halifax's hall struggled on for most of a century, its space rented out to assorted activities including religious meetings, parade gatherings, choral celebrations, and fireworks displays. The town finally took it over in 1863 and for a while used it as a produce and fish market. In 1928 the hall was classified as an "ancient monument," and the fish were banished. Finally, in 1976 Piece Hall was converted into a center for the sale of arts and crafts.

Controversy over who actually designed it has never been resolved. Whether it was the work of architect Thomas Bradley, the brothers Samuel and John Hope, or all three, the designer(s) brought to the job a certain Italian influence. Part of what is a basement level on the east comes out of the sloping ground as a three-sided Tuscan arcade. The middle level is a gallery of rusticated square piers. And round Tuscan columns ring the top level. The ideal piazza designs of the great Renaissance architects Leon Battista Alberti and Andrea Palladio seem to have set the standard for the overall dimensions and scale if not the shape: the courtyard proportions of 4:5 can be compared to Palladio's ideal of 2:3 and Alberti's 1:2. The systems used to establish Piece Hall's detailed proportions probably came from Palladio and carpenters' pattern books.

Its floor has been an object of care and attention. It is covered in dressed stone and well-trimmed grass that slopes eastward with the existing grade. In its simple, straightforward way, Piece Hall is, as architect-scholar Philip Smithies put it, "a wholly admirable marriage of business and architecture."

After World War II, the city of Halifax built an enclosed Victorian-design mall that competes for traffic with Piece Hall, and a well-planned network of pedestrian streets further serves the town's shops. The success of these efforts has left very little commerce for Piece Hall; a Friday-and-Saturday market is the only regular use of the open center. Only about half the stalls that open onto the multilevel arcades are occupied, and the long-term use of Piece Hall must again present questions for Halifax's city fathers.

How to define Piece Hall remains a question. It is certainly more than a courtyard; it approaches being a square. Although closed at night, it is open to the public all day every day. Three arched openings serve pedestrians, and the height of one has been adjusted to admit trucks. There is pedestrian cross traffic, and some people come expressly to shop. The walls' deep arcades provide the visual interest of the space as they come alive under the movement of the sun. Despite the hall's sketchy past, uncertain future, and defiance of categorization, the architecture itself exerts a strong attraction and provides sufficient reward—a fine urban space.

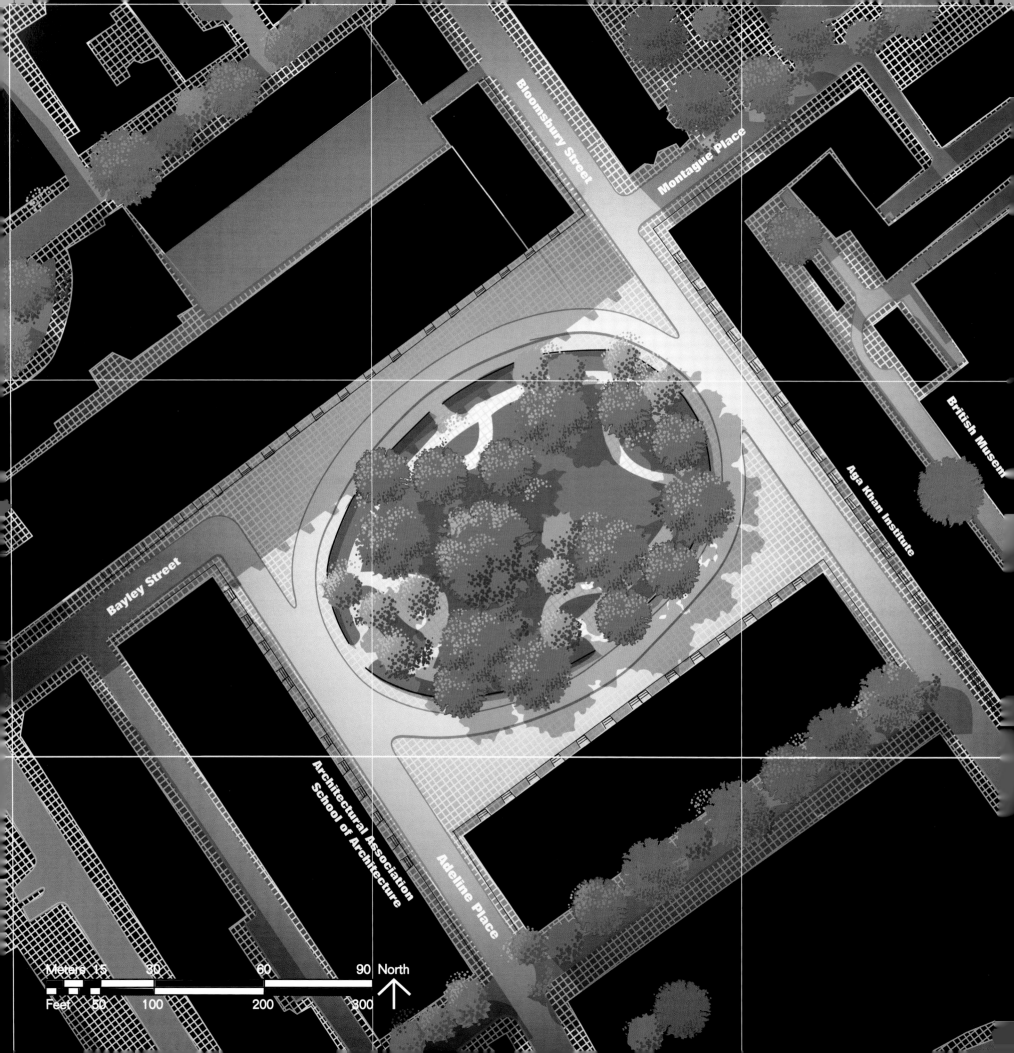

Bloomsbury Street

Montague Place

British Museum

Aga Khan Institute

Bayley Street

Architectural Association
School of Architecture

Adeline Place

Meters 15   30   60   90   North

Feet 50   100   200   300   ↑

BEDFORD SQUARE

London

PLAN DIMENSIONS	RATIO OF WIDTH TO LENGTH	AREA	TYPICAL HEIGHT TO SKYLINE	HIGHEST POINT	RATIO OF WIDTH TO SKYLINE HEIGHT	ANGLE OF VIEW FROM THE SHORT SIDE TO THE SKYLINE	KEY DATE
378 × 518 ft (115 × 158 m)	1 to 1 (approx. square)	4.5 acres (1.8 ha)	65 ft (20 m)	top of towering trees	6 to 1	10°	1775, start of construction

Source of drawing data: Cadastral information from the ordnance survey of Great Britain

For a sense of place and historic atmosphere, Bedford Square can't be beat. My fondness for this most balanced of all London squares began decades ago, when I spent a year at number 36—the Architectural Association School of Architecture. Since then the sidewalks have been widened, providing almost as gracious a pedestrian setting as the car-free squares of Italy and Germany do. In the winter, when the leaves are gone, this great room—identified by architectural historian Andrew Byrne as London's first and only "perfect, symmetrical" square—presents itself with strength and clarity. Ivory-framed walls of black masonry look as sumptuous as velvet wall covering. Polished brass hardware and plaques sparkle ornamentally. Crossing Bedford Square's paths proves that this space wears very well.

When London was remaking itself after the Great Fire of 1666, Britain was blessed with some very good architects, including Inigo Jones; Sir Christopher Wren; the brothers John, Robert, and James Adam; and Sir John Soane. It also had many wealthy owner-developers who saw the advantage of using good architecture to sell or rent row houses on their land holdings. One of them, John Russell, the fourth Duke of Bedford, followed the lead of Inigo Jones (1573–1654), who had been inspired by the bastides of France (see page 130), and introduced residential squares to London. They soon became a widespread fashion. In 1766, Russell proposed Bedford Square, but he died before his vision was realized. His widow saw the wisdom of the plan and told a surveyor, Robert Palmer, to press on with developing the square. But life was not simple, and several wars—including a nasty rebellion in America— kept upsetting the economic stability that favored land development. As business was recovering, a new building code in 1774, aimed mostly at preventing another conflagration, was enacted. It stipulated many aspects of what could and couldn't be done in the construction of housing in a fast-expanding London, including the brilliant architectural move of pushing wooden window frames to the back of brick walls. It not only kept fire from spreading but created strong, deep shadows.

The planning of Portland Place by James and Robert Adam in the late eighteenth century had set a standard for all that was to follow. The prevailing style was Georgian, the term applied to the Palladian Renaissance architecture that predominated in Britain through the consecutive reigns of four kings George—from 1714 through 1830.

No one architect is credited with the design of Bedford Square. We know, however, that Robert Palmer did hire a builder's son named Thomas Leverton from his hometown in Essex, and a special house at number 1, quite different from the rest of the square, is generally credited to Leverton. We also know that the builders were named Robert Crews and William Scott. Work elsewhere by the Adam brothers certainly influenced the general character of Bedford Square.

Whoever was responsible, Bedford Square has been beautifully maintained and has hardly changed since it was built. It remains in the eyes of most Londoners the best example of the Georgian squares in their city.

Walking around the gated garden at its elliptical center you might feel a little awed by the square's near perfection, but the mood is comfortable and friendly. All four sides are made up of terraced houses built as residences, although institutions have taken over most of this high-priced space.

1 The view through the garden is inviting but the gates are locked to all but residents. 2 The northwest terrace appears to be identical to all of the other three and is in fact very similar. But there are differences in window height and surround, balcony arrangement, width of pavilion, and cornice placement. 3 A pavilion doorway is crowned with keystone and voussoirs. 4 Stretched across the southeast terrace, the elements in common with the others make up a façade of subtle complexity above regular areaways. The windows are set in a deep reveal required by the Building Act after the Great Fire. 5 The areaways in front of the buildings make for a strong architectural base for the houses and pavilions above. 6 This "classic" bay is marked by its painted cornice rail.

At the center of each side a light-colored pavilion punctuates the row of dark brick structures; along with slight variations in the roof railings, the pavilions give the illusion of a unified palace of sorts. Although there are just enough small variations to give the square a human touch, the walls of Bedford Square are essentially uniform in terms of color and material.

The bricks were originally what Londoners call gray, but two and a half centuries of coal smoke and soot have turned them black. The actual color of the brick is a sort of yellow beige that was considered to be better than the ordinary red; the pale original brick can still be seen, clean, in many modern buildings around London. But Bedford Square likes its black brick so much that some of it has apparently been painted the color of the sooty stain. The Danish architect and town planner Steen Eiler Rasmussen wrote, "These blackened walls formed an effective background for the light details of painted stone. . . . There was no question of imitation but only of obtaining an elegant textural effect by combining smooth and rough elements."

All the doors except a few are painted glossy black. The door and window frames and muntins are painted the same light ivory as is used on the stone and occasional plaster. So many layers of paint have built up that you can hardly tell where one material ends and another begins. The original paint may even have been white before weathering darkened it.

The masonry under Bedford Square's paint is a uniquely durable terra-cotta first produced in 1760 by Mrs Coade's Artificial Stone Company. The precast heroic heads and wormy quoins that surround each doorway appear elsewhere in London; they were advertised for general use in a catalog known to most builders. The miscellaneous ironwork of each entry stair, lamppost, bench, and the central garden railing (bright green when I was a student) are equally black thanks to a restoration. Traffic on Bloomsbury Street moves slowly through the eastern side of the square, but the new curbing of the square itself has managed to discourage motorists in the twenty-first century.

Bedford Square raises questions common to many British squares. The dense, tall trees of the central garden—do they enhance or destroy the space that is so beautifully defined? Must the garden be under lock and key? If there were no trees, Britain's squares would look more Italian. Fewer trees, unfenced, among which you could walk would make the square French. What, then, would a British square be? One answer has to be: Bedford Square.

1 This doorway is narrower, its door is blue, and its areaway bridge is elegantly tiled. 2 The restraint and austerity of the Palladian years are reflected in the "artificial stone" produced by the Coade Company. It was sold and installed elsewhere in London but never as consistently as at Bedford Square. Compared to Portland stone, which it was to imitate, it has weathered rather better. 3 The north corner is closed nicely by the trees that extend along Montague Place. 4 The east corner is closed by House No. 1 with a unique central doorway that required a special interior stairway now serving the Aga Khan University. 5 This mildly elaborate variant relies on sidelights, plants, and shrubs to mark its identity. 6 The pediment of the southeast pavilion groups four columns above a single doorway. (The facing pavilion, #2 on page 188, has five columns and two doorways.) 7 The component parts of Bedford Square are very few and simple: black brick, wood and masonry trim painted in ivory, and black painted ironwork.

Glenfinlas Street

Bute House
(First Minister's Residence)

George Street

West Register House

Roxburghe Hotel

Hope Street

Meters 15   30   60   90 North

Feet   50   100   200   300

CHARLOTTE SQUARE

Edinburgh

PLAN DIMENSIONS	RATIO OF WIDTH TO LENGTH	AREA	TYPICAL HEIGHT TO SKYLINE	HIGHEST POINT	RATIO OF WIDTH TO SKYLINE HEIGHT	ANGLE OF VIEW FROM ANY SIDE TO THE SKYLINE	KEY DATE
525 × 525 ft (160 × 160 m)	1 to 1 (square)	6.3 acres (2.5 ha)	50 ft (15 m)	100 ft (30 m), top of the church dome	10 to 1	6°	1792, publication of Robert Adam's plan

Source of drawing data: Information from the ordnance survey of Great Britain; and Mr. John Butters, keeper of the Charlotte Square garden gate

Although it is subject to the British practice of locking gardens within city squares—usually because the gardens are privately owned—Charlotte is a splendid square. The calm dignity of its forms and the disciplined color of its materials enclose a space of significant quality. Its garden is a patch of the greenery for which Edinburgh is deservedly famous. Cars may drive into but not easily through the space, thanks to traffic engineers. Since visitors don't normally have access to the garden, few people loll about, but the square's residents and office workers are properly proud of their good luck to pass regularly through the space. Charlotte Square vies with Bedford Square as Britain's most quintessential Georgian square; both are among the best urban spaces in Europe.

In 1767, the young Scottish architect James Craig (1744–1795) won a competition for the planning of a new quarter of the city of Edinburgh to be laid out on a rise, the Mound, above the old city. The city's northern edge had just been extended by the draining of the Nor' Loch, and the fill had been used to create the Princes Street Gardens and a causeway to the Mound. Craig's plan for the New Town is a subtle grid that is brilliant in its design, execution, and maintenance. Three streets define the New Town along an east–west axis: the broad George Street at its center with the one-sided Princes and Queen streets looking south toward the fortified Edinburgh Castle and north across the gardens. The master plan is anchored at either end of George Street by a square: St. Andrew's to the east (rather badly botched as a transportation center) and Charlotte at the west, still reigning supreme. (Originally, the two squares were named for the patron saints of Scotland and England, St. Andrew and St. George; the latter was renamed in 1785 for Queen Charlotte, wife of King George III.)

Development of the New Town moved steadily, starting in the east. When the time came to complete the western end, the city fathers asked one of Scotland's best-known architects, Robert Adam (1728–1792), to submit detailed designs. Adam's 1791 proposal for the north side of the square grouped row houses into an articulated terrace, reflecting his experience in designing great country houses; they also showed Adam's familiarity with John Wood's successful pavilions at Bath (see page 176). Lots on the north side went up for sale in 1792, just a few days after Adam's death.

Adam's church, on which he had labored mightily, looking for a major public building to crown his accomplishments, was never built. His draw-ings show the building as a square, stand-alone structure of considerable complexity. When the time came to build it, it seemed too expensive, so the job went to another local architect, Robert Reid (1774–1856), who had earned distinction working for the crown. The church that did get built incorporates some of Adam's ideas, but most critics agree that it is a faint echo of what should have climaxed the west end of George Street. Around 1960 the church was found to be crumbling from dry rot, but parishioners and the public were unable or unwilling to pay for its restoration. As a compromise, the city of Edinburgh took it over for storage of municipal archives and the church was deconsecrated, despite the cross that still tops its cupola.

Like most of the New Town, all the buildings on Charlotte Square are of a cream-colored sandstone called Craigleith, and all are at least inspired by Robert Adam's designs. The north side is in fact his, and, since it serves as Bute House, the residence of Scotland's First Minister, it has been kept in particularly fine condition. The other three sides were shaped in deference to Adam and to the building regulations imposed on the entire New Town. The Roxburghe Hotel occupies part of the south corner of the east side, and its flower boxes and elegant metalwork set a very good example. One wishes such excellence for the entire square.

Following the death of Prince Albert in 1861, Queen Victoria ordered a sculptural group placed in his honor at the center of the garden. The pompous monument necessitated the destruction of many trees and was an unwelcome imposition on Edinburgh. It was nonetheless installed in 1865. Visitors now can see it up close for three weeks each August, when the garden is open to the public for the annual Edinburgh Book Festival; the rest of the time, you have to view it through a wrought-iron fence.

If Robert Adam had lived to control the building of all Charlotte Square's four sides, and if Edinburgh's finances had been sufficient to execute his church to St. George, the space might have been even better than it is. But we shouldn't complain.

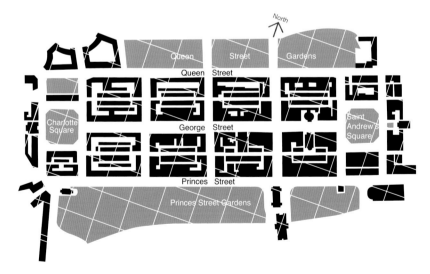

Edinburgh's new town was laid out as one of the world's finest urban designs and has been developed very much according to its original plan. Charlotte Square remains its jewel at the west end of George Street and is best appreciated in its context.

1 The porticos on either side of the West Register House add to the architectural interest of its side of the square and recall its days as a church. 2 The north terrace seen to the right on entry from George Street is the only pavilion actually designed by Robert Adam and is the residence of Scotland's First Minister. 3 The rich texture of local limestone is heightened by brightly painted wood trim and occasional flower boxes. 4 The former church is far away on arrival at the square, and the garden with its memorial is vast.

CHARLOTTE SQUARE

1 Charlotte Square, as seen from George Street, is marked by the dome and its mass of trees. 2 Buildings are largely screened from view within the garden including that sporting its dome. 3 The entry from George Street is bracketed by identical pavilions that make up the eastern side of the square. This one is to the north. 4 Stairs give access to each first floor by crossing a lightwell that serves the basement. This one belongs to the hotel with its window boxes. 5 The Albert Memorial can only be appreciated from within the garden, and that is probably just as well. 6 The entry to the residence of the First Minister shows the fine hand of Scotland's preeminent architect that inspired, but was not equaled, on the other three sides of Charlotte Square. 7 Subtle changes in the plane of the façade imply the wings of Adam's country houses. 8 The southern pavilion on the eastern side, like its twin (#3 this page), was inspired by Robert Adam but designed by others.

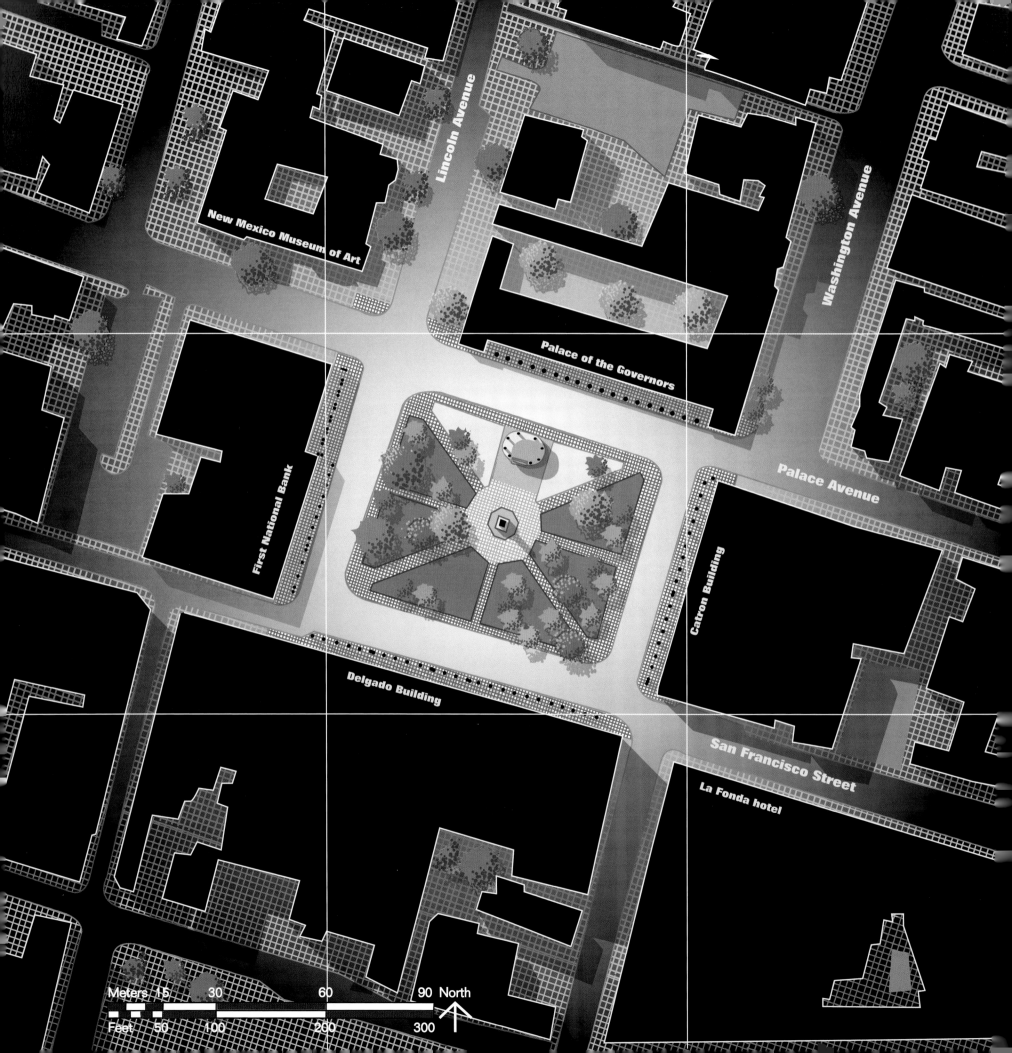

New Mexico Museum of Art

Lincoln Avenue

Washington Avenue

Palace of the Governors

Palace Avenue

First National Bank

Catron Building

Delgado Building

San Francisco Street

La Fonda hotel

Meters 15 30 60 90 North

Feet 50 100 200 300

THE PLAZA AT SANTA FE

New Mexico

PLAN DIMENSIONS	RATIO OF WIDTH TO LENGTH	AREA	TYPICAL HEIGHT TO SKYLINE	HIGHEST POINT	RATIO OF WIDTH TO SKYLINE HEIGHT	ANGLE OF VIEW FROM ANY SIDE TO THE SKYLINE	KEY DATE
275 × 328 ft (84 × 100 m)	1 to 1 (approx. square)	2.0 acres (0.8 ha)	35 ft (10 m)	50 ft (15 m), roof of the adjacent La Fonda Hotel	8 to 1	7°	1610, start of construction of the original Palace of the Governors

Source of drawing data: Cadastral quads from the city of Santa Fe

The Plaza at Santa Fe succeeds in attracting all the tourists for whom it was designed. Its skyline is on the low side, but its space is otherwise well contained at the four corners of a grid plan. Its trees provide welcome shade from New Mexico's high-desert sun, and the square is well furnished and finished with wood siding and posts, benches, a bandstand, a memorial monument, and pleasant paving. These elements give it a very American feel and evoke memories of western movies. Like many of Europe's greatest squares, it has been in constant flux and subject to frequent improvement right up to the end of the twentieth century. Because of the circumstances surrounding its construction, the authenticity of the plaza has been somewhat controversial.

In 1609 the Spanish viceroy appointed a governor for New Mexico with instructions to found a new capital at Santa Fe. The governor, in turn, directed that a gubernatorial headquarters building be erected. From the time of its completion, the Palace of the Governors has been occupied by assorted rulers and residents, including Native Americans, Christian clergymen, Mexicans, Anglos (both Union and Confederate), as well as the original Spaniards.

According to Professor Chris Wilson at the University of New Mexico, "Instructions clearly echoed the town planning ordinances of the Laws of the Indies. Compiled in 1573 by King Philip II of Spain, the Laws codified seventy years of Spanish town planning experience in the Americas, and drew from a variety of European sources: Roman and Renaissance planning theory from Vitruvius to Alberti.... [T]he Laws of the Indies provided specific, practical instructions for maintaining friendly relations with natives, selecting a town site, laying out a grid of streets with a central plaza...the Laws shaped virtually every city in the Spanish domain."

There is no reason to doubt the claim made in 1901 by the then-territorial governor that "the Palace is the oldest public building and the most historic edifice in the United States." But how much of what we see today even resembles the structures that have been built and rebuilt on this spot? Maps dating back to 1766 show some building on the north side of a very typical Spanish plaza. Starting in 1867 photographs show the building with and without its arcade, and with and without the adobe enclosures that today anchor either end of the arcade. Written records describe buildings of greatly varying size and splendor. In Rosemary Nusbaum's edition of the papers of southwestern archeologist, photographer, and first director of the Mesa Verde National Monument, Jesse Nusbaum, is this account from 1831: "[N]either is the Governors' Palace in Santa Fe anything more than a mud building, fifteen feet high, with a mud covered portico, supported by rough pine pillars." The palace is featured, nevertheless, in the stories of Billy the Kid. If the Palace of the Governors that we visit with pleasure today serves its role as the historical museum of New Mexico, does it matter if it is authentic?

That is the question that critics posed about Santa Fe for a century. If, like "colonial" Williamsburg, Santa Fe is largely a tourist attraction reconstructed in the 1920s and 1930s by some talented architects, the same can be said of Rhodes and San Gimignano in the hands of Mussolini's designers (see pages 100 and 56). We can, however, judge what we see today in deciding whether the plaza deserves its reputation as one of America's greatest squares. It certainly demonstrates the power of architectural detail on a public space.

Historian Marc Simmons notes convincingly that the plaza probably originally extended for two city blocks, all the way to the Cathedral of St. Francis on the east. Since almost all Spanish colonial squares had the town's principal church on one side, and early documents refer to Santa Fe's plaza as a military parade ground (*plaza de armas*), it was undoubtedly large enough to accommodate the review of troops. Sometime in the 1820s a customs house was built on the south side of Palace Avenue, and soon the plaza was cut in half by the row of commercial buildings that followed.

Two important buildings by the two principal designers of the present Santa Fe—John Gaw Meem and the architectural firm Rapp and Rapp—define the plaza but don't face onto it; they occupy adjacent lots on the northwest and southeast kitty-corners.

Rapp and Rapp, famous for their movie theaters throughout the United States, had designed the New Mexico Building for the 1915–16 Panama-California Exposition in San Diego, basing it on New Mexico's grand old Acoma Mission building. The building proved to be such a success that it was largely re-created in 1916 at the corner of Santa Fe's Palace and Lincoln streets, where it serves today as a fine arts museum. It presents many of the best architectural features of what is known as Santa Fe style—a fashion that grew out of lively discussions during World War I proposing a picturesque eclecticism based on native American pueblos.

At the opposite corner of San Francisco and Washington streets is the great hotel, La Fonda, designed in 1920 by Rapp and Rapp as part of the Fred Harvey chain for the Santa Fe railroad and added to in 1927 by Meem, an engineer-architect who came to Santa Fe in 1924 for tuberculosis treatment, and stayed. Leaving the hotel on San Francisco Street and looking left, you can see the gracious entry to the plaza on its diagonal axis. As you proceed to the square, the Palace of the Governors appears, forming the northern boundary. Its elegant arcade (*portales* in Spanish) shelters the wares of the best Native American jewelry makers in town and savvy shoppers who know where to find them. The bold columns, caps, and beams that define this space date from 1913, when the building was extensively renovated by Jesse Nusbaum and turned into today's museum and government building. The broad adobe cornice that tops the arcade and the adobe enclosures that anchor the façade at both ends also date from this time. It is handsome and looks far better than any of its predecessors shown in photos.

The other three sides of the plaza are a random mix of commercial buildings dating from the 1860s almost to the present. The façades are of varying heights and styles, depending on what was fashionable when they were built; they include Greek Revival, Carpenter Gothic, Italianate with cast-iron columns and pressed metal cornices, and Richardsonian Romanesque. But they are visually unified by the addition of their own portales—a simple but powerful architectural gesture suggested by Meem in 1930 (though not completed until 1966). The arcade is what makes the plaza we know today.

The other unifying element is the brown brick paving of most of the square. The plaza is also enhanced, and visitors are welcomed, by a diagonal pattern of paths and by green benches, lighting standards, and trees that had to be hauled down out of the mountains to the treeless desert site. A central Civil War monument features an obelisk that recalls those so often appearing in Roman squares. A classic, very American, metal bandstand completes the square.

Rapp and Rapp and John Gaw Meem may well have visited some of the European squares that bear at least a family resemblance to their plaza. More to the point, they all came to New Mexico in search of a romantic exception to the typical America of the early twentieth century. They were encouraged by merchants looking for tourists who could be serviced, after 1880, by the new railroad connection of the Atchison, Topeka and Santa Fe (even though the main line passes through Albuquerque and never reached Santa Fe).

Walking around the plaza, you find the space well contained and comfortable. Prominent views of the fine arts museum and La Fonda, which establish the square's Spanish colonial–Pueblo architectural character, visually close the openings at the southeast and northwest corners. The arcaded shop fronts recall America's frontier days, and the irregularities of the plaza lend vitality.

1 Gerald Cassidy's painting *The End of the Santa Fe Trail* shows the cathedral behind an imaginative square. 2 The Victorian bandstand, between the monument and the palace, seems to be the most American element of the plaza. 3 The Governors' Palace on the left looks out at the bandstand and the Civil War monument. 4 The best gift shop in town huddles under the Governors' arcade. 5 The New Mexico Museum of Art is a reconstruction of the Rapp and Rapp Exposition building.

203

Pinckney Street

West Cedar Street

Mount Vernon Street

Willow Street

Meters 15   30   60   90 North

Feet   50   100   200   300

LOUISBURG SQUARE

Boston

PLAN DIMENSIONS	RATIO OF WIDTH TO LENGTH	AREA	TYPICAL HEIGHT TO SKYLINE	HIGHEST POINT	RATIO OF WIDTH TO SKYLINE HEIGHT	ANGLE OF VIEW FROM THE SHORT SIDE TO THE SKYLINE	KEY DATE
125 × 360 ft (38 × 110 m)	1 to 3	1 acre (0.4 ha)	50 ft (15 m)	65 ft (20 m), top of several penthouses	2 to 1	21°	1833, start of construction

Source of drawing data: Beacon Hill cadastral information from the city of Boston

One of the smallest sites discussed in this book, Louisburg Square has something special that justifies its inclusion: its original elegant proportions and quiet dignity maintained for almost two centuries in private hands without public support or control. The homes that define the four sides of the square, the leafy park at its center, even the streets that flank the square are monuments to high quality, good taste, and unflagging care.

The beauty of Louisburg Square consists of the simplicity of its form and the quality of its materials. It has just enough variety in the detailing of its doorways to enrich the music of the place. One might argue that, like London's Bedford and Edinburgh's Charlotte squares, Louisburg Square isn't really public, since its garden, enclosed by a wrought iron fence, is locked to all but the residents. But with that technicality aside, Louisburg Square is unquestionably worth our consideration. Cars drive by slowly because Louisburg Square's streets are narrow; people walk by slowly, because it is a remarkable expression of good urban design and the good life.

According to the inscription on a bronze plaque attached to the fence, and with the name of the venerable Boston neighborhood where it is located,

> Louisburg (pronounced Lewisberg) square is a private residential park. It was laid out in 1826 by the Mount Vernon proprietors on pasture land purchased from John Singleton Copley. The houses were built from 1833 to 1847, and the statues of Aristides, to the south, and Columbus, to the north, were erected in 1850. The name is thought to commemorate the 1745 battle of Louisburg, during which an army of New England volunteers captured Cape Breton Island from the French. —Beacon Hill

The city register adds to this history that the original deed to Harrison Gray Otis et al. designated that "the square and streets parallel to it shall be forever reserved and kept open," and the streets were to be "deeded to the City of Boston whenever the city shall accept them."

The square was set near the highest point remaining on Beacon Hill after it was reduced in height at the end of the eighteenth century to permit manageable slopes for the streets that were being installed. The streets are paved with some of the finest patterns of cobblestone still to be found in America. The dates of the houses place the buildings at a moment when the Federal style was passing into the Greek Revival. Red brick was plentiful, so it dominates both the walls and the sidewalks of the square. And the houses have the bay windows that Boston has made its own.

The speed with which the square was built and the care with which it has been maintained have helped guarantee an elegant uniform set of building façades that recall—and even rival—those of Paris's Place des Vosges (see page 136). Although the square is not very wide—hardly more than most New York City avenues—the visual closure at either end gives it the feel of a rounder space. Trees crowd the garden, giving it an appropriately residential scale, as is the case with the Circus at Bath and most of the Georgian squares of London. The public crowds the sidewalks, but the residents don't seem to be bothered.

1 As seen along its eastern side, the square includes buildings from many eras, tied together by its common palette of materials. 2 Antique and modern are mixed in the street furniture of this historic square. 3 Wrought-iron railings and granite steps add class to the local brickwork. 4 The square as seen from Mt. Vernon Street on the south is anything but level. 5 Cobbles come in all shapes and sizes and meld well with red brick sidewalks. 6 Classic Greek is brought forward into the sunlight. 7 Vines are used as architectural garlands.

LOUISBURG SQUARE

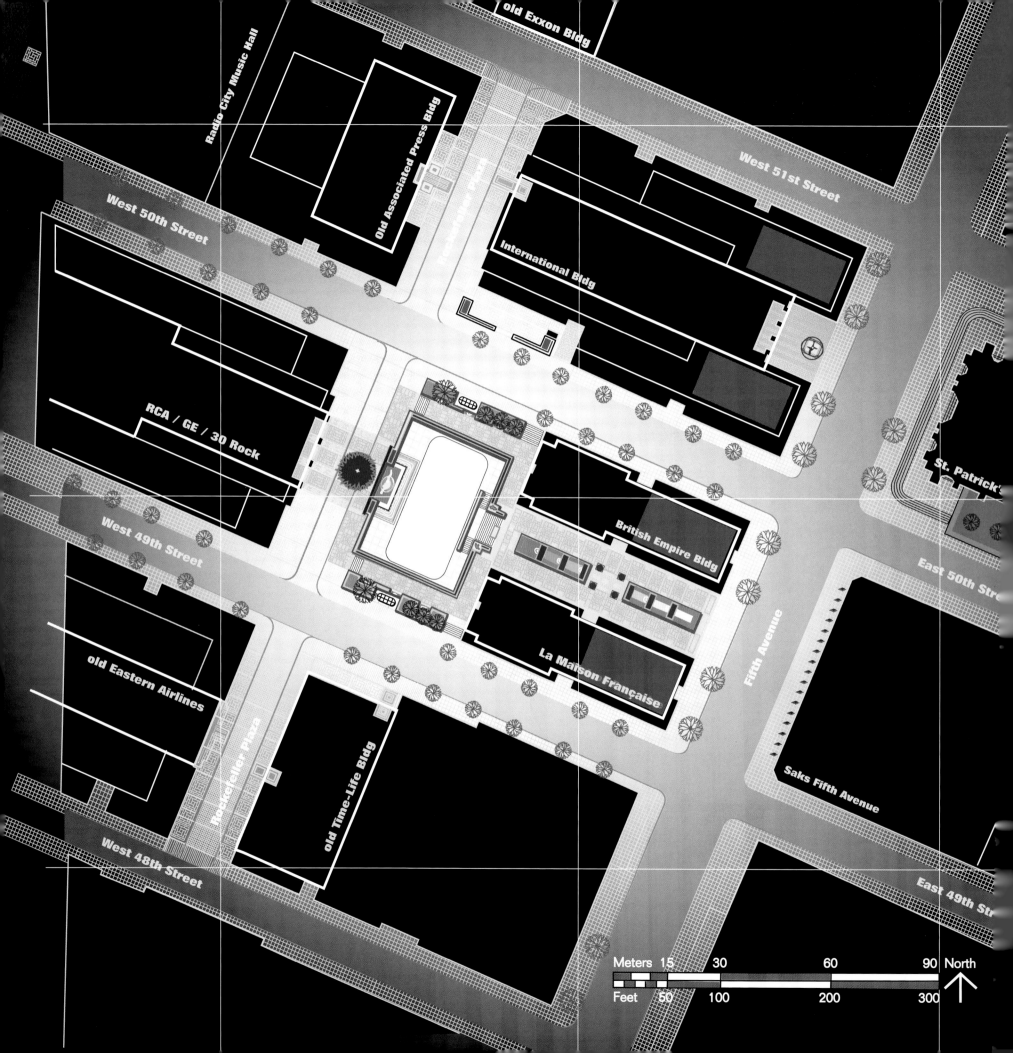

old Exxon Bldg

Radio City Music Hall

West 51st Street

Old Associated Press Bldg

West 50th Street

International Bldg

West 49th Street

RCA / GE / 30 Rock

St. Patrick's

British Empire Bldg

old Eastern Airlines

La Maison Française

East 50th Str

Rockefeller Plaza

old Time-Life Bldg

Fifth Avenue

Saks Fifth Avenue

West 48th Street

East 49th Str

Meters 15   30   60   90   North

Feet   50   100   200   300

ROCKEFELLER PLAZA
New York

PLAN DIMENSIONS	RATIO OF WIDTH TO LENGTH	TYPICAL HEIGHT TO SKYLINE	HIGHEST POINT	RATIO OF WIDTH TO SKYLINE HEIGHT	ANGLE OF VIEW FROM BASE OF 30 ROCK TO SKYLINE	FROM ENTRANCE TO SAKS FIFTH AVENUE TO TOP OF 30 ROCK	KEY DATE
200 × 380 ft (60 × 115 m)	1 to 2	95 ft (30 m)	850 ft (260 m), top of 30 Rock	2 to 1	27°	60°	1928, first plans of Rockefeller Center
AREA 1.7 acres (0.7 ha)							

Source of drawing data: Design layouts provided by realtor-developers Tishman Speyer, and Beyer Blinder Belle Architects & Planners LLP

Most of Manhattan Island embodies a very special kind of architectural life in which the two sides of its gridded streets—the block—are more closely related than the backyards that elsewhere might represent neighborliness. It should come as no surprise, therefore, that New York's greatest square is a mega-block bracketed by a number of those streets. Rockefeller Plaza, at the heart of the eighteen-building Rockefeller Center complex, is not usually thought of as a square, but it meets virtually every criterion of such a great urban space: containment, human scale, beauty, and enjoyment. The tall buildings that form its walls cast long shadows that restrict the view of the sky, but they establish a luxurious sense of enclosure.

Most of the plaza is off-limits to cars, buses, and trucks; and the traffic bordering it on West 49th and 50th streets—both vehicular and pedestrian—is usually so heavy that it moves slowly. While most people in the plaza at any one time have come with a purpose—to shop, skate, visit Radio City Music Hall, etc.—their experience, framed by the vision of brilliant designers and developers, touches the spirit. The writer Daniel Okrent reported that Gertrude Stein called the view across Rockefeller Plaza "the most beautiful thing I have ever seen, ever seen, ever seen."

Visitors to Rockefeller Plaza who enter it from Fifth Avenue follow a broad esplanade that slopes subtly downhill between buildings occupied partly by British and French commercial interests. This promenade, aptly named the Channel Gardens, is defined by relatively low, seven-story buildings, which do their formative job nicely. At the west end of the Channel Gardens, the plaza opens out and a grand staircase leads down to a second, sunken plaza overlooked by the Greek god Prometheus, a sculpture by Paul Manship (1886–1966). When Rockefeller Center was new, eager shoppers were meant to flow like a river to the lower plaza, into its surrounding shops, and across it to a vast underground network of stores and services. But the lower-level businesses attracted too few customers and were replaced by restaurants. In the summer, a forest of table parasols completely fills the space. When in use as a skating rink, which has occupied the plaza in wintertime since 1936, the original lower plaza can be better seen and appreciated.

Most stunning, however, is the view to the west beyond the sunken plaza and straight to the top of my favorite skyscraper. First called the RCA Building (for the Radio Corporation of America) and now the GE (General Electric) Building, it has always been known by the locals as 30 Rock from its address on a private street that runs from West 48th Street to West 51st Street midblock between Fifth and Sixth Avenues. The building is clad in piers of shot-sawn Indiana limestone, their striated surfaces alternating with stacks of dark gray windows and aluminum spandrels on a roughly five-foot module. The restricted palette of material and hue amounts to a monumental success that establishes the architectural vocabulary for the entire space.

Rockefeller Plaza's complicated but successful ground plan has one of its boundaries across one of the city's busiest thoroughfares: Fifth Avenue. There the façade of Saks Fifth Avenue forms the plaza's eastern wall—500 feet (150 meters) from Saks to 30 Rock. To the north, John D. Rockefeller Jr., for whom the plaza is named, got the Eastern States Standard Oil company (now Exxon) to build a tower defining the end of the street that forms one wing of

1 30 Rockefeller Plaza, seen from Fifth Avenue through the Channel Gardens formed by the Maison Française and the British Empire Building, is Gertrude Stein's "most beautiful thing." 2 According to Daniel Okrent, Lee Lawrie cribbed Genius from William Blake for the entry to 30 Rock. 3 30 Rock in the early morning mist from West 50th Street dominates the plaza at its base to the left. 4 Another decorative incision by the architects' favorite sculptor, Lee Lawrie, above the south entry to the British Empire Building, represents Mercury in the language of Art Deco with reference to Grant Wood. 5 The grand staircase was originally designed to draw pedestrians down to the lower plaza encircled by shops that have since closed. 6 The towers forming the plaza are, from left to right, 30 Rock, the old Associated Press Building, Warner Communications, and the International Building, with the British Empire and La Maison Française forming the entry along the Channel Gardens to the right. (The white intruder on the right is on the other side of Fifth Avenue.)

the plaza. On the south, however, years of negotiation failed to bring about the acquisition of West 48th Street's midblock, and the plaza peters out over a line of old buildings, remnants of a neighborhood known for its flophouses and speakeasies—825 feet (250 meters) from Exxon to the far side of 48th Street.

Rockefeller Center began in the financially heady days of the late 1920s. Born of a plan to establish a new home for the Metropolitan Opera on midtown property owned by Columbia University, it died when financier Otto Kahn's grand scheme collapsed with the stock market. Little was left but the idea of architect Benjamin Wistar Morris and his society-architect friends, including Joseph Urban, Ralph Walker, and Ely Jacques Kahn, of the opera's forecourt edged by commercial structures.

John D. Rockefeller Jr. assumed the financing of the center in 1928. He was thereafter guided by real estate genius John R. Todd, who eventually assembled the design team, adding Harvey Wiley Corbett, Wallace Harrison, and Raymond Hood to the roster. These out-of-work superstars formed a group called Associated Architects, and they collaborated remarkably well in realizing Rockefeller Center. In his book *Delirious New York*, architect Rem Koolhaas proclaimed Rockefeller Center "a masterpiece without a genius."

If the story behind the architectural design of Rockefeller Center is principally one of great organizers such as Corbett and Harrison, its fine design hand was, if not that of a genius, that of Raymond Hood (1881–1934). Hood won the Chicago Tribune competition of 1922 with a Gothic pastiche that gave no hint of his later masterworks in New York for American Radiator, McGraw-Hill, and the Daily News. Hood's stripes of light and dark gray at 30 Rock create a great crag of a building that seems to shed sheets of masonry like some exfoliating peak. Once you are inside the plaza, its embracing sense of enclosure resembles a mountain pass or some great woods with splendid tree trunks.

The years 1929 to 1940 marked the high-water mark in America of Art Deco; this style is frozen in time at Rockefeller Center by the austerity demanded during World War II—frozen but honored and maintained as almost nowhere else. The center is outstanding for the quality of its architectural details: its bronze tree grates, patterned paving, luxurious elevator cabs, and restrained commercial signage have paid dividends in terms of rentals, rates of occupancy, and simple pride of ownership and presence. As we look back at Art Deco today, it is often marked by exaggeration and excess, but in the hands of someone as good as Ray Hood, its disciplined beauty shines.

Since the glorious first ten years of Rockefeller Center, sequential owners have done a good job of preserving what they inherited. The only problem, and it is a serious one, has been in not knowing where to stop. Trees are welcome along the side streets and Fifth Avenue, but they crowd the relatively small plaza when they are placed within the confines of its 49th and 50th street boundaries. The closely spaced line of sixty flagpoles (one for each of the then United Nations) has encircled the lower plaza since 1950. While the flags add life and color to the almost uniform stone gray of the buildings, they are so dense and active in their movement that they make seeing the true space of the square nearly impossible.

These small and, I hope, temporary drawbacks aside, we are the lucky beneficiaries of ten short years in art and architecture when everything came together at Rockefeller Plaza—inspiration, talent, taste, money, and craftsmanship.

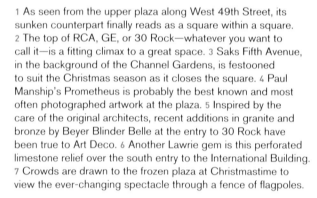

1 As seen from the upper plaza along West 49th Street, its sunken counterpart finally reads as a square within a square. 2 The top of RCA, GE, or 30 Rock—whatever you want to call it—is a fitting climax to a great space. 3 Saks Fifth Avenue, in the background of the Channel Gardens, is festooned to suit the Christmas season as it closes the square. 4 Paul Manship's Prometheus is probably the best known and most often photographed artwork at the plaza. 5 Inspired by the care of the original architects, recent additions in granite and bronze by Beyer Blinder Belle at the entry to 30 Rock have been true to Art Deco. 6 Another Lawrie gem is this perforated limestone relief over the south entry to the International Building. 7 Crowds are drawn to the frozen plaza at Christmastime to view the ever-changing spectacle through a fence of flagpoles.

ROCKEFELLER PLAZA

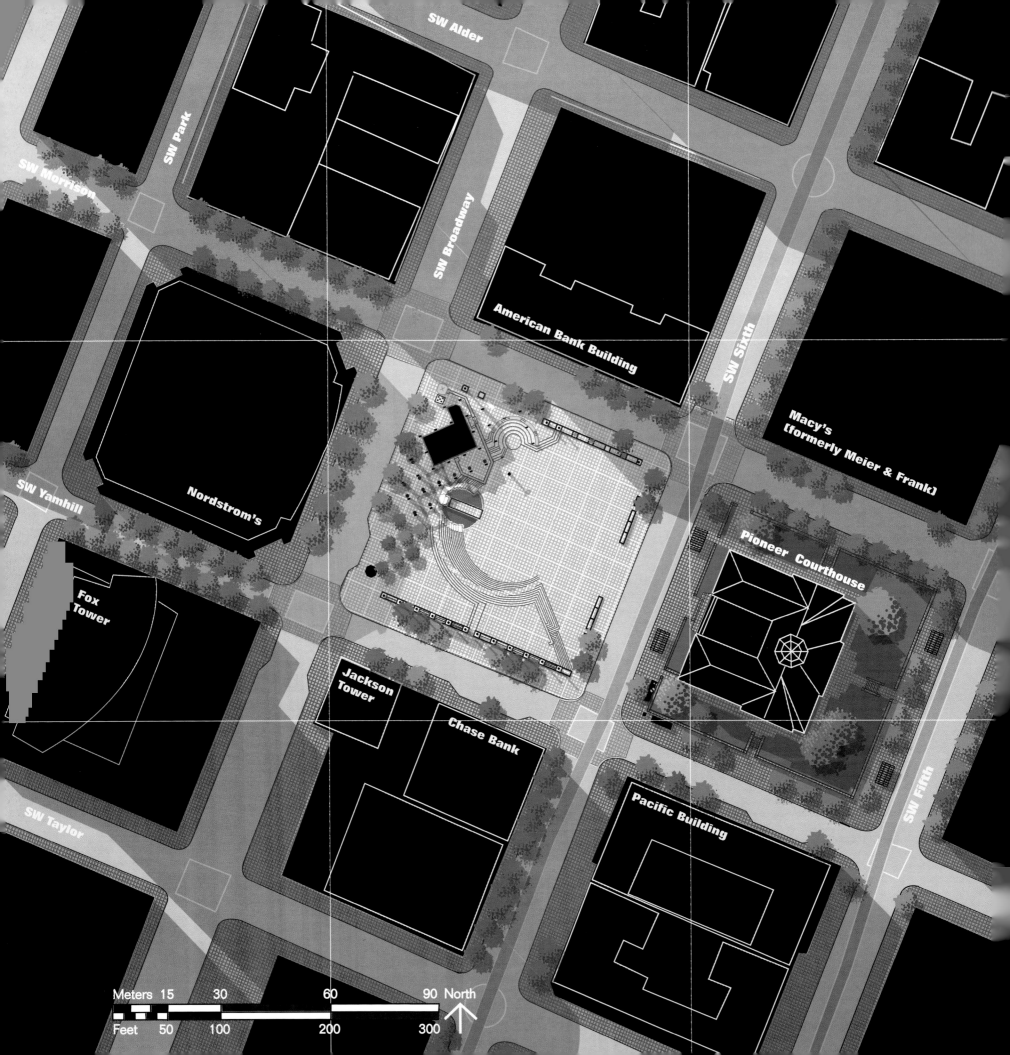

SW Alder

SW Park

SW Morrison

SW Broadway

American Bank Building

SW Sixth

Macy's
(formerly Meier & Frank)

SW Yamhill

Nordstrom's

Pioneer Courthouse

Fox
Tower

Jackson
Tower

Chase Bank

SW Fifth

SW Taylor

Pacific Building

Meters 15   30   60   90 North

Feet   50   100   200   300

PIONEER COURTHOUSE SQUARE

Portland, Oregon

PLAN DIMENSIONS	RATIO OF WIDTH TO LENGTH	AREA	TYPICAL HEIGHT TO SKYLINE	HIGHEST POINT	RATIO OF WIDTH TO SKYLINE HEIGHT	ANGLE OF VIEW FROM THE SHORT SIDE TO THE SKYLINE	KEY DATE
318 × 353 ft (97 × 108 m), street side to facing street side	1 to 1 (approx. square)	2.5 acres (1.0 ha) street to street; 0.9 acres (0.36 ha) within the 200-foot-wide property lines	80 ft (25 m), parapet of Nordstrom's building	355 ft (108 m), top of adjacent Fox Tower	4 to 1	15°	1981, start of construction

Source of drawing data: Details of the plan from Pioneer Courthouse Square Inc.

Many of the world's great squares have been cut right into the middle of a city's urban fabric. Often the purpose has been to set off an important building. But rarely have squares been created solely as a space for walkers—all walkers, as is the case with Pioneer Courthouse Square. Europe has had its kings and dukes; Portland has its citizens. Pioneer Courthouse Square, a veritable newcomer, could not have been built without the inspiration of a fine designer, nor maintained without a great client: the city of Portland. Productive criticism from citizen groups, national awards, and praise in the press have suggested gradual additions and changes, and most have been to the good. The square is today an immensely popular feature of a beautiful city. The result of government support at every level—federal, state, and, above all, municipal—it is a model of good detailed planning and urban care that is all too rare in the United States.

This very square square in the middle of downtown Portland takes its name from the first public building built in the American northwest. The courthouse, completed in 1875, is the eastern wall of the square. Workaday department stores and office buildings form the other three walls.

Planning the square was a long and sometimes painful process that resulted in an open design competition in 1979. Discussion of a new square began before the last of many previous occupants of the space was demolished in the late 1960s. On the site had stood Portland's first public school, built in 1858, and a grand hotel designed by the notable McKim, Mead & White in 1890 for the arrival of the railroad. Various schemes for parking facilities to serve the customers of the Meier and Frank (now Macy's) department store came and went. When an eleven-story parking structure was proposed in the late 1960s, cool heads prevailed. Portland's Downtown Plan (1972–74) said simply that space was needed to bring more people, not more cars, to downtown.

The program that was finally issued for the architectural competition—the work of many talented architects, planners, and politicians—was a very good one, but it grew out of controversy. Should the square be covered or open? How to handle the diagonal fifteen-foot fall from west to eastern corners? These decisions were left to the competitors to resolve. Plans for a new public transit system to encircle the spot added impetus to the development.

Five finalists were finally chosen from the one hundred sixty-two submissions, four of them well-known firms based elsewhere: the winner was local, Will Martin. He and his colleagues brought a bright, lighthearted attitude toward design and, with very minor changes, the square was built to their initial design. Sadly, it proved to be Martin's last project; he died in a plane crash just after the square was completed.

Pioneer Courthouse Square is a square within a square surrounded by relatively low-speed vehicular traffic. Since nothing could be done about the buildings that form its outer walls, attention in the square concentrates on its sloping floor and interior features. Some of these echo European public spaces: a coffee shop; concrete chessboards; waterfalls flanking a bridge that crosses a pool (and leads to an underground tourist office); and food stalls and trinket sellers, protected by glass canopies supported by stoa columns of the classical orders. Trees and pergolas shade the tables where visitors can eat a snack—particularly some famous burritos. Red brick sidewalks and bronze statuary appear on all the nearby streets and are used throughout the square to good effect. The network of brick-paved streets that has extended outward pulls you into the square.

By all odds the square's most dramatic and successful feature is a brick amphitheater nested in the northwest corner. Its steps provide seats for visitors, readers, people just pausing for a rest, audiences for open-air concerts, and meeting participants. Most pleasing is the sculptural finesse with which the steps intersect the ramp that accommodates baby strollers and wheelchairs. The broad bank of steps continues its descent to expose the façade of an underground shop. Originally occupied by a branch of Powell's, the Northwest's principal bookstore, the space has proved to be a difficult corner to exploit commercially. New occupants have finally moved in—the NBC-TV affiliate, KGW, which since early 2009 has broadcast from it as a newsroom, "the studio in the square."

Following the lead of many of its European market precedents, the square has been kept mostly empty so it can be used all year long by temporary stands, stages, rolling displays, and a Christmas tree. Pacific Ocean currents soften Portland winters, and this great outdoor room has so far withstood attempts to close it in against the weather. The fact that most Portland buses and trolleys, plus a new light-rail route, either originate in or pass by the square means that practically everyone gets a glimpse of what's going on there, which encourages pedestrian use.

If at times Pioneer Courthouse Square seems too busy, there are always opportunities to make adjustments in a city that treats its living room with obvious love and respect. This space, cited by the Project for Public Spaces as one of the twelve best urban public places in North America, will continue to give joy to Portland's citizenry and visitors.

1 Many of the square's bricks are engraved with the names of donors. 2 The entry to the underground Visitor Information Center is bracketed by waterfalls leading to a pool. 3 The square runs downhill from the lip of the amphitheater toward surrounding office buildings and the namesake Courthouse on the right. 4 The principal elements are seen against the brick façade of Nordstrom, the color of which is very similar to the floorscape of the square. The steps circle south along food kiosks sheltered by glass canopies.

SUMMARY DATA

NAME OF SQUARE	CITY	DATE	PLAN DIMENSIONS			AREA		TYPICAL SKYLINE			
					WIDTH TO LENGTH RATIO			HEIGHT		WIDTH TO HEIGHT RATIO	
			FEET	METERS		ACRES	HA	FEET	METERS		ANGLE
Piazza Navona	Rome	85	180x845	55x257	1:5	3.5	1.4	65	20	3:1	20°
Piazza della Rotonda	Rome	120	200x220	61x67	1:1	1.0	0.4	65	20	3:1	18°
Piazza delle Erbe	Verona	1172	138x475	42x145	1:3	1.4	0.5	65	20	2:1	25°
& Piazza dei Signori	Verona	1476	118x210	36x64	1:2	0.6	0.2	50	15	2:1	22°
Piazza San Marco	Venice	1063	230x560	70x171	1:2	3.0	1.3	80	25	3:1	20°
& Piazzetta	Venice	1536	160x290	48x88	1:2	1.0	0.4	80	25	2:1	27°
Campo dei Santi Giovanni e Paolo	Venice	1230	200x410	60x125	1:2	0.9	0.4	50	15	3:1	14°
Piazza del Santo	Padua	1232	330x330	100x100	1:1	2.0	0.8	65	20	5:1	11°
Piazza del Campo	Siena	1292	328x395	100x120	1:1	2.9	1.2	95	30	3:1	17°
Piazza della Cisterna	San Gimignano	1273	130x280	40x85	1:2	0.9	0.4	65	20	2:1	27°
& Piazza del Duomo	San Gimignano	1239	200x200	61x61	1:1	0.9	0.4	65	20	3:1	18°
Piazza Vecchia	Bergamo	1300	115x230	35x70	1:2	0.6	0.2	65	20	2:1	30°
& Piazza del Duomo	Bergamo	1444	66x132	20x40	1:2	0.2	0.1	115	40	1:2	64°
Piazza della Signoria	Florence	1299	295x395	90x120	1:1	2.0	0.8	65	20	4:1	12°
Piazza della Santissima Annunziata	Florence	1421	207x246	63x75	1:1	1.2	0.5	50	15	4:1	14°
Campo de' Fiore	Rome	1514	148x368	45x112	1:2	1.2	0.5	80	25	2:1	29°
& Piazza Farnese	Rome	1514	174x243	53x74	1:1	1.0	0.4	95	30	2:1	30°
Piazza del Campidoglio	Rome	1534	164x262	50x80	1:2	1.0	0.4	70	22	2:1	24°
Piazza San Pietro	Rome	1656	690x790	210x240	1:1	12.5	5.0	65	20	10:1	6°
Piazza di Spagna	Rome	1623	230x850	70x260	1:3	2.5	1.0	65	20	4:1	16°
Fountain Square of Hippocrates	Rhodes	1507	100x120	30x36	1:1	0.3	0.1	30	10	4:1	18°
Old Town Square	Prague	1338	395x460	120x140	1:1	4.2	1.7	65	20	6:1	10°
Old Town Square	Telč	1354	165x985	50x300	1:6	1.8	0.8	65	20	3:1	22°
Münsterplatz	Freiburg	1360	368x410	112x125	1:1	3.4	1.4	50	15	7:1	8°
Münsterplatz	Ulm	1377	295x395	90x120	1:1	2.6	1.1	65	20	4:1	12°
Place des Cornières	Monpazier	1285	135x154	41x47	1:1	0.5	0.2	35	10	4:1	14°
Place des Vosges	Paris	1612	468x468	143x143	1:1	5.0	2.0	65	20	7:1	8°
Place Vendôme	Paris	1699	410x453	124x140	1:1	4.2	1.7	65	20	6:1	9°
Jardin du Palais-Royal	Paris	1782	304x738	93x225	1:2	5.0	2.0	50	15	6:1	9°
Place Stanislas	Nancy	1755	333x393	102x120	1:1	3.0	1.3	65	20	5:1	11°
Plaza Mayor	Salamanca	1755	265x265	80x80	1:1	1.5	0.6	50	15	6:1	11°
Praça do Comércio	Lisbon	1755	575x605	175x185	1:1	8.0	3.2	65	20	9:1	6°
The Circus	Bath	1754	318 (diam)	97 (diam)	1:1	1.8	0.7	50	15	6:1	9°
Piece Hall	Halifax	1775	230x288	70x88	1:1	1.5	0.6	35	10	7:1	8°
Bedford Square	London	1775	378x518	115x158	1:1	4.5	1.8	65	20	6:1	10°
Charlotte Square	Edinburgh	1792	525x525	160x160	1:1	6.3	2.5	50	15	10:1	6°
The Plaza	Santa Fe	1610	275x328	84x100	1:1	2.0	0.8	35	10	8:1	7°
Louisburg Square	Boston	1833	125x360	38x110	1:3	1.0	0.4	50	15	2:1	21°
Rockefeller Plaza	New York	1928	200x380	60x115	1:2	1.7	0.7	95	30	2:1	27°
Pioneer Courthouse Square	Portland, OR	1981	318x353	97x108	1:1	2.5	1.0	80	25	4:1	15°
AVERAGES			**265x410**	**80x125**	**1:1.5**	**2.5**	**1.0**	**65**	**20**	**4:1**	**17°**

Notes to the Data

DATE Approximate time of the start or completion of construction

PLAN DIMENSIONS Reasonably accurate except for averages due to irregularities

AREA Approximate calculations have been rounded to the nearest decimal tenth

SKYLINE Parapet, peak, or other edge that separates the space from the sky

HEIGHT approximate and rounded to the nearest multiple of five

RATIOS and **ANGLES** rounded to whole numbers

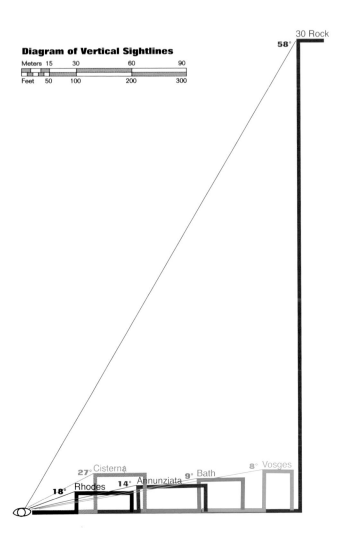

After looking at the drawings that illustrate forty squares, reviewing and averaging their dimensions, and making aesthetic judgments, one might ask if there are any conclusions that can be drawn. Mine are that not much has changed during the 120 years since Camillo Sitte began his comparisons in 1890 and since Zucker added his 60 years ago. All but two of the squares that I have written about (Rockefeller Plaza and Pioneer Courthouse Square) were known to Sitte; only the latter has appeared since Zucker's time. On the other hand, two candidates for the judgment of "great" within one century fall exactly in the same proportion as forty within the twenty centuries preceding it.

In scanning the plans in this book, you may be surprised, as I was, to find that the squares are far more similar than different in shape and overall size. Why this uniformity?

For one thing, Sitte was right in suggesting that normal architectural details start to lose their legibility at a distance of 200 feet (60 meters), and the average width of our squares is 265 feet (80 meters). Human vision has remained more or less the same over all these years.

Another interesting observation is that the comfort edge of our cone of vision is about 25° above horizontal; things higher than that require lifting the head. The top of a wall has importance and is easily seen from a point that is twice as far away as it is high, but it seems insignificant at a much greater distance.

Before the elevator, the walls of squares usually topped out at the height of a four-story walk-up, or about 65 feet (20 meters), suggesting that the distance of easy viewing of its top is about 130 feet (40 meters). This is just about the distance from the center of our average square to its surrounding walls. It's true that the walls of squares have been gradually rising in height since the arrival of the elevator, but architects often stop using elegant stone above the fourth floor since no one notices it over that height. (The columns in St. Peter's change from marble to marbleized plaster at about that point.)

When you stand in the middle of an ideal square, therefore, its architectural detailing will start to disappear if it is more than 200 feet (60 meters) away, and its ceiling of sky may appear to be just about right if it meets the walls at some height between 65 and 100 feet (20–30 meters.) Does this suggest why most great squares, thus far, are between 250 and 400 feet (80 and 120 meters) in width? It is worth considering.

BIBLIOGRAPHY

Bacon, Edmund. *Design of Cities*. New York: Viking Press, 1967.

Ballon, Hilary. *The Paris of Henri IV*. Cambridge, MA: MIT Press, 1991.

Baker, Geoffrey H. *Design Strategies in Architecture: An Approach to the Analysis of Form*. New York: Van Nostrand Reinhold, 1989.

Blumenfeld, Hans. *The Modern Metropolis: Its Origins, Growth, Characteristics, and Planning*. Cambridge, MA: MIT Press, 1967.

Borsi, Franco, and Geno Pampaloni. *Monumenti d'Italia, Le Piazze*. Novara: Istituto Geografico de Agostini, 1987.

Buckley, Alexandra, Stephanie Crandell, and Ann Girand. *Pioneer Courthouse Square Celebration*. Portland, OR: City of Portland, 1991.

Buchanan, Colin, and Ministry of Transport. *Traffic in Towns: A Study of the Long Term Problems of Traffic in Urban Areas*. London: Penguin Books, 1963.

Byrne, Andrew. *Bedford Square: An Architectural Study*. London: Athlone Press, 1990.

Caccin, Angelo M. O. *Basilica of Saints John and Paul*. Venice: Edizioni d'Arte Marconi, 1992.

Carmona, Matthew, Tim Heath, Taner Oc, and Steve Tiesdell. *Public Places—Urban Spaces*. Oxford: Architectural Press, 2003.

Cerver, Francisco Asensio, and Michael Webb. *City Squares and Plazas*. New York: Hearst Books International, 1997.

Childs, Mark C. *Squares: A Public Place Guide for Urbanists*. Albuquerque: University of New Mexico Press, 2004.

Coste, Michel. *Monpazier, les clés d'une bastide*. Monpazier: Librarie du Château, 2002.

Cullen, Gordon. *Townscape*. New York: Reinhold, 1961.

De Chiara, Joseph, and Lee Koppelman. *Urban Planning and Design Criteria*. New York: Van Nostrand Reinhold, 1975.

Dörfler, Herbert, and Reinhold Ambruster-Mayer. *Ulm, Charming City at the Danube*. Trans. by Gandalf Gamdschi. Ulm: Schöning Verlag, 2006.

Dubourg, Jacques. *Histoire des Bastides: les villes neuvres du Moyen Âge*. Luçon: Sud Ouest, 2002.

Dunn, John B. *Piece Hall Guide*. Halifax, UK: Metropolitan Borough of Calderdale, 1981.

Fabbri, Patrizia. *Verona*. Verona: Casa Editrice Bonechi, 2003.

Feraboli, Maria Teresa, and Angela Arnone. *City Squares of the World*. Vercelli: White Star, 2007.

Fletcher, Sir Banister. *A History of Architecture on the Comparative Method*. London: Scribner, 1943.

Forsyth, Michael, and Stephen Bird. *Bath*. New Haven, CT: Yale University Press, 2003.

Gehl, Jan, and Lars Gemzoe. *New City Spaces*. Copenhagen: Danish Architectural Press, 2000.

Giedion, Sigfried. *Space, Time, and Architecture: The Growth of a New Tradition*. Cambridge, MA: Harvard University Press, 1967.

Giomi, Luciano. *San Gimignano, Town of Beautiful Towers*. Florence: Foto Fontanelli, 2006.

Gromort, Georges. *Choix des Plans de Grandes Compositions Exécutées*. 3rd ed. Paris: Vincent & Fréal, 1944.

Hegemann, Werner, Elbert Peets, and Alan J. Plattus. *The American Vitruvius: An Architects' Handbook of Civic Art*. New York: Princeton Architectural Press, 1922.

Hernandez, María Leticia Sánchez. *All Salamanca*. Trans. by R. Lockay. Barcelona: Editorial Escudo de Oro S.A., 1997.

Howard, Deborah. *Venice & the East: The Impact of the Islamic World on Venetian Architecture 1100–1500*. New Haven, CT: Yale University Press, 2000.

Jacobs, Allan B. *Great Streets*. Cambridge, MA: MIT Press, 1993.

Jenkins, Eric J. *To Scale: One Hundred Urban Plans*. NewYork: Routledge, 2007.

Kidder Smith, G. E. *Italy Builds: Its Modern Architecture and Native Inheritance*. New York: Reinhold, 1955.

Kostof, Spiro. *The City Shaped*. Boston: Little Brown, 1991.

———. *City Assembled: Elements of Urban Form Throughout History*. Boston: Little Brown, 1992.

Kratinova, Vlasta, Bohumil Samek, and Milos Stehlik. *Telč: Historic Town of South Moravia*. Prague: Odeon, 1992.

Krinsky, Carole. *Rockefeller Center*. New York: Oxford Press, 1978.

Lasansky, D. Medina. *The Fascist Redesign of San Gimignano*. Chicago: Journal of the Society of Architectural Historians, 2004.

Lees-Milne, James. *Saint Peter's: the Story of Saint Peter's Basilica in Rome*. London: Hamish Hamilton, 1967.

Longo, Gianni. *Great American Public Spaces*. New York: Urban Initiatives, 1996.

Luttrell, Anthony. *The Town of Rhodes: 1306–1356*. Rhodes: Office for the Medieval Town, 2003.

Martin, Philippe, and François Pupil. *Nancy from the Middle Ages to the 21st Century*. Metz: Éditions Serpenoise, 2005.

Manoussou, Katerina. *Medieval Town of Rhodes, Restoration Works 1985–2000*. Rhodes: Ministry of Culture, 2001.

Musée Carnavalet. *Le Palais Royal*. Paris: Musée Carnavalet, 1988.

Norman, Diuana. *Siena, Florence, and Padua: Art, Society, and Religion 1280–1400*. New Haven: Yale University Press, 1995.

Novelli, Italo, ed. *Atlante di Roma*. Venice: Marsilio Editori, 1991.

Nusbaum, Rosemary. *The City Different and the Palace*. Santa Fe, NM: The Sunstone Press, 1978.

Okrent, Daniel. *Great Fortune: The Epic of Rockefeller Center*. New York: Viking, 2003.

Orefice, Gabriella, Mario Fondelli, and Oberdan Armanni. *Atlante di Firenze: The Form of the Historic Center*. Venice: Marsilio Editori, 1994.

Perocco, Guido. *The Basilica of Saint Mark and the Gold Altarpiece*. Venice: Storti Edizioni, 1994.

Prunet, Pierre, Nicolas Detry, Max Querrien, and Giovanni Carbonara. *Architecture et restauration*. Paris: Passion, 2000.

Rasmussen, Steen Eiler. *Experiencing Architecture*. Cambridge: The MIT Press, 1959.

Ravanelli, Renato. *Bergamo—the History—the Art*. Bergamo: Grafica & Arte, 2003.

Reps, John W. *The Making of Urban America*. Princeton, NJ: Princeton University Press, 1965.

Rhodes Ministry of Culture. *Restoration Works (1985–2000)*. Rhodes: City of Rhodes, 2001.

Rowe, Colin, and Fred Koetter. *Collage City*. Cambridge, MA: MIT Press, 1984.

Salerno, Luigi. *Piazza di Spagna*. Rome: Mauro Editore, 1967.

Schama, Simon. *Landscape and Memory*. New York: Vintage Books, 1995.

Sitte, Camillo. *Der Städtebau nach seinen küntieischen Grundsätzen*. Vienna: 1889; New York: Reinhold, 1945.

Smithies, Philip. *The Architecture of the Halifax Piece Hall, 1775–1779*. Halifax: Stott Brothers Ltd., 1988.

Staňková, Jaroslava, Jiři Štursa, and Svatopluk Voděra. *Prague: Eleven Centuries of Architecture*. Prague: PAV Publisher, 1992.

Stutz, Bruce. *Resurrecting Lisbon*. www.NewScientist.com News Service, 22 October 2005.

Summerson, John. *Georgian London*. New York: Pleiades, 1945.

Trachtenburg, Marvin. *Dominion of the Eye: Urbanism, Art, and Power in Early Modern Florence*. Cambridge, MA: Cambridge University Press, 1997.

Trachtenberg, Marvin, and Isabelle Hyman. *Architecture, from Prehistory to Post-Modernism*. New York: Prentice Hall, 1986.

Tunnard, Christopher, and Boris S. Pushkarev. *Man-Made America*. New Haven: Yale University Press, 1963.

Tyrwhitt, Jaqueline, Josep Luis Sert, Ernesto N. Rogers, and Sigfried Giedion. *CIAM [8]: The Heart of the City: Towards the Humanism of Urban Life*. London: L. Humphries, 1952.

Webb, Michael, and Francisco Asensio Cerver. *Redesigning City Squares and Plazas: Urban Landscape Architecture*. New York: Hearst Books International, 1997.

Wilson, Chris. *The Myth of Santa Fe: Creating a Modern Regional Tradition*. Albuquerque: University of New Mexico Press, 1997.

Zucker, Paul. *Town and Square*. New York: Columbia University Press, 1959.

INDEX

CREDITS

Except as listed here, by page and figure number, all drawings and photographs are by the author.

Avery Architectural & Fine Arts Library, Columbia University, New York— 25: 5; 139: 4, 5; 149: 4, 7; 175: 7.
Ian Arnott, Architect, Edinburgh— 95:1; 196: 3; 197: 6.
The Image Works for Roger-Viollet and the Musée Carnavalet, Paris— 143: 5; 49: 8; 153: 5; 155: 2, 5; 157: 3.
Mario Jossa, Architecte, Paris— 147: 1; 149: 6.
New Mexico Museum of Art, Santa Fe – 203: 1.
Susan R Witter, New York— 167: 5; 169: 7.
Wikimedia Commons – 95: 4.